PENGUIN BOOKS

677

CHARLES LAMB AND ELIA

EDITED BY J. E. MORPURGO

CHARLES LAMB
AND ELIA

*

EDITED BY
J. E. MORPURGO

PENGUIN BOOKS
HARMONDSWORTH · MIDDLESEX

Specially edited for Penguin Books and first published 1948

To
C. N. K. M.

MADE AND PRINTED IN GREAT BRITAIN
FOR PENGUIN BOOKS, LTD, BY WYMAN & SONS, LTD,
LONDON, FAKENHAM AND READING

CONTENTS

PART II · HE SERVES UP HIS FRIENDS

ACKNOWLEDGEMENT

All editors of Lamb must acknowledge their indebtedness to E. V. Lucas, Thomas Hutchinson and Edmund Blunden. In my own case, the editorial indebtedness to Mr Blunden has been increased by the advice that he has given me and the kindness that he has always shown to me.

INTRODUCTION

Seldom can it be said of a writer that he is better known
than his works. Shakespeare has had myriad commentators
but few biographers. Millions know that Milton wrote
Paradise Lost, thousands have read it, but only hundreds
know more of the unquiet life of the poet than the fact that
he went blind at the age of forty-two. The Greeks, who for
the most part cannot read his works, cherish the memory
of Byron, but it is the earnest champion of liberty whose
name they inscribe in their calendar of national heroes,
and the 'martyr' of Missolonghi has only a facial resem-
blance to the author of *Mazeppa*. The personality of Browning has gained acquaintances from the efforts of the contemporary stage and cinema, but these intermediaries are
crabbed with apocryphal tendencies and their Browning is
but a coloured and romanticized print of that great pepper-
pot of titillating exclamations. As a studied portrait of the
man it is no more accurate than was the free-hand impression of wit and brilliance, modelled upon the one *bon mot*
that made Browning's fame with the unread, before the
intervention of Mr. Frederic March. Charles Dickens, next
to Shakespeare the most omnipresent of English writers, had
an almost Elian gift for egotistic projection, and, unlike
Shakespeare, has been at once cursed and blessed by a procession of pilgrim-biographers, yet, even to the reading
public, the man Dickens is an unappreciated stranger,
overshadowed by friends made from his introduction : Cop-
perfield, Oliver Twist, Pickwick and the Wellers.

Two literary men stand pre-eminent as authors who are
as well known as (and even better known than) their writings : Samuel Johnson and Charles Lamb. Whereas Johnson
beat his ponderous way to fame over the deflated bodies of
his victims, aided and at times driven by the sycophantic

artistry of Boswell, Lamb's life has become universal
property both from his own autobiographical genius
(often mischievously perverted) and from the greatness
of the circle of genius that looked to him as to its
focus.

The reader of Johnson may sometimes wonder if he deserved his Boswell; the reader of Lamb is confident that he
merited the praise of Coleridge: 'His genius is talent, and
his talent is genius, and his heart is as whole and one as his
head'; of Thomas Barnes: 'You have written about Shakespear finer than any one ever did in the world', of Landor:
'He leaves behind him ... the love of friends without a
single foe'; and of Wordsworth: 'O, he was good if e'er a
good man lived.' Johnson's powers won him admirers and
enemies; Lamb, from his skill and for himself gained friends
who could yet admire the great artist who was their simple
friend.

Often, as Lamb wrote, his own tortured yet cheerful
character overpowered his imagination so that his self-
portrait is more striking than his creations. His friends, each
from his own genius, contributed their footnotes to his autobiography, and his works, rearranged in the reader's mind,
punctuated by his letters and interspersed with the com-
ments of Coleridge, Hood, De Quincey, Hazlitt, Leigh
Hunt and Crabb Robinson give almost all that can be
known of his day by day existence, his likes and dislikes,
his passions and his reserve. The student who selects carefully, watching warily for the deliberate false scent, can
reconstruct the whole of the life, person and character of
Charles Lamb.

Loved by his friends and reverenced by his admirers as a
creature *sui generis* there was, nevertheless, something
about Lamb that appeals to the English love of convention.
He was essentially middle class, born away from the handi-
cap of poverty and never achieving the disgrace of riches.
As unadventurous practically as he was daring in imagination, he worked for thirty years as a clerk in the East
India House. He lived, all of his life, in London or its
suburbs, venturing only once to the Continent, where

according to Coventry Patmore, his conversational French was so conventionally English that a waiter brought him a brandy instead of the egg that Lamb imagined he had ordered – an error that would not have angered Charles Lamb.

He shared the half-humorous mistrust of Scotsmen common among his countrymen: 'I have been trying all of my life to like Scotsmen, and am obliged to desist from the experiment in despair.' With the possible exception of Walter Scott, his Northern contemporaries despised him in return. Christopher North, after his early attacks, was sufficiently converted to persuade Lamb to add his consequential ammunition to the heavy blast of *Blackwood's*, but Carlyle insisted, even thirty years after Lamb's death, that his talk was 'contemptibly small, indicating wondrous ignorance and shallowness', and never recanted his first unperceptive account: 'Charles Lamb, I sincerely believe to be in some considerable degree insane. A more pitiful, rickety, gasping, staggering Tom Fool I do not know. ... Poor England, when such a despicable abortion is named genius!'

Conservative in his love of familiar things, friends, books, and places, so that 'the disappearance of the old clock from St Dunstan's Church drew tears from him', he was nevertheless ardent to reform wrongs done or wrongs intended, and on the rare occasions when he entered the political ring – already overcrowded with ability – he hit at corruption with as much zest as Leigh Hunt or Thomas Barnes. It was Hunt who went to prison for the outspoken attacks on the Prince of Wales written by him and published in his paper *The Examiner*, but Lamb's lampoon in the same paper, 'The Triumph of the Whale', must have helped to arouse the anger of the Prince:

> 'Say what appellation suits?
> By his bulk and by his size,
> By his oily qualities,
> This (or else my eyesight fails)
> This should be the Prince of Whales'

and of the Prince's party:

> 'Every fish of generous kind
> Scuds aside or slinks behind;
> But about his presence keep
> All the monsters of the deep;
> Crooked dolphins they surround him;
> Dog-like seals they fawn around him.
> Following hard the progress mark
> Of the intolerant salt sea-shark;
> For his solace and relief
> Flat fish are his courtiers chief.
> Last and lowest in his train
> Ink-fish (libellers of the main)
> Their black liquor shed in spite.'

Engrossed, as they were at times, with the philosophical
and political unrest of their day, Coleridge, Wordsworth,
Byron and Shelley are in some essentials, through the
transient causes of their interest, dated, but Lamb, who stood
for the most part outside contemporary affairs, is timeless
and of all time.   He seldom referred to the outstanding
phenomenon of his age, the Emperor Napoleon ('I heard
he is small, even less than me, who am less than the least of
the Apostles' and 'I should not mind standing barehead at
his table to do him service in his fall. They should give him
Hampton Court or Kensington'). He shared Coleridge's
mistrust of Pitt, but not its wordiness, and, though he lived
through the great political events of 1832, he spared them
both comment and ink.

His mind centred on the sixteenth and seventeenth
centuries. *John Woodvil* is a dubious imitation, but his
friendly acquaintance with Elizabethan and Caroline
writers, and the natural ease with which he borrowed their
style and their phrases, turning them into living literature
that is neither plagiarist nor archaic, makes him more the
contemporary of 'old Tom Browne' than of Byron. Lamb's
life lasted fifty-nine years but his memory spanned three
centuries. It is no wonder then that the longevity of his
spirit supports him, human till to-day.

'Shy of all imposing appearances, of all assumptions of self-importance, of all adventitious ornaments', disdaining 'all the vulgar artifices of authorship, all the cant of criticism and helps to notoriety', Lamb's essential bourgeoisie could not and cannot be slurred by the accusation of Bohemianism so often hurled at the English artist by reason of his art and its imagined un-English associations. 'Tripe and cow-heels were to him delicacies – rare dainties', and in a man of such immaculate taste the Englishman can always allow certain eccentricities.

Even his faults are the faults that win censure from prigs but strengthen the affections of the multitude, which, like Lamb himself, prefers a man 'who is as he ought not to be'. In common with most heavy smokers, he was always on the point of abjuring the habit: 'This very night I am going to leave off Tobacco! Surely there must be some other world in which this unconquerable purpose shall be realized.' He was over-fond of alcohol and an inveterate 'pub-crawler': Whenever the opportunity occurred 'he had a humorous method of testing the friendship of his visitors, it was, whether in their walks with him they would taste the tap of mine Host at the Horseshoe, or at the Rose and Crown or at the Rising Sun', but the *Confessions of a Drunkard* should be taken with water, and Carlyle was so consistently mistaken in Lamb that it is unnecessary and uncharitable to place too much credence upon his puritanical condemnation: 'He is now a confirmed shameless drunkard; *asks* vehemently for gin and water in strangers' houses, tipples till he is utterly mad, and is only not thrown out of doors because he is too much despised for taking such trouble with him.' Lamb himself has demonstrated that his commercial superiors at the East India House were not gentle with clerks who succumbed to liquor, and had his proclivity to drunkenness been so free as is insinuated it is doubtful if he would have been allowed to remain in the service of the East India House for thirty-three years, and certain that he would not have been granted the generous pension of four hundred and fifty pounds a year had his intemperance been so obvious as to demand the attention of the Whitehall-like dignitaries of the East India Company.

The whimsical nature of his conversation and of some of his writing has brought upon him the accusation of sentimentality, even of effeminacy, but this essentially mild man (with his typically masculine weaknesses) could be blisteringly rude to bores, utterly unsentimental with false art, and viciously unkind to those who offended his conception of the sanctity of friendship. Happy with children, happiest with men, only a few women held his affection, his sister Mary (Bridget Elia of *Blakesmoor in H—shire*), their adopted daughter Emma Isola, Dorothy Wordsworth, and the actress Fanny Kelly to whom he proposed unsuccessfully at the age of forty ('what a lass to go a-gipsying through the world with!'). Hester Savory, to whom he gave the immortality of one of his laments, was often seen but never addressed by him. Ann Simmons, Anna of the sonnets and Alice W—n of the essays, lingered so long in his imagination as 'what might have been' that it almost appears as if he fell in love with her as with a memory of his own creation; the author becoming enamoured of one of his own characters until she becomes more real to him than the woman who was the original of the character; the sculptor forgetting the inspiring model in his love for the clay into which he has breathed life.

Through all of his work and in every action of his adult life was throbbing a fear of madness. Insanity to him was much more than a mental disease, it was an abstract conception of calamity. He had, himself, one experience of dementia, but it came before Mary Lamb's act of matricide forced him to devote his life to her care, resigning voluntarily his natural inclination towards marriage so that he might stay 'wedded to the fortune of my sister and my poor old father'. When, in the first of his letters to Coleridge, he wrote of his own lapse, he could write cheerfully enough: 'The six weeks that finished last year and began this, your very humble servant spent very agreeably in a madhouse at Hoxton. I am got somewhat rational, and don't bite anyone. But mad I was; and many a vagary my imagination played

with me, enough to make a volume.' A few months later
the hideous death of his mother made nightmare terror
of the idea of mental failure. Not only was he weighed
down with the sad presence and the frequent relapses of
the sister whom he loved so well, but the memory of his
own insanity became doubly horrible, for itself and for the
fear that a recurrence in him might leave Mary without
cherisher and supporter.

This obsession obtruded the name of insanity again and
again into his work. The narrative of *Rosamund Gray* is
broken by soliloquy: 'False things are told concerning thee,
fair planet, for I will ne'er believe that thou canst take a
perverse pleasure in distorting the brains of us poor mortals.
Lunatics! Moonstruck. Calumny invented, and folly took
up these names.' Seeking for words to describe the condition
of Don Quixote after Sancha has lost faith in his master,
Lamb finds them immediately: 'a treatable lunatic'.
'Madness', 'lunacy', 'insanity', 'imbecility', these are the
words that beat the discordant recurring theme in the
sweet symphony of Lamb's brain.

Sadness, even gloom, were never far away. It is not only
the plot that makes his early and unsuccessful novel, *Rosamund Gray*, read like an advance evocation of Thomas Hardy.
The desperate repetition 'All, all are gone, the old familiar
faces' in the best known of his poems, cuts with tragic knife
the cord of his self-restraint.

He wrote quietly, and, in general, cheerfully, yet his
quality of lightness and pleasure, like his indulgence in all
good things – books, pictures, food, drink and friendship
– is symptomatic of his quest for compensation for the tragic
shacklings of his misfortune. It is as if he were happy to
shame his own misery and all-interested to spite the monotony of routine. 'I had been,' he wrote to Coleridge on one
typical occasion, 'in a sad quandary of spirits but a Pipe
and some generous Port and *King Lear* had their effects as
solaces. I went to bed pot-valiant.'

It is not surprising that John Webster 'found his first
recognition at the pious and fortunate hands of Charles
Lamb', for few critics can have had such instinctive and

personal sympathy for Webster's consciousness of tragedy and for his ability ' to touch a soul to the quick, to play upon fear as much as it can bear, to wean and weary a life till it is ready to drop, and then step in with mortal instruments to take its last forfeit'.

Hovering ' as one between earth and heaven, neither hoping much nor fearing anything', Lamb had no use for the facile consolations offered by the Churches. He was no anti-Christian, but he abhorred bigotry, and, needing something more immediate than a promissory note on Heaven to hold his mind from bitterness, found his comfort in humour. In his humour is that tempering quality of tragedy that is common to all great humorists. His jester's motley he wore consciously, masking himself as Edax or Crito, subduing his own identity in Pensilis or Burton Junior, writing of Charles Lamb as if he were a chance acquaintance, even, on occasion, stealing the person, though not the personality of Coleridge, and finding, finally, the satisfaction of escaping the burdensome sadness of life as Lamb in the cheerful pen-life of Elia.

The Essays of Elia are Lamb's most popular writings. They are forced upon school-children with an insistence that is almost justifiable, for he who does not discover *Roast Pig* could well have been spared the pains of learning to read. But it was as ' the first to draw the public attention to the old English dramatists' that he wished to be remembered. The echoing voice of Elia is heard in Leigh Hunt, in Thackeray (who took upon himself the canonization of Saint Charles), in Stevenson, Chesterton, Montague, Lynd and, grossly distorted, in the gossip-writers of the daily press. Elia influenced the writers; and, through their printed homage, won pedagogues and the love or passionate hatred of schoolboys; but Charles Lamb reinstated readers in their own domain, resurrecting for them the beauties of the English Renaissance, saving and salving Webster, Ben Jonson, Beaumont and Fletcher, Marlowe, Middleton – even Shakespeare himself – after the neglect and ill-usage that they had received from the hooks of the pretentious Augustan iconoclasts.

Continually Lamb denied his scholarship, contrasting it, as he must have contrasted it from their schooldays, with the depth of learning of his greatest friend, Coleridge, yet Lamb's diversity of knowledge is awesome. As Edmund Blunden, a fellow-Blue and a devoted and exquisite commentator has noted, 'Lamb is a master of his Bible, of his classical mythology, of writers on heraldry, of medieval geographers, of Elizabethan drama and Caroline poetry, of general biography, of the standard novelists, of the commentators'. To complete his paraphernalia of ability must be added a knowledge of music and of stage technique, a fine appreciation of painting, a well-grounded understanding of philosophy, and (despite his detractors who confuse religion and Church dogma), of the essentials of true Christianity.

His very scholarship has dulled many editions of his works, for whereas Lamb could use his knowledge without emphasizing the ignorance of his readers, his editors have insisted on a supply of explanatory footnotes, dragging the eye joltingly from the body of the text to the bottom of the page, wrenching the mind from Lamb's familiarity that is above incidental knowledge, adding unimportant information on details, but diverting from the deliberate casualness with which Lamb proceeds to his real conclusions.

To attempt to assess Lamb as a stylist is to defy critical tenets, for his English rambles, stammers as his speech, runs and falters. He knows not concision though he is a master of precision. He chases an insignificant idea into significance and makes of an interloping inspiration a literary occasion. He is archaic and yet never 'precious'. His writing is often amorphous, for his prose style is rebellion against the formalism of his immediate predecessors, as is the habit of verse adopted by his friends Coleridge and Wordsworth.

His first literary efforts were in verse, and he had a vicious, almost bad-tempered vigour in writing treasonable rhymes, but of his poetry only *The Old Familiar Faces* and *Hester* are fit company for the work of his great contemporaries. Nevertheless his poetic powers were sufficient to draw from

Coleridge a protest at his momentary renunciation of versifying after his mother's death:

> 'Dear Charles! Whilst yet thou wert a babe, I ween
> That Genius plunged thee in that wizard fount
> High Castalie: and (sureties of thy faith)
> That Pity and Simplicity stood by,
> And promised for thee, that thou shouldst renounce
> The world's low cares and lying vanities,
> Steadfast and rooted in the Heavenly Muse,
> And washed and sanctified to Poesy.'

A failure as a playwright, his dramatic efforts added to his academic knowledge, and gave to his criticism an element of practical appreciation that is rare save among exponents.

Himself, his letters and his essays are his greatness. They must be judged together; the works as the offspring of the man's life – the letters and the essays often the babe and the grown man of the same idea – full of the same inventiveness and amiability, weighted and yet never made ponderous by the same learning, blessed with the same technique (and lack of technique).

May 1947

PART I

MR CHARLES LAMB

IN THE DAYS OF MY CHILDHOOD

Charles Lamb was born in 1775, in the Temple, where his father
was the personal servant of Samuel Salt.

To his father's employer Lamb owed a great deal. It was
through Salt's influence, though not on his presentation, that
he went to Christ's Hospital, and Salt, one of those kind but
dilatory creatures who always delighted Charles Lamb; a man
'who never dressed for dinner but he forgot his sword'; applied himself
continually in the interest of the Lambs. *'Though indolent and
procrastinating to the last degree'*, it was he who placed John Lamb,
Charles's elder brother, in the South Sea House, and it was he
who, just before his death, helped to obtain for Charles a position
in the service of the East India House (though again, he was
not the actual sponsor).

Lamb's early childhood he described frequently and fluently;
it is remarkable that such detail should have remained in his
memory of the years before he went to Christ's Hospital. Of
Samuel Salt and of the environment in which he was brought
up he wrote in *The Old Benchers of the Inner Temple* and in *My
First Play*. His early schooling he had under Betsy Chambers
(Mrs Reynolds – later one of his two pensioners)

> 'prim Betsy Chambers
> Decayed in her members
> No longer remembers
> Things as she once did.'

and in the academy of William Bird, *'in the main a humane and
judicious master'*, where his sister Mary had preceded him, and
where she had been taught by that Captain Starkey who,
living and dying *'a broken bulrush'*, gave Lamb the model for
one of his contributions to William Hone's *Everyday Book*.

But of all the influences in Lamb's early life, none, save the
companionship of his sister, was more potent than his visits to
his Hertfordshire relatives – to his great-aunt Gladman at
Mackery End and to his grandmother Field, housekeeper to
the Plumers at Blakesware (Blakesmoor).

Blakesmoor in H—shire

I do not know a pleasure more affecting than to range at will over the deserted apartments of some fine old family mansion. The traces of extinct grandeur admit of a better passion than envy: and contemplations on the great and good, whom we fancy in succession to have been its inhabitants, weave for us illusions, incompatible with the bustle of modern occupancy, and vanities of foolish present aristocracy. The same difference of feeling, I think, attends us between entering an empty and a crowded church. In the latter it is chance but some present human frailty – an act of inattention on the part of some of the auditory – or a trait of affectation, or worse, vainglory, on that of the preacher, puts us by our best thoughts, disharmonizing the place and the occasion. But wouldst thou know the beauty of holiness? – go alone on some week-day, borrowing the keys of good Master Sexton, traverse the cool aisles of some country church: think of the piety that has kneeled there – the congregations, old and young, that have found consolation there – the meek pastor – the docile parishioner. With no disturbing emotions, no cross conflicting comparisons, drink in the tranquillity of the place, till thou thyself become as fixed and motionless as the marble effigies that kneel and weep around thee.

Journeying northward lately, I could not resist going some few miles out of my road to look upon the remains of an old great house with which I had been impressed in this way in infancy. I was apprised that the owner of it had lately pulled it down; still I had a vague notion that it could not all have perished – that so much solidity with magnificence could not have been crushed all at once into the mere dust and rubbish which I found it.

The work of ruin had proceeded with a swift hand indeed, and the demolition of a few weeks had reduced it to – an antiquity.

I was astonished at the indistinction of everything. Where had stood the great gates? What bounded the court-yard? Whereabout did the out-houses commence? A few bricks only lay as representatives of that which was so stately and so spacious.

Death does not shrink up his human victim at this rate. The burnt ashes of a man weigh more in their proportion.

Had I seen these brick-and-mortar knaves at their process of destruction, at the plucking of every panel I should have felt the varlets at my heart. I should have cried out to them to spare a plank at least out of the cheerful storeroom, in whose hot window-seat I used to sit and read Cowley, with the grass-plot before, and the hum and flappings of that one solitary wasp that ever haunted it about me – it is in mine ears now, as oft as summer returns; or a panel of the yellow-room.

Why, every plank and panel of that house for me had magic in it. The tapestried bedrooms – tapestry so much better than painting – not adorning merely, but peopling the wainscots – at which childhood ever and anon would steal a look, shifting its coverlid (replaced as quickly) to exercise its tender courage in a momentary eye-encounter with those stern bright visages, staring reciprocally – all Ovid on the walls, in colours vivider than his description. Actæon in mid sprout, with the unappeasable prudery of Diana; and the still more provoking and almost culinary coolness of Dan Phœbus, eel-fashion, deliberately divesting of Marsyas.

Then, that haunted room – in which old Mrs Battle died – whereinto I have crept, but always in the daytime, with a passion of fear; and a sneaking curiosity, terror-tainted, to hold communication with the past. *How shall they build it up again?*

It was an old deserted place, yet not so long deserted but that the traces of the splendour of past inmates were everywhere apparent. Its furniture was still standing – even to the tarnished gilt leather battledores, and crumbling feathers of shuttlecocks in the nursery, which told that children had once played there. But I was a lonely child, and had the range at will of every apartment, knew every nook and corner, wondered and worshipped everywhere.

The solitude of childhood is not so much the mother of

thought as it is the feeder of love, of silence, and admiration.
So strange a passion for the place possessed me in those
years, that, though there lay – I shame to say how few roods
distant from the mansion – half hid by trees, what I judged
some romantic lake, such was the spell which bound me to
the house, and such my carefulness not to pass its strict and
proper precincts, that the idle waters lay unexplored for me;
and not till late in life, curiosity prevailing over elder devotion, I found, to my astonishment, a pretty brawling brook
had been the Lacus Incognitus of my infancy. Variegated
views, extensive prospects – and those at no great distance
from the house – I was told of such – what were they to me,
being out of the boundaries of my Eden? So far from a wish
to roam, I would have drawn, methought, still closer the
fences of my chosen prison, and have been hemmed in by a
yet securer cincture of those excluding garden walls. I could
have exclaimed with the garden-loving poet –

> Bind me, ye woodbines, in your twines;
> Curl me about, ye gadding vines;
> And oh so close your circles lace,
> That I may never leave this place;
> But, lest your fetters prove too weak,
> Ere I your silken bondage break,
> Do you, O brambles, chain me too,
> And, courteous briars, nail me through.[1]

I was here as in a lonely temple. Snug firesides – the
low-built roof – parlours ten feet by ten – frugal boards, and
all the homeliness of home – these were the condition of my
birth – the wholesome soil which I was planted in. Yet,
without impeachment to their tenderest lessons, I am not
sorry to have had glances of something beyond, and to have
taken, if but a peep, in childhood, at the contrasting accidents of a great fortune.

To have the feeling of gentility, it is not necessary to have
been born gentle. The pride of ancestry may be had on
cheaper terms than to be obliged to an importunate race
of ancestors; and the coatless antiquary in his unemblazon-

[1] Marvell, on Appleton House, to the Lord Fairfax.

ed cell, revolving the long line of a Mowbray's or De Clifford's pedigree, at those sounding names may warm himself into as gay a vanity as those who do inherit them. The claims of birth are ideal merely, and what herald shall go about to strip me of an idea? Is it trenchant to their swords? can it be hacked off as a spur can? or torn away like a tarnished garter?

What, else, were the families of the great to us? what pleasure should we take in their tedious genealogies, or their capitulatory brass monuments? What to us the uninterrupted current of their bloods, if our own did not answer within us to a cognate and corresponding elevation?

Or wherefore, else, O tattered and diminished 'Scutcheon that hung upon the time-worn walls of thy princely stairs, 'Blakesmoor'! have I in childhood so oft stood poring upon thy mystic characters – thy emblematic supporters, with their prophetic 'Resurgam' – till, every dreg of peasantry purging off, I received into myself Very Gentility? Thou wert first in my morning eyes; and of nights hast detained my steps from bedward, till it was but a step from gazing at thee to dreaming on thee.

This is the only true gentry, by adoption; the veritable change of blood, and not as empirics have fabled, by transfusion.

Who it was by dying that had earned the splendid trophy, I know not, I inquired not; but its fading rags, and colours cobweb-stained, told that its subject was of two centuries back.

And what if my ancestor at that date was some Damœtus – feeding flocks, not his own, upon the hills of Lincoln – did I in less earnest vindicate to myself the family trappings of this once proud Ægon? repaying by a backward triumph the insults he might possibly have heaped in his lifetime upon my poor pastoral progenitor.

If it were presumption so to speculate, the present owners of the mansion had least reason to complain. They had long forsaken the old house of their fathers for a newer trifle; and I was left to appropriate to myself what images I could pick up, to raise my fancy, or to soothe my vanity.

I was the true descendant of those old W——s, and not the present family of that name, who had fled the old waste places.

Mine was that gallery of good old family portraits, which as I have gone over, giving them in fancy my own family name, one – and then another – would seem to smile, reaching forward from the canvas, to recognize the new relationship; while the rest looked grave, as it seemed, at the vacancy in their dwelling, and thoughts of fled posterity.

That Beauty with the cool blue pastoral drapery, and a lamb – that hung next the great bay window – with the bright yellow H——shire hair, and eye of watchet hue – so like my Alice! – I am persuaded she was a true Elia – Mildred Elia, I take it.

Mine too, 'Blakesmoor', was thy noble Marble Hall, with its mosaic pavements, and its Twelve Cæsars – stately busts in marble – ranged round; of whose countenances, young reader of faces as I was, the frowning beauty of Nero, I remember, had most of my wonder; but the mild Galba had my love. There they stood in the coldness of death, yet freshness of immortality.

Mine, too, thy lofty Justice Hall, with its one chair of authority, high-backed and wickered, once the terror of luckless poacher, or self-forgetful maiden – so common since, that bats have roosted in it.

Mine, too, – whose else? – thy costly fruit-garden, with its sun-baked southern wall; the ampler pleasure-garden, rising backwards from the house in triple terraces, with flower-pots now of palest lead, save that a speck here and there, saved from the elements, bespake their pristine state to have been gilt and glittering; the verdant quarters backwarder still; and, stretching still beyond, in old formality, thy firry wilderness, the haunt of the squirrel, and the day-long murmuring wood-pigeon, with that antique image in the centre, God or Goddess I wist not; but child of Athens or old Rome paid never a sincerer worship to Pan or to Sylvanus in their native groves, than I to that fragmental mystery.

Was it for this, that I kissed my childish hands too fer-

vently in your idol-worship, walks and windings of 'Blakesmoor'! for this, or what sin of mine, has the plough passed
over your pleasant places? I sometimes think that as men,
when they die, do not die all, so of their extinguished
habitations there may be a hope – a germ to be revivified.

ELIA.

London Magazine, September 1824.

AND IN MY JOYFUL SCHOOLDAYS

To have had charge of the schooling of Lamb, Coleridge,
Leigh Hunt, Thomas Barnes, Bishop Middleton of Calcutta,
Henry Meyer (who painted the best known portraits of his
three greatest schoolfellows) and John Colborne (who led the
cavalry at Waterloo) is glory enough for a schoolmaster. That
so many of his pupils should have become men of letters, all
of them with a tendency towards reminiscence, has enshrined
James Boyer in the minds of readers who know little of the school
over which he presided.

In an age of great floggers, Boyer stands pre-eminent; and
Coleridge's valediction '*Poor J. B.! may all his faults be forgiven;
and may he be wafted to bliss by little cherub boys, all head and wings,
with no bottoms to reproach his sublunary infirmities*' has overcast
the fact that Coleridge also bore testimony to Boyer's power
'*as an educer no less than educator of the intellect*' and that Lamb
lauded him for his '*great merits as an instructor*'.

Of the school which Lamb entered at the age of seven, there
is ample description in his own essays *Christ's Hospital, Five and
Thirty Years Ago* and *Recollections of Christ's Hospital*, and in
Coleridge's *Biographia Literaria*, but perhaps the most attractive
is in Leigh Hunt's *Autobiography*. Leigh Hunt entered the
school a few years after Lamb had left, but his outline of the
peculiar nature of that institution would apply equally well to
Lamb's day, or to our own.

'*Perhaps there is not a foundation in the country so truly English,
taking that word to mean what Englishmen wish it to mean – something
solid, unpretending, of good character and free to all. More boys are to
be found in it, who issue from a greater variety of ranks, than in any
school in the kingdom ... the boys themselves had no sort of feeling of the*

difference of one another's ranks out of doors. The cleverest boy was the noblest, let his father be who he might.'

The affection of Blues for their old school is famous and almost notorious. That it should have won the loyalty of three such diverse persons as Coleridge, Lamb and Leigh Hunt is sufficient testimony to its merit, and all three recognized the influence that Christ's Hospital had exercised over their mental development. *'I am grateful to Christ's Hospital'*, wrote Leigh Hunt in a passage that might be a paraphrase of either of his great contemporaries, *'for having bred me up in old cloisters, for its making me acquainted with the languages of Homer and Ovid, and for its having seemed to me, on the whole, a well-trained and cheerful boyhood. It pressed no superstition upon me. It did not hinder my growing mind from making what excursions it pleased into the wide and healthy regions of general literature … There was nothing prohibited but what might have been prohibited by all good fathers.'*

With Lamb, as with Leigh Hunt, the intellectual curiosity that the school encouraged was not the only *'benefit that he received in this place'*. Throughout his life many of his friends were Blues; not all of them Blues of his own generation.

George Dyer, of whom Hunt wrote that *'his life was one unbroken dream of learning and goodness'*, had left Christ's Hospital in 1774, the year before Lamb was born, and was probably first seen by Lamb as by Leigh Hunt when *'passing through the schoolroom (where no other person in town clothes ever appeared) to consult books in the library'*. Himself a prolific hack writer and a poet of fluency and little merit, but as Lamb's friend, correspondent and subject of the essay *Amicus Redivivus* (as well as Hazlitt's *On the Look of a Gentleman*) he has gained immortality.

By Lamb's own testimony part of his respect for Dyer, as for Coleridge, arose from the fact that Dyer had left Christ's Hospital, a Grecian. It is too facile to explain Grecians as the Sixth Form of any other school. They are more godlike, and for their learning and the apparent certainty of their future, far more to be reverenced. In 1831, Lamb admitted that *'writing to you* [George Dyer] *or to Coleridge, besides affection, I feel a reverential deference as to Grecians still'*, and in earlier days this reverence must have been even stronger towards Coleridge who was at school with him, a Grecian when Lamb was but a Deputy Grecian – *'keeping his soaring way above the Great Erasmians'*, yet far beneath the Grecians.

The names of Coleridge and Lamb slip naturally into companionship, and, save for one break, they were friends, and
close friends, throughout their lives. They knew each other at
school, and, it is generally believed that Coleridge gave to
Lamb not only his friendship, but that degree of patronage
which is the prerogative of Grecians towards those who show
intellectual promise.

Other Blues were among Lamb's friends and correspondents
– the two le Grices (Charles Valentine – co-Grecian with
Coleridge, a humorist of some ability and the translator of
Longus – and Samuel), James White, acknowledged author of
the *Falstaff Letters* and donor of the yearly dinner to chimney
sweeps described in the Elia essay *The Praise of Chimney-Sweepers,*
the dogged faithful Favell, who like Sam le Grice '*exchanged
Alma Mater for the camp*', and as a military surgeon died in the
West Indies, Thomas Barnes, who as editor, '*was afterwards
identified with the sudden and striking increase of* The Times *newspaper
in fame and influence*', but who '*might assuredly have made himself a
name in wit and literature*' and another, but less successful journalist, Robert Allen, who shared Lamb's experiences as provider
of paragraphs for the daily press. (See p. 47, *Newspapers Thirty-
Five Years Ago.*)

Valentine le Grice gave to Thomas Talfourd, Lamb's biographer, a description of Lamb at school:

'*Lamb was an amiable, gentle boy, very sensible and keenly observing,
indulged by his schoolfellows and by his master on account of his infirmity
of speech. His countenance was mild, his complexion clear brown, with an
expression which might lead you to think that he was of Jewish descent.
His eyes were not each of the same colour; one was hazel, the other had
specks of grey in the iris, mingled as we see red spots in the blood stone.
His step was plantigrade, which made his walk slow and peculiar, adding
to the staid appearance of his figure. I never heard his name mentioned
without the addition of Charles, although, as there was no other boy of
the name of Lamb, the addition was unnecessary; but there was an
implied kindness in it, and it was a proof that his gentle manners excited
that kindness.*'

In the more intimate of his school essays Lamb wrote so
feelingly of the awfulness of conditions at school, anywhere, at
the end of the eighteenth century that it is often assumed that
his was a miserable boyhood. To refute this all that is really
necessary is the one reference to '*my joyful schooldays*', but the
refutation is emphasized by the numerous loving allusions to

Christ's Hospital in his essays and letters, and by the alacrity with which he sprang to the defence of the school. When it was attacked in the Press in 1813, Lamb replied with the following essay contributed to the *Gentleman's Magazine*:

Recollections of Christ's Hospital

To comfort the desponding parent with the thought that, without diminishing the stock which is imperiously demanded to furnish the more pressing and homely wants of our nature, he has disposed of one or more, perhaps, out of a numerous offspring, under the shelter of a care scarce less tender than the paternal, where not only their bodily cravings shall be supplied, but that mental *pabulum* is also dispensed which he hath declared to be no more necessary to our sustenance, who said, that 'not by bread alone man can live'; for this Christ's Hospital unfolds her bounty. Here neither, on the one hand, are the youth lifted up above their family, which we must suppose liberal though reduced; nor, on the other hand, are they liable to be depressed below its level by the mean habits and sentiments which a common charity-school generates. It is, in a word, an institution to keep those who have yet held up their heads in the world from sinking; to keep alive the spirit of a decent household when poverty was in danger of crushing it; to assist those who are the most willing, but not always the most able, to assist themselves; to separate a child from his family for a season, in order to render him back hereafter with feelings and habits more congenial to it than he could even have attained by remaining at home in the bosom of it. It is a preserving and renovating principle, an antidote for the *res angusta domi*, when it presses, as it always does, most heavily upon the most ingenuous nature.

This is Christ's Hospital; and whether its character would be improved by confining its advantages to the very lowest of the people, let those judge who have witnessed the looks, the gestures, the behaviour, the manner of their play with one another, their deportment towards strangers, the whole aspect and physiognomy of that vast assemblage of boys on the London foundation who freshen and make alive again with their sports the else mouldering cloisters of the old Grey Friars — which strangers who have never witnessed, if they pass through Newgate Street or by Smithfield, would do well to go a little out of their way to see.

For the Christ's Hospital boy feels that he is no charity-boy; he feels it in the antiquity and regality of the foundation to which he belongs; in the usage which he meets with at school, and the treatment he is accustomed to out of its bounds; in the respect, and even kindness, which his well-known garb never fails to procure him in the streets of the metropolis; he feels it in his education, in that measure of classical attainments which every individual at that school, though not destined to a learned profession, has it in his power to procure — attainments which it would be worse than folly to put it in the reach of the labouring classes to acquire: he feels it in the numberless comforts, and even magnificences, which surround him; in his old and awful cloisters, with their traditions; in his spacious schoolrooms, and in the well-ordered, airy, and lofty rooms where he sleeps; in his stately dining-hall, hung round with pictures by Verrio, Lely, and others, one of them surpassing in size and grandeur almost any other in the kingdom[1]; above all, in the very extent and magnitude of the body to which he belongs, and the consequent spirit, the intelligence, and public conscience, which is the result of so many various yet wonderfully combining members. Compared with this last-named advantage, what is the stock of information (I do not here speak of book-learning, but of that knowledge which boy receives from boy), the mass of collected opinions, the intelligence in common, among the few and narrow members of an ordinary boarding-school?

[1] By Verrio, representing James the Second on his throne, surrounded by his courtiers (all curious portraits), receiving the mathematical pupils at their annual presentation, a custom still kept up on New-Year's-day at Court.

The Christ's Hospital or Blue-coat boy has a distinctive
character of his own, as far removed from the abject
qualities of a common charity-boy as it is from the disgusting
forwardness of a lad brought up at some other of the public
schools. There is pride in it, accumulated from the circumstances which I have described as differencing him from
the former; and there is a *restraining modesty*, from a sense of
obligation and dependence, which must ever keep his
deportment from assimilating to that of the latter. His very
garb, as it is antique and venerable, feeds his self-respect;
as it is a badge of dependence, it restrains the natural
petulance of that age from breaking out into overt acts of
insolence. This produces silence and a reserve before strangers, yet not that cowardly shyness which boys mewed up
at home will feel, he will speak up when spoken to, but the
stranger must begin the conversation with him. Within his
bounds he is all fire and play; but in the streets he steals
along with all the self-concentration of a young monk.
He is never known to mix with other boys, they are a sort of
laity to him. All this proceeds, I have no doubt, from the
continual consciousness which he carries about him of the
difference of his dress from that of the rest of the world,
with a modest jealousy over himself, lest, by over-hastily
mixing with common and secular playfellows, he should
commit the dignity of his cloth. Nor let anyone laugh at
this; for, considering the propensity of the multitude, and
especially of the small multitude, to ridicule anything unusual in dress above all, where such peculiarity may be
construed by malice into a mark of disparagement — this
reserve will appear to be nothing more than a wise instinct
in the Blue-coat boy. That it is neither pride nor rusticity,
at least that it has none of the offensive qualities of either,
a stranger may soon satisfy himself by putting a question
to any of these boys: he may be sure of an answer couched
in terms of plain civility, neither loquacious nor embarrassed.
Let him put the same question to a parish-boy, or to one
of the trencher-caps in the —— cloisters, and the impudent
reply of the one shall not fail to exasperate, any more than
the certain servility and mercenary eye to reward which he

will meet with in the other, can fail to depress and sadden him.

The Christ's Hospital boy is a religious character. His school is eminently a religious foundation; it has its peculiar prayers, its services at set times, its graces, hymns, and anthems, following each other in an almost monastic closeness of succession. This religious character in him is not always untinged with superstition. That is not wonderful when we consider the thousand tales and traditions which must circulate with undisturbed credulity amongst so many boys, that have so few checks to their belief from any intercourse with the world at large, upon whom their equals in age must work so much, their elders so little. With this leaning towards an over-belief in matters of religion, which will soon correct itself when he comes out into society, may be classed a turn for romance above most other boys. This is to be traced in the same manner to their excess of society with each other and defect of mingling with the world. Hence the peculiar avidity with which such books as *The Arabian Nights' Entertainments*, and others, of a still wilder cast, are, or at least were in my time, sought for by the boys. I remember when some half-dozen of them set off from school, without map, card, or compass, on a serious expedition to find out *Philip Quarl's Island*.

The Christ's Hospital boy's sense of right and wrong is peculiarly tender and apprehensive. It is even apt to run out into ceremonial observances, and to impose a yoke upon itself beyond the strict obligations of the moral law. Those who were contemporaries with me at that school thirty years ago will remember with what more than Judaic rigour the eating of the fat of certain boiled meats[1] was interdicted. A boy would have blushed, as at the exposure of some heinous immorality to have been detected eating that forbidden portion of his allowance of animal food, the whole of which, while he was in health, was little more than sufficient to allay his hunger. The same or even greater refinement was shown in the rejection of certain kinds of

[1] Under the denomination of *gags*.

B

sweet cake. What gave rise to these supererogatory penances, these self-denying ordinances, I could never learn,[1] they certainly argue no defect of the conscientious principle. A little excess in that article is not undesirable in youth, to make allowance for the inevitable waste which comes in maturer years. But in the less ambiguous line of duty, in those directions of the moral feelings which cannot be mistaken or depreciated, I will relate what took place in the year of 1785, when Mr Perry, the steward, died. I must be pardoned for taking my instances from my own times. Indeed the vividness of my recollections, while I am upon this subject, almost brings back those times; they are present to me still. But I believe that in the years which have elapsed since the period which I speak of, the character of the Christ's Hospital boy is very little changed. Their situation in point of many comforts is improved; but that which I ventured before to term the *public conscience* of the school, the pervading moral sense, of which every mind partakes, and to which so many individual minds contribute, remains, I believe, pretty much the same as when I left it. I have seen within this twelvemonth almost the change which has been produced upon a boy of eight or nine years of age upon being admitted into that school; how, from a pert young coxcomb, who thought that all knowledge was comprehended within his shallow brains, because a smattering of two or three languages and one or two sciences were stuffed into him by injudicious treatment at home, by a mixture with the wholesome society of so many schoolfellows, in less time than I have spoken of, he has sunk to his own level, and is contented to be carried on in the quiet orb of modest self-knowledge in which the common mass of that unpre-

[1] I am told that the late steward, Mr Hathaway, who evinced on many occasions a most praiseworthy anxiety to promote the comfort of the boys, had occasion for all his address and perseverance to eradicate the first of these unfortunate prejudices, in which he at length happily succeeded, and thereby restored to one-half of the animal nutrition of the school those honors which painful superstition and blind zeal had so long conspired to withhold from it.

sumptuous assemblage of boys seem to move; from being a
little unfeeling mortal, he has got to feel and reflect. Nor
would it be a difficult matter to show how, at a school like
this, where the boy is neither entirely separated from home
nor yet exclusively under its influence, the best feelings, the
filial, for instance, are brought to a maturity which they
could not have attained under a completely domestic
education; how the relation of parent is rendered less tender
by unremitted association, and the very awfulness of age is
best apprehended by some sojourning amidst the comparative levity of youth; how absence, not drawn out by
too great extension into alienation or forgetfulness, put an
edge upon the relish of occasional intercourse, and the boy
is made the better *child* by that which keeps the force of that
relation from ebbing felt as perpetually pressing on him;
how the substituted paternity, into the care of which he is
adopted, while in everything substantial it makes up for the
natural in the necessary omission of individual fondness
and partialities, directs the mind only the more strongly to
appreciate that natural and first tie, in which such weaknesses are the bond of strength, and the appetite which
craves after them betrays no perverse palate. But these
speculations rather belong to the question of the comparative
advantage of a public over a private education in general. I
must get back to my old favourite school; and to that which
took place when our old and good steward died.

And I will say, that when I think of the frequent instances
which I have met with in children of a hard-heartedness, a
callousness, and insensibility to the loss of relations, even
of those who have begot and nourished them, I cannot but
consider it as a proof of something in the peculiar conforma-
tion of that school, favourable to the expansion of the best
feelings of our nature, that, at the period which I am notic-
ing, out of five hundred boys there was not a dry eye to be
found among them, nor a heart that did not beat with
genuine emotion. Every impulse to play, until the funeral
day was past, seemed suspended throughout the school;
and the boys, lately so mirthful and sprightly, were seen
pacing their cloisters alone, or in sad groups standing about,

few of them without some token, such as their slender means could provide, a black riband or something, to denote respect and a sense of their loss. The time itself was a time of anarchy, a time in which all authority (out of school-hours) was abandoned. The ordinary restraints were for those days superseded, and the gates, which at other times kept us in, were left without watchers. Yet, with the exception of one or two graceless boys at most, who took advantage of that suspension of authority to *skulk out,* as it was called, the whole body of that great school kept rigorously within their bounds, by a voluntary self-imprisonment, and they who broke bounds, though they escaped punishment from the master, fell into a general disrepute among us, and, for that which at any other time would have been applauded and admired as a mark of spirit, were consigned to infamy and reprobation: so much *natural government* have gratitude and the principles of reverence and love, and so much did a respect to their dead friend prevail with these Christ's Hospital boys above any fear which his presence among them when living could ever produce. And if the impressions which were made on my mind so long ago are to be trusted, very richly did their steward deserve this tribute. It is a pleasure to me even now to call to mind his portly form, the regal awe which he always contrived to inspire, in spite of a tenderness and even weakness of nature that would have enfeebled the reins of discipline in any other master; a yearning of tenderness towards those under his protection, which could make five hundred boys at once feel towards him each as to their individual father. He had faults, with which we had nothing to do; but with all his faults, indeed, Mr Perry was a most extraordinary creature. Contemporary with him, and still living, though he has long since resigned his occupation, will it be impertinent to mention the name of our excellent upper grammar-master, the Rev. James Boyer? He was a disciplinarian, indeed, of a different stamp from him whom I have just described; but now the terrors of the rod, and of a temper a little too hasty to leave the more nervous of us quite at our ease to do justice to his merits in those days, are long since over, ungrateful were we if we should refuse our testimony to that unwearied assiduity with which he attended to the particular improvement of each of us. Had we been the offspring of the first gentry in the land, he could not have been instigated by the strongest views of recompense and regard to have made himself a greater slave to the most laborious of all occupations than he did for us sons of charity, from whom, or from our parents, he could expect nothing. He has had his reward in the satisfaction of having discharged his duty, in the pleasurable consciousness of having advanced the respectability of that institution to which, both man and boy, he was attached; in the honours to which so many of his pupils have successfully aspired at both our Universities; and in the staff with which the Governors of the Hospital at the close of his hard labours, with the highest expressions of the obligations the school lay under to him, unanimously voted to present him.

I have often considered it among the felicities of the constitution of this school, that the offices of steward and schoolmaster are kept distinct, the strict business of education alone devolving upon the latter, while the former has the charge of all things out of school, the control of the provisions, the regulation of the meals, of dress, of play, and the ordinary intercourse of the boys. By this division of management, a superior respectability must attach to the teacher while his office is unmixed with any of these lower concerns. A still greater advantage over the construction of common boarding-schools is to be found in the settled salaries of the masters, rendering them totally free of obligation to any individual pupil or his parents. This never fails to have its effect at schools where each boy can reckon up to a hair what profit the master derives from him, where he views him every day in the light of a caterer, a provider for the family, who is to get so much by him in each of his meals. Boys will see and consider these things; and how much must the sacred character of preceptor suffer in their minds by these degrading associations! The very bill which the pupil carries home with him at Christmas, eked out, perhaps, with elaborate though necessary minuteness, in-

structs him that his teachers have other ends than the mere
love to learning in the lessons which they give him; and
though they put into his hands the fine sayings of Seneca or
Epictetus, yet they themselves are none of those disinter-
ested pedagogues to teach philosophy *gratis*. The master,
too, is sensible that he is seen in this light; and how much
this must lessen that affectionate regard to the learners
which alone can sweeten the bitter labour of instruction,
and convert the whole business into unwelcome and un-
interesting task work, many preceptors that I have conversed with on the subject are ready, with a sad heart, to
acknowledge. From this inconvenience the settled salaries
of the masters of this school in great measure exempt them;
while the happy custom of choosing masters (indeed every
officer of the establishment) from those who have received
their education there, gives them an interest in advancing
the character of the school, and binds them to observe a
tenderness and a respect to the children, in which a stranger
feeling that independence which I have spoken of might
well be expected to fail.

In affectionate recollection of the place where he was
bred up, in hearty recognition of old schoolfellows met with
again after the lapse of years, or in foreign countries, the
Christ's Hospital boy yields to none; I might almost say he
goes beyond most other boys. The very compass and magnitude of the school, its thousand bearings, the space it takes
up in the imagination beyond the ordinary schools, im-
presses a remembrance, accompanied with an elevation of
mind, that attends him through life. It is too big, too
affecting an object, to pass away quickly from his mind.
The Christ's Hospital boy's friends at school are commonly
his intimates through life. For me, I do not know whether
a constitutional imbecility does not incline me too obstinate-
ly to cling to the remembrance of childhood; in an inverted
ratio to the usual sentiments of mankind, nothing that I
have been engaged in since seems of any value or importance, compared to the colours which imagination gave to
everything then. I belong to no *body corporate* such as I then
made a part of. And here, before I close, taking leave of

the general reader, and addressing myself solely to my old
schoolfellows, that were contemporaries with me from the
year 1782–9, let me have leave to remember some of those
circumstances of our school which they will not be unwilling to have brought back to their minds.

And first, let us remember, as first in importance in our
childish eyes, the young men (as they almost were) who,
under the denomination of *Grecians*, were waiting the expira-
tion of the period when they should be sent, at the charges
of the Hospital, to one or other of our Universities, but more
frequently to Cambridge. These youths, from their superior
acquirements, their superior age and stature, and the few-
ness of their numbers (for seldom above two or three at a
time were inaugurated into that high order), drew the eyes
of all, and especially of the younger boys, into a reverent
observance and admiration. How tall they used to seem to
us! how stately would they pace along the cloisters! while
the play of the lesser boys was absolutely suspended, or its
boisterousness at least allayed, at their presence! Not that
they ever beat or struck the boys – that would have been
to have demeaned themselves – the dignity of their persons
alone ensured them all respect. The task of blows, of
corporal chastisement, they left to the common monitors, or
heads of wards, who, it must be confessed, in our time had
rather too much license allowed them to oppress and misuse
their inferiors; and the interference of the Grecian, who
may be considered as the spiritual power, was not unfrequently called for to mitigate by its mediation, the heavy,
unrelenting arm of this temporal power, or monitor. In
fine, the Grecians were the solemn Muftis of the school.
Eras were computed from their time; it used to be said,
Such or such a thing was done when S — or T — was
Grecian.

As I ventured to call the Grecians the Muftis of the school,
the King's boys,[1] as their character then was, may well
pass for the Janissaries. They were the terror of all the
other boys; bred up under that hardy sailor, as well as

[1] The mathematical pupils, bred up to the sea, on the foundation of Charles the Second.

excellent mathematician, and co-navigator with Captain Cook, William Wales. All his systems were adapted to fit them for the rough element which they were destined to encounter. Frequent and severe punishments, which were expected to be borne with more than Spartan fortitude, came to be considered less as inflictions of disgrace than as trials of obstinate endurance. To make his boys hardy, and to give them early sailor habits, seemed to be his only aim; to this everything was subordinate. Moral obliquities, indeed, were sure of receiving their full recompense, for no occasion of laying on the lash was ever let slip; but the effects expected to be produced from it were something very different from contrition or mortification. There was in William Wales a perpetual fund of humour, a constant glee about him, which, heightened by an inveterate provincial-ism of North Country dialect, absolutely took away the sting from his severities. His punishments were a game at patience, in which the master was not always worst con-tented when he found himself at times overcome by his pupil. What success this discipline had, or how the effects of it operated upon the after lives of these King's boys, I cannot say: but I am sure that, for the time, they were absolute nuisances to the rest of the school. Hardy, brutal, and often wicked, they were the most graceless lump in the whole mass: older and bigger than the other boys (for, by the system of their education, they were kept longer at school by two or three years than any of the rest, except the Grecians), they were a constant terror to the younger part of the school, and some who may read this, I doubt not, will remember the consternation into which the juven-ile fry of us were thrown when the cry was raised in the cloisters that *the first order was coming* – for so they termed the first form or class of those boys. Still these sea-boys answered some good purposes in the school. They were the military class among the boys, foremost in athletic exercises, who extended the fame of the prowess of the school far and near; and the apprentices in the vicinage, and sometimes the butchers' boys in the neighbouring market, had sad occa-sion to attest their valour.

The time would fail me if I were to attempt to enumerate all those circumstances, some pleasant, some attended with some pain, which, seen through the mist of distance, come sweetly softened to the memory. But I must crave leave to remember our transcending superiority in those invigorating sports, leap-frog, and basting the bear; our delightful excursions in the summer holidays to the New River, near Newington, where, like otters, we would live the long day in the water, never caring for dressing ourselves when we had once stripped; our savoury meals afterwards, when we came home almost famished with staying out all day without our dinners; our visits at other times to the Tower, where by ancient privilege, we had free access to all the curiosities; our solemn processions through the city at Easter, with the Lord Mayor's largess of buns, wine, and a shilling, with the festive questions and civic pleasantries of the dispensing Aldermen, which were more to us than all the rest of the banquet; our stately suppings in public, where the well-lighted hall, and the confluence of well-dressed company who came to see us, made the whole look more like a concert or assembly than a scene of a plain bread-and-cheese collation; the annual orations upon St Matthew's Day, in which the senior scholar, before he had done, seldom failed to reckon up, among those who had done honour to our school by being educated in it, the names of those accomplished critics and Greek scholars, Joshua Barnes and Jeremiah Markland (I marvel they left out Camden while they were about it). Let me have leave to remember our hymns and anthems and well-toned organ; the doleful tune of the burial anthem, chanted in the solemn cloisters upon the seldom-occurring funeral of some schoolfellow; the festivities at Christmas, when the richest of us would club our stock to have a gaudy day, sitting round the fire, replenished to the height with logs, and the penniless, and he that could contribute nothing, partook in all the mirth, and in some of the substantialities of the feasting; the carol sung by night at that time of the year, which when a young boy, I have so often lain awake to hear from seven (the hour of going to bed) till ten, when it was sung by the older boys and monitors, and have listened to it, in their rude chanting, till I have been transported in fancy to the fields of Bethlehem, and the song which was sung at that season by the angels' voices to the shepherds.

Nor would I willingly forget any of those things which administered to our vanity. The hem-stitched bands and town-made shirts, which some of the most fashionable among us wore; the town-girdles, with buckles of silver or shining stone; the badges of the sea-boys; the coats, or superior shoe-strings of the monitors; the medals of the markers (those who were appointed to hear the Bible read in the wards on Sunday morning and evening), which bore on their obverse in silver, as certain parts of our garments carried in meaner metal, the countenance of our founder, that godly and royal child, King Edward the Sixth, the flower of the Tudor name – the young flower that was untimely cropped as it began to fill our land with its early odours – the boy-patron of boys – the serious and holy child who walked with Cranmer and Ridley – fit associate in those tender years for the bishops and future martyrs of our Church to receive, or (as occasion sometimes proved) to give instruction.

Gentleman's Magazine, June 1813

STRANGE FACE OF CALAMITY

Lamb left Christ's Hospital at the age of fifteen, and took a post in the office of Joseph Paice '*of Bread Street Hill ... the only pattern of consistent gallantry I have met with*'. Paice was also a director of the South Sea Company and on September 1st, 1791, Lamb entered the Examiners' Office at the South Sea House; his salary half a guinea a week.

He only served the South Sea Company for five months, but thirty years later when he was invited to contribute to the *London Magazine*, it was of those five months that he wrote his first Elia essay, *The South Sea House*: of the clerks who '*partook of the genius of the place*', of the throng of merchants, the beadles, doorkeepers, '*directors seated in form on solemn days (to proclaim a dead dividend)*'.

He complained that there was not much of the man of business in his nature, and that '*living accounts and accountants puzzled*' him, but he was to spend most of his life on an office stool. From the South Sea House he passed on to the service of the East India Company.

His love for good company developed in the years that followed. Many nights he spent '*drinking late, sitting late*' with Coleridge and Jem White. He was writing poetry and falling in love with Ann Simmons.

That Mary Lamb suffered from occasional bouts of serious illness is borne out by a poem that Coleridge sent to Lamb in December, 1794:

> In fancy (well I know)
> In business wandering far and local cares,
> Thou creepest round a dear-loved sister's bed
> With noiseless step, and watchest the faint look,
> Soothing each pang with fond solicitude,
> And tenderest tones medicinal of love ...

and on Wednesday, September 22nd, 1796, she developed signs of mania. Early next morning she lost her reason completely and, picking up a table knife, stabbed her mother to death.

The *Morning Chronicle* of September 26th has the story most accurately, though it makes no reference to the presence of Charles at the hideous scene:

'*On Friday afternoon the coroner and a respectable jury sat on the body of a lady in the neighbourhood of Holborn, who died in consequence of a wound from her daughter the preceding day. It appeared by the evidence adduced, that while the family were preparing for dinner, the young lady seized a case knife laying on the table, and in a menacing manner pursued a little girl, her apprentice, round the room; on the eager calls of her helpless infirm mother to forbear, she renounced her first object, and with loud shrieks approached her parent.*

'*The child by her cries quickly brought up the landlord of the house, but too late — the dreadful scene presented to him the mother lifeless, pierced to the heart, on a chair, her daughter yet wildly standing over her with the fatal knife, and the venerable old man, her father, weeping by her side, himself bleeding at the forehead from the effects of a severe blow he received from one of the forks she had been madly hurling about the room.*

'For a few days prior to this the family had observed some symptoms of insanity in her, which had so much increased on the Wednesday evening, that her brother early next morning went in quest of Dr Pitcairn — had that gentleman been met with, the fatal catastrophe had, in all probability, been prevented.

'It seems the young lady had been once before, in her earlier years, deranged, from the harassing fatigues of too much business. — As her carriage towards her mother was ever affectionate in the extreme, it is believed that to the increased attentiveness, which her parents' infirmities called for by day and night, is to be attributed the present insanity of this ill-fated young woman.

'It has been stated in some of the Morning Papers, that she has an insane brother also in confinement — this is without foundation.

'The jury of course brought in their Verdict, Lunacy.'

Lamb himself described the event in a letter to Coleridge five days later:

                    To S. T. Coleridge   September 27, 1796

My dearest friend,

White, or some of my friends, or the public papers, by this time may have informed you of the terrible calamities that have fallen on our family. I will only give you the outlines : — My poor dear, dearest sister, in a fit of insanity, has been the death of her own mother. I was at hand only time enough to snatch the knife out of her grasp. She is at present in a madhouse, from whence I fear she must be moved to an hospital. God has preserved to me my senses : I eat, and drink, and sleep, and have my judgement, I believe, very sound. My poor father was slightly wounded, and I am left to take care of him and my aunt. Mr Norris, of the Bluecoat School, has been very kind to us, and we have no other friend; but, thank God, I am very calm and composed, and able to do the best that remains to do. Write as religious a letter as possible, but no mention of what is gone and done with. With me 'the former things are passed away', and I have something more to do than to feel.

God Almighty have us all in his keeping!

                                        C. LAMB.

Mention nothing of poetry: I have destroyed every vestige

of past vanities of that kind. Do as you please, but if you publish, publish mine (I give free leave) without name or initial, and never send me a book, I charge you.

Your own judgement will convince you not to take any notice of this yet to your dear wife. You look after your family; I have my reason and strength left to take care of mine. I charge you, don't think of coming to see me. Write. I will not see you if you come. God Almighty love you and all of us!

The court, with considerable benignity, allowed Charles to undertake the guardianship of his sister. To this task he devoted the rest of his life and in return he had the love and solicitude of Mary's periods of sanity.

Only once did a double calamity force him to open despair:

To S. T. Coleridge   Monday, May 12th, 1800

My dear Coleridge,

I don't know why I write, except from the propensity misery has to tell her griefs. Hetty died on Friday night, about eleven o'clock, after eight days' illness; Mary, in consequence of fatigue and anxiety, is fallen ill again, and I was obliged to remove her yesterday. I am left alone in a house with nothing but Hetty's dead body to keep me company. Tomorrow I bury her, and then I shall be quite alone, with nothing but a cat to remind me that the house has been full of living beings like myself. My heart is quite sunk, and I don't know where to look for relief. Mary will get better again; but her constantly being liable to such relapses is dreadful, nor is it the least of our evils that her case and all our story is so well known around us. We are in a manner *marked*. Excuse my troubling you; but I have nobody by me to speak to me. I slept out last night, not being able to endure the change and the stillness. But I did not sleep well, and I must come back to my own bed. I am going to try and get a friend to come and be with me to-morrow. I am completely shipwrecked. My head is quite bad. I almost wish that Mary were dead. – God bless you! Love to Sara and Hartley.

C. LAMB.

PARAGRAPH SPINNER

Lamb's novel, *Rosamund Gray*, was published during 1798. At the time it received very poor notices, though later Shelley was to write of it: '*What a lovely thing is his* Rosamund Gray! *How much knowledge of the sweetest and deepest parts of our nature in it!*' Some of his poems had already been printed with the Coleridge collections of 1796 and 1797, and he had started work on his play *John Woodvil*.

He had among his friends some of the most progressive English writers, Coleridge, Wordsworth, Southey and Hazlitt, and he had made many useful contacts: the actor Kemble, for example, who tried to place *John Woodvil* at Drury Lane; but his contacts did not help him to earn much money. Mary was a considerable expense to him and his salary at the East India House probably not more than one hundred and thirty pounds a year. To solve his financial difficulties he turned, as writers will, to popular journalism.

His efforts were not altogether happy, either for Lamb or for his editors. His political lampoons, and particularly his attack on Sir James Mackintosh, were so vicious that they choked the life out of his first paper, the *Albion*. The epigram appeared in August 1801:

> Though thou'rt like Judas, an apostate black,
> In the resemblance one thing thou dost lack:
> When he had gotten his ill-purchased pelf,
> He went away, and wisely hanged himself:
> This thou may'st do at last; yet much I doubt,
> If thou hast any bowels to gush out!

In the same month Fenwick, the editor (Bigod of the *Two Races of Men*) was forced to stop the publication of his paper.

After the *Albion*, Lamb tried the *Morning Chronicle*, where, according to Southey '*more than two-thirds of his materials are superciliously rejected*'. Early in 1802 he wrote some paragraphs and some dramatic criticism for the *Morning Post* (Coleridge was also a contributor), and although he suffered once more from an unsympathetic editor, one essay, *The Londoner*, did come from his association with Daniel Stuart (see p. 148).

Disappointment at the refusal of the managers to accept *John*

Woodvil for production was added to his disgust with Stuart who rejected most of his paragraphs, particularly those '*that are personal, where my forte lies*'. Early in 1802 he published *John Woodvil*, at his own expense, and at the same time left the *Morning Post*. But, when in 1803, Stuart gave up the editorship of the *Morning Post*, Lamb became its chief jester.

In 1831 when he wrote the story of his journalistic efforts, Lamb was inaccurate both in dates and facts. It was thirty and not thirty-five years since his days as a newspaperman, and untrue that he had passed from the *Post* to the *Albion*, but the newspaper fashion of the first years of the nineteenth century is as accurately described in this essay as in any history of the Press. Even more clear is the certain memory of his own feeling of frustration as a hack-writer; frustration that was so irritating that Mary Lamb could write, when finally Charles lost his freelance income in 1804: '*What we dreaded as an evil has proved a great blessing, for we have both strangely recovered our health and spirit since this has happened.*'

Newspapers Thirty-five Years Ago

Dan Stuart once told us, that he did not remember that he ever deliberately walked into the Exhibition at Somerset House in his life. He might occasionally have escorted a party of ladies across the way that were going in, but he never went in of his own head. Yet the office of the *Morning Post* newspaper stood then just where it does now – we are carrying you back, reader, some thirty years or more – with its gilt-globe-topt front facing that emporium of our artists' grand Annual Exposure. We sometimes wish that we had observed the same abstinence with Daniel.

A word or two of D. S. He ever appeared to us one of the finest-tempered of editors. Perry, of the *Morning Chronicle*, was equally pleasant, with a dash, no slight one either, of the courtier. S. was frank, plain, and English all over. We have worked for both these gentlemen.

It is soothing to contemplate the head of the Ganges; to trace the first little bubblings of a mighty river,

With holy reverence to approach the rocks,
Whence glide the streams renowned in ancient song.

Fired with a perusal of the Abyssinian Pilgrim's explora-
tory ramblings after the cradle of the infant Nilus, we well
remember on one fine summer holyday (a 'whole day's
leave' we called it at Christ's Hospital) sallying forth at rise
of sun, not very well provisioned either for such an under-
taking, to trace the current of the New River – Middletonian
stream! – to its scaturient source, as we had read, in meadows by fair Amwell. Gallantly did we commence our solitary quest – for it was essential to the dignity of a 'Discovery'
that no eye of schoolboy, save our own, should beam on the
detection. By flowery spots, and verdant lanes skirting
Hornsey, Hope trained us on in many a baffling turn; endless, hopeless meanders, as it seemed; or as if the jealous
waters had *dodged* us, reluctant to have the humble spot of
their nativity revealed; till spent, and nigh famished, before
set of the same sun, we sate down somewhere by Bowes
Farm near Tottenham, with a tithe of our proposed labours
only yet accomplished; sorely convinced in spirit, that that
Brucian enterprise was as yet too arduous for our young
shoulders.

Not more refreshing to the thirsty curiosity of the traveller is the tracing of some mighty waters up to their shallow
fontlet, than it is to a pleased and candid reader to go back
to the inexperienced essays, the first callow flights in authorship, of some established name in literature; from the Gnat
which preluded to the *Æneid*, to the Duck which Samuel
Johnson trod 'on.

In those days, every Morning Paper, as an essential
retainer to its establishment, kept an author, who was bound
to furnish daily a quantum of witty paragraphs. Sixpence a
joke – and it was thought pretty high too – was Dan
Stuart's settled remuneration in these cases. The chat of the
day – scandal, but, above all, *dress* – furnished the material.
The length of no paragraph was to exceed seven lines.
Shorter they might be, but they must be poignant.

A fashion of *flesh*, or rather *pink*-coloured hose for the ladies,
luckily coming up at the juncture when we were on our
probation for the place of Chief Jester to S.'s Paper, established our reputation in that line. We were pronounced a

'capital hand'. O the conceits which we varied upon *red*
in all its prismatic differences! from the trite and obvious
flower of Cytherea, to the flaming costume of the lady that
has her sitting upon 'many waters'. Then there was the
collateral topic of ankles. What an occasion to a truly chaste
writer, like ourself, of touching that nice brink, and yet
never tumbling over it, of a seemingly ever approximating
something 'not quite proper'; while, like a skilful posture-
master, balancing betwixt decorums and their opposites, he
keeps the line, from which a hair's-breadth deviation is
destruction; hovering in the confines of light and darkness,
or where 'both seem either'; a hazy uncertain delicacy;
Autolycus-like in the Play, still putting off his expectant
auditory with 'Whoop, do me no harm, good man!' But
above all, that conceit arrided us most at that time, and
still tickles our midriff to remember, where, allusively to
the flight of Astræa – *ultima Cœlestûm terras reliquit* – we pronounced – in reference to the stockings still – that 'Modesty,
taking her final leave of mortals, her last Blush was visible
in her ascent to the Heavens by the tract of the glowing
instep'. This might be called the crowning conceit: and was
esteemed tolerable writing in those days.

But the fashion of jokes, with all other things, passes away;
as did the transient mode which had so favoured us. The
ankles of our fair friends in a few weeks began to reassume
their whiteness, and left us scarce a leg to stand upon. Other
female whims followed, but none, methought, so pregnant,
so invitatory of shrewd conceits, and more than single
meanings.

Somebody has said, that to swallow six cross-buns daily
consecutively for a fortnight, would surfeit the stoutest
digestion. But to have to furnish as many jokes daily, and
that not for a fortnight, but for a long twelvemonth, as we
were constrained to do, was a little harder exaction. 'Man
goeth forth to his work until the evening' – from a reason-
able hour in the morning, we presume it was meant. Now,
as our main occupation took us up from eight till five every
day in the city; and as our evening hours, at that time of
life, had generally to do with anything rather than business,

it follows, that the only time we could spare for this manu-
factory of jokes – our supplementary livelihood, that supplied us in every want beyond mere bread and cheese –
was exactly that part of the day which (as we have heard of
No Man's Land) may be fitly denominated No Man's
Time; that is, no time in which a man ought to be up, and
awake, in. To speak more plainly, it is that time of an hour,
or an hour and a half's duration, in which a man, whose
occasions call him up so preposterously, has to wait for his
breakfast.

O those head-aches at dawn of day, when at five, or half-
past five in summer, and not much later in the dark seasons,
we were compelled to rise, having been perhaps not above
four hours in bed – (for we were no go-to-beds with the
lamb, though we anticipated the lark oft-times in her rising
– we like a parting cup at midnight, as all young men did
before these effeminate times, and to have our friends about
us – we were not constellated under Aquarius that watery
sign, and therefore incapable of Bacchus, cold, washy,
bloodless – we were none of your Basilian watersponges,
nor had taken our degrees at Mount Ague – we were right
toping Capulets, jolly companions, we and they) – but to
have to get up, as we said before, curtailed of half our fair
sleep, fasting, with only a dim vista of refreshing bohea in
the distance – to be necessitated to rouse ourselves at the
detestable rap of an old hag of a domestic, who seemed to
take a diabolical pleasure in her announcement that it was
'time to rise'; and whose chappy knuckles we have often
yearned to amputate, and string them up at our chamber
door, to be a terror to all such unseasonable rest-breakers
in future —

'Facil' and sweet, as Virgil sings, had been the 'descend-
ing' of the over-night, balmy the first sinking of the heavy
head upon the pillow; but to get up, as he goes on to say,

– revocare gradus, superasque evadere ad auras –

and to get up, moreover, to make jokes with malice pre-
pended – there was the 'labour', there the 'work'.

No Egyptian taskmaster ever devised a slavery like to that,
our slavery. No fractious operants ever turned out for half
the tyranny which this necessity exercised upon us. Half a
dozen jests in a day (bating Sundays too), why, it seems
nothing! We make twice the number every day in our lives
as a matter of course, and claim no Sabbatical exemptions.
But then they come into our head. But when the head has
to go out to them — when the mountain must go to
Mahomet—

Reader, try it for once, only for a short twelvemonth.

It was not every week that a fashion of pink stockings
came up; but mostly, instead of it, some rugged untractable
subject; some topic impossible to be contorted into the
risible; some feature, upon which no smile could play; some
flint, from which no process of ingenuity could procure a
scintillation. There they lay; there your appointed tale of
brick-making was set before you, which you must finish,
with or without straw, as it happened. The craving dragon
— *the Public* — like him in Bel's Temple — must be fed, it
expected its daily rations; and Daniel, and ourselves, to do
us justice, did the best we could on this side bursting him.

While we were wringing out coy sprightliness for the *Post*,
and writhing under the toil of what is called 'easy writing',
Bob Allen, our *quondam* schoolfellow, was tapping his im-
practicable brains in a like service for the *Oracle*. Not that
Robert troubled himself much about wit. If his paragraphs
had a sprightly air about them, it was sufficient. He carried
this nonchalance so far at last, that a matter of intelligence,
and that no very important one, was not seldom palmed
upon his employers for a good jest; for example sake —
'*Walking yesterday morning casually down Snow Hill, who should
we meet but Mr Deputy Humphreys! we rejoice to add, that the
worthy Deputy appeared to enjoy a good state of health. We do not
remember ever to have seen him look better.*' This gentleman so
surprisingly met upon Snow Hill, from some peculiarities in
gait or gesture, was a constant butt for mirth to the small
paragraph-mongers of the day; and our friend thought that
he might have his fling at him with the rest. We met A.
in Holborn shortly after this extraordinary rencounter,

which he told with tears of satisfaction in his eyes, and chuckling at the anticipated effects of its announcement next day in the paper. We did not quite comprehend where the wit of it lay at the time; nor was it easy to be detected, when the thing came out advantaged by type and letterpress. He had better have met anything that morning than a Common Council Man. His services were shortly after dispensed with, on the plea that his paragraphs of late had been deficient in point. The one in question, it must be owned, had an air, in the opening especially, proper to awaken curiosity; and the sentiment, or moral, wears the aspect of humanity and good neighbourly feeling. But somehow the conclusion was not judged altogether to answer to the magnificent promise of the premises. We traced our friend's pen afterwards in the *True Briton*, the *Star*, the *Traveller*, – from all which he was successively dismissed, the Proprietors having 'no further occasion for his services.' Nothing was easier than to detect him. When wit failed, or topics ran low, there constantly appeared the following – '*It is not generally known that the three Blue Balls at the Pawnbrokers' shops are the ancient arms of Lombardy. The Lombards were the first money-brokers in Europe.*' Bob has done more to set the public right on this important point of blazonry, than the whole College of Heralds.

The appointment of a regular wit has long ceased to be a part of the economy of a Morning Paper. Editors find their own jokes, or do as well without them. Parson Este, and Topham, brought up the set custom of 'witty paragraphs' first in the *World*. Boaden was a reigning paragraphist in his day, and succeeded poor Allen in the *Oracle*. But, as we said, the fashion of jokes passes away; and it would be difficult to discover in the biographer of Mrs Siddons, any traces of that vivacity and fancy which charmed the whole town at the commencement of the present century. Even the prelusive delicacies of the present writer – the curt 'Astræan allusion' – would be thought pedantic and out of date, in these days.

From the office of the *Morning Post* (for we may as well exhaust our Newspaper Reminiscences at once) by change

of property in the paper, we were transferred, mortifying
exchange! to the office of the *Albion* Newspaper, late Rack-
strow's Museum, in Fleet-street. What a transition – from a
handsome apartment, from rosewood desks and silver ink-
stands, to an office – no office, but a *den* rather, but just
redeemed from the occupation of dead monsters, of which
it seemed redolent – from the centre of loyalty and fashion,
to a focus of vulgarity and sedition! Here in murky closet,
inadequate from its square contents to the receipt of the
two bodies of Editor and humble paragraph-maker, together at one time, sat in the discharge of his new editorial
functions (the 'Bigod' of Elia) the redoubted John Fenwick.

F., without a guinea in his pocket, and having left not
many in the pockets of his friends whom he might command,
had purchased (on tick, doubtless) the whole and sole
Editorship, Proprietorship, with all the rights and titles
(such as they were worth) of the *Albion* from one Lovell; of
whom we know nothing, save that he had stood in the pillory
for a libel on the Prince of Wales. With this hopeless concern – for it had been sinking ever since its commencement,
and could now reckon upon not more than a hundred subscribers – F. resolutely determined upon pulling down the
Government in the first instance, and making both our
fortunes by way of corollary. For seven weeks and more did
this infatuated democrat go about borrowing seven-shilling
pieces, and lesser coin, to meet the daily demands of the
Stamp Office, which allowed no credit to publications of
that side in politics. An outcast from politer bread, we
attached our small talents to the forlorn fortunes of our
friend. Our occupation now was to write treason.

Recollections of feelings – which were all that now remained from our first boyish heats kindled by the French
Revolution, when, if we were misled, we erred in the company of some who are accounted very good men now –
rather than any tendency at this time to Republican doctrines – assisted us in assuming a style of writing, while the
paper lasted, consonant in no very under tone to the right
earnest fanaticism of F. Our cue was now to insinuate,
rather than recommend, possible abdications. Blocks, axes,

Whitehall tribunals, were covered with flowers of so cunning a periphrasis – as Mr Bayes says, never naming the *thing* directly – that the keen eye of an Attorney-General was insufficient to detect the lurking snake among them. There were times, indeed, when we sighed for our more gentleman-like occupation under Stuart. But with change of masters it is ever change of service. Already one paragraph, and another, as we learned afterwards from a gentleman at the Treasury, had begun to be marked at that office, with a view of its being submitted at least to the attention of the proper Law Officers – when an unlucky, or rather lucky epigram from our pen, aimed at Sir J[ames] M[ackintosh] who was on the eve of departing for India to reap the fruits of his apostasy, as F. pronounced it (it is hardly worth particularizing), happening to offend the nice sense of Lord (or, as he then delighted to be called, Citizen) Stanhope, deprived F. at once of the last hopes of a guinea from the last patron that had stuck by us; and breaking up our establishment, left us to the safe, but somewhat mortifying, neglect of the Crown Lawyers. It was about this time, or a little earlier, that Dan Stuart made that curious confession to us, that he had 'never deliberately walked into an Exhibition at Somerset House in his life'.

By the Author of ELIA.

Englishman's Magazine, October 1831.

THE PHANTOM CLOUD OF ELIA

The end of his newspaper connections did not deter Lamb from literary effort.

Mr H., his rather too-clever farce, was accepted for Drury Lane in 1806, shown to a well-papered house for one night and then died; its author dancing in its funeral procession (see p. 214), and, incidentally, showing great fortitude, for the damning of *Mr H.* meant the failure of two years work, a year's hopes and the loss of a promised three hundred pounds.

In the same year Mary Lamb began *The Tales from Shakespeare*. That they were originally her project is evidenced by Charles's letter to Manning on May 10th, 1806, in which he wrote, '*she is doing for Godwin's bookseller twenty of Shakspear's plays, to be made into children's tales. Six are already done by her, to wit,* The Tempest, Winter's Tale, Midsummer Night, Much Ado, Two Gentlemen of Verona, *and* Cymbeline. The Merchant of Venice *is in forwardness. I have done* Othello *and* Macbeth, *and mean to do all the tragedies. I think it will be popular among the little people. Besides money. It is to bring in 60 guineas. Mary has done them capitally, I think you'd think*'.

In a letter to Wordsworth that accompanied presentation volumes of the *Tales*, Lamb admits his responsibility for 'Lear, Macbeth, Timon, Romeo, Hamlet, Othello, *for occasionally a tail piece or correction of grammar, for none of the cuts and all of the spelling*'.

The *Tales* published, Lamb began the *Adventures of Ulysses*, basing his story on Chapman's translation of *The Odyssey*, and this too found a publisher in 1807.

To *Ulysses* followed '*Specimens of English Dramatic Poets contemporary with Shakespear*'.

In the introduction to this work, '*the first to draw the public attention to the old English dramatists*', Lamb writes:

'The kind of extracts which I have sought after have been, not so much passages of wit and humour, though the old plays are rich in such, as scenes of passion, sometimes of the deepest quality, interesting situations, serious descriptions, that which is more nearly allied to poetry than to wit, and to tragic rather than to comic poetry. The plays which I have made choice of have been, with few exceptions, those which treat of human life and manners, rather than masques and Arcadian pastorals, with their train of abstractions, unimpassioned deities, passionate mortals, Claius and Medorus, and Amintas and Amarillis. My leading design has been to illustrate what may be called the moral sense of our ancestors: to show in what manner they felt when they placed themselves by the power of imagination in trying situations, in the conflicts of duty and passion, or the strife of contending duties, what sort of loves and enmities theirs were, how their griefs were tempered and their full-swollen joys abated: how much Shakespear shines in the great men his contemporaries, and how far in his divine mind and manners he surpassed them and all mankind.

'Another object which I had in making these selections was to bring together the most admired scenes in Fletcher and Massinger, in the estimation of the world the only dramatic poets of that age who are entitled to be considered after Shakespear, and to exhibit them in the same volume with the more impressive scenes of old Marlowe, Heywood, Webster, Ford, and others, to show what we have slighted, while beyond all proportion we have cried up one or two favourite names. ...

'The reader will not fail to observe the frequent instances of two or more persons joining in the composition of the same play (the noble practice of those times), that of most of the writers contained in these selections it may be strictly said they were contemporaries. The whole period, from the middle of Elizabeth's reign to the close of the reign of Charles I, comprises a space of little more than half a century, with which time nearly all that we have of excellence in serious dramatic composition was produced; if we except the *Samson Agonistes* of Milton.'

His intention was admirably executed and Lamb's reputation as a critic was assured.

But he was still a clerk at the East India office, his literary ambition still unfulfilled and his income still slender.

Mary, with the help of Charles, tried writing for children once again, but Charles could not be satisfied with work such as *Poetry for Children*. '*Sometimes I think of drama, but I have no head for playmaking, I can do the dialogue and that's all, I am quite aground for a plan, and I must do something for money. Not that I have immediate wants but I have prospective ones.*'

Still seeking to '*rattle his pocket at the foul fiend*' he wrote advertising copy for the principal London lottery, and then in 1810 stepped forth, an essayist at last, in Leigh Hunt's *Reflector*.

In the four numbers of the *Reflector* appeared two of his finest critical essays — those on Hogarth and on Shakespeare's tragedies (see p. 233) — *On the Inconveniences of Being Hanged* and the *Notes on Fuller. The Londoner* (see p. 148 and *On the Melancholy of Tailors*,

prepared for the *Reflector* had to find other markets, but the habit
of essay-writing was formed (it continued in 1813 with the first
version of *Confessions of a Drunkard*) and though eight years
elapsed before Elia was born, eight years in which Lamb wrote
political epigrams when he wrote at all, Elia was already
conceived.

In 1820, Baldwin and Cradock established the *London Magazine*
with the intent '*to catch, condense, and delineate the spirit of things
generally, and, above all of the present time*' and its first editor, John
Scott, had the genius to secure both Lamb and Hazlitt as col-
laborators in this task.

It was hoped that the *London* might subdue the predominant
and conservative influence of the Edinburgh journal *Blackwoods*.
John Scott himself fell victim to this struggle; killed in a duel of
purely literary origin.

For the four years that followed Scott's death the *London* was
owned by Keats' publishers, Taylor and Hessey, and edited by
John Taylor himself. Despite his failings as an editor, Taylor
did succeed in making of those years four of the most glorious in
the history of English magazine publishing.

Lamb, disguised in a transparent mask as Elia, was one of
his most regular contributors, and his consistent pre-eminence
is all the more noteworthy in that his rivals in the pages of the
London included Hazlitt, de Quincey, Hood, Hartley, Coleridge,
Cary, Clare, and even, with some posthumous poems, John
Keats.

When, in 1825, the *London* changed hands once more, Lamb
deserted, but for the *London* he had written most of his best-
known and best-loved work.

His reasons for the choice of the pseudonym Elia cannot be
ascertained with any certainty. Some assert that it was intended
as an anagram of '*a lie*', but he himself, in a letter that may have
been a typically Elian diversion, claimed that he had stolen the
name from another clerk who was also a writer.

Lamb wrote much of himself, and yet little of his work as an
essayist. But at the end of 1822, perhaps from a sense of disappointment that Elia had only made one hundred and seventy
pounds for Charles Lamb, and perhaps from temporary bore-
dom with his creation, he put him to death – prematurely, for the
resurrected Elia had three very vigorous years of life before
him. His epitaph he wrote in an essay that is both autobiography and literary analysis.

A Character of the Late Elia

By a Friend

This gentleman, who for some months past had been in a declining way, hath at length paid his final tribute to Nature. He just lived long enough (it was what he wished) to see his papers collected into a volume. The pages of the *London Magazine* will henceforth know him no more.

Exactly at twelve last night his queer spirit departed, and the bells of Saint Bride's rang him out with the old year. The mournful vibrations were caught in the dining-room of his friends, T[aylor] and H[essey], and the company, assembled there to welcome in another first of January, checked their carousals in mid-mirth and were silent. Janus wept. The gentle P[ratt], in a whisper, signified his intention of devoting an elegy; and Allan C[unningham], nobly forgetful of his countrymen's wrongs, vowed a memoir to his manes full and friendly as a 'Tale of Lyddalcross'.

To say truth, it is time he were gone. The humour of the thing, if there was ever much in it, was pretty well exhausted; and a two years and a half's existence has been a tolerable duration for a phantom.

I am now at liberty to confess that much which I have heard objected to my late friend's writings was well founded. Crude they are, I grant you, a sort of unlicked, incondite things, villainously pranked in an affected array of antique modes and phrases. They had not been *his* if they had been other than such, and better it is that a writer should be natural in a self-pleasing quaintness than to affect a naturalness (so called) that should be strange to him. Egotistical they have been pronounced by some who did not know that what he tells us as of himself was often true only (historically) of another, as in his third essay (to save many instances), where, under the *first person* (his favourite figure), he shadows forth the forlorn estate of a country boy placed at a London school, far from his friends and connections, in direct opposition to his own early history. If it be egotism to imply and twine with his own identity the griefs and affections of another, making himself many, or reducing many unto himself, then is the skilful novelist, who all along brings his hero or heroine speaking of themselves, the greatest egotist of all, who yet has never, therefore, been accused of that narrowness. And how shall the intenser dramatist escape being faulty, who doubtless, under cover of passion uttered by another, oftentimes gives blameless vent to his most inward feelings, and expresses his own story modestly?

My late friend was in many respects a singular character. Those who did not like him hated him, and some, who once liked him, afterwards became his bitterest haters. The truth is, he gave himself too little concern about what he uttered, and in whose presence. He observed neither time nor place, and would ever out with what came uppermost. With the severe religionist he would pass for a free-thinker, while the other faction set him down for a bigot, or persuaded themselves that he belied his sentiments. Few understood him, and I am not certain that at all times he quite understood himself. He too much affected that dangerous figure – irony. He sowed doubtful speeches and reaped plain, unequivocal hatred. He would interrupt the gravest discussion with some light jest, and yet, perhaps, not quite irrelevant in ears that could understand it. Your long and much talkers hated him. The informal habit of his mind, joined to an inveterate impediment of speech, forbade him to be an orator, and he seemed determined that no one else should play that part when he was present. He was *petit* and ordinary in his person and appearance. I have seen him sometimes in what is called good company, but where he has been a stranger, sit silent, and be suspected for an odd fellow, till, some unlucky occasion provoking it, he would stutter out some senseless pun (not altogether senseless, perhaps, if rightly taken), which has stamped his character for the evening. It was hit or miss with him, but, nine times out of ten, he contrived by his device to send away a whole company of his enemies. His conceptions rose kindlier than his utterance, and his happiest impromptus had the appearance of effort. He has been accused of trying to be witty, when in truth he was but struggling to give his poor thoughts articulation. He chose his companions for some individuality of character which they manifested. Hence not many persons of science, and few professed *literati*, were of his counsels. They were, for the most part, persons of an uncertain fortune, and as to such people commonly nothing is more obnoxious than a gentleman of settled (though moderate) income, he passed with most of them for a great miser. To my knowledge this was a mistake. His *intimados*, to confess a truth, were, in the world's eye, a ragged regiment. He found them floating on the surface of society, and the colour, or something else in the weed, pleased him. The burrs stuck to him, but they were good and loving burrs for all that. He never greatly cared for the society of what are called good people. If any of these were scandalized (and offences were sure to arise), he could not help it. When he had been remonstrated with for not making more concessions to the feelings of good people, he would retort by asking, what one point did these good people ever concede to him? He was temperate in his meals and diversions, but always kept a little on this side of abstemiousness. Only in the use of the Indian weed he might be thought a little excessive. He took it, he would say, as a solvent of speech. Marry! as the friendly vapour ascended, how his prattle would curl up sometimes with it! The ligaments which tongue-tied him were loosened, and the stammerer proceeded a statist!

I do not know whether I ought to bemoan or rejoice that my old friend is departed. His jests were beginning to grow obsolete and his stories to be found out. He felt the approach of age, and, while he pretended to cling to life, you saw how slender were the ties left to bind him. Discoursing with him latterly on this subject, he expressed himself with a pettishness which I thought unworthy of him. In our walks about his suburban retreat (as he called it) at Shacklewell, some children belonging to a school of industry had met us, and bowed and courtesied, as he thought, in an especial manner to *him*. 'They take me for a visiting governor,' he muttered earnestly. He had a horror, which he carried to a foible, of looking like anything important and parochial. He thought that he approached nearer to that stamp daily. He had a general aversion from being treated like a grave or respectable character, and kept a wary eye upon the advances of age that should so entitle him. He herded always, while it was possible, with people younger than himself. He did not conform to the march of time, but was dragged along in the procession. His manners lagged behind his years. He was too much of the boy-man. The *toga virilis* never sat gracefully on his shoulders. The impressions of infancy had burnt into him, and he resented the impertinence of manhood. These were weaknesses; but, such as they were, they are a key to explicate some of his writings.

He left little property behind him. Of course, the little that is left (chiefly in India bonds) devolves upon his cousin Bridget. A few critical dissertations were found in his *escritoire*, which have been handed over to the editor of this magazine, in which it is to be hoped they will shortly appear, retaining his accustomed signature.

He has himself not obscurely hinted that his employment lay in a public office. The gentlemen in the export department of the East India House will forgive me if I acknowledge the readiness with which they assisted me in the retrieval of his few manuscripts. They pointed out in the most obliging manner the desk at which he had been planted for forty years, showed me ponderous tomes of figures, in his own remarkably neat hand, which, more properly than his few printed tracts, might be called his 'Works'. They seemed affectionate to his memory, and universally commended his expertness in book-keeping. It seemed he was the inventor of some ledger which should combine the precision and certainty of the Italian double entry (I think they called it) with the brevity and facility of some newer German system; but I am not able to appreciate the worth of the discovery. I have often heard him express a warm regard for his associates in office, and how fortunate he considered himself in having his lot thrown in amongst them. There is more sense, more discourse, more shrewdness, and even talent, among these clerks (he would say), than in twice the number of authors by profession that I have conversed with. He would brighten up sometimes

upon the 'old days of the India House', when he consorted
with Woodroffe, and Wissett, and Peter Corbet (a descendant and worthy representative, bating the point of sanctity,
of old facetious Bishop Corbet) ; and Hoole, who translated
Tasso ; and Bartlemy Brown, whose father (God assoil him
therfore!) modernized Walton ; and sly, warm-hearted old
Jack Cole (King Cole they called him in those days), and
Campe and Fombelle, and a world of choice spirits, more
than I can remember to name, who associated in those days
with Jack Burrell, (the *bon vivant* of the South Sea House),
and little Eyton (said to be a *facsimile* of Pope – he was a
miniature of a gentleman), that was cashier under him,
and Dan Voight of the Custom House, that left the famous
library.

Well, Elia is gone, for aught I know, to be reunited with
them, and these poor traces of his pen are all we have to
show for it. How little survives of the wordiest authors! Of
all they said or did in their lifetime, a few glittering words
only! His essays found some favourers as they appeared
separately. They shuffled their way in the crowd well
enough singly : how they will *read* now they are brought
together, is a question for the publishers, who have thus
ventured to draw out into one piece his 'weaved-up follies'.

PHIL-ELIA.

London Magazine, January, 1823. Reprinted, with some considerable omissions, in the collected *Last Essays of Elia*, 1833.

BY DUTY CHAINED

The India Office in Whitehall has a collection of portraits of the
soldiers, statesmen and administrators who created the Indian
Empire. In this collection hangs one picture of a mere office
worker who never achieved the pretension of an office to himself :
Charles Lamb, Clerk in the India House, 1792–1825.

Through all of his most active years as a writer, Lamb served
in the Accountants Department of the East India Company.

Despite his frequent complaint of overwork, the East India

Company seems to have been a lenient taskmaster, and in the intervals of entering up accounts and drafting official letters, Lamb kept up his own correspondence (mostly on East India House notepaper), talked to his colleagues and received visitors.

Not even in his commercial life could Lamb resign himself to discipline, and at least one of his retorts to an office superior merits a place in his work as, perhaps, the most outrageous example of impertinence in the history of business relations. Lamb, rebuked by one of his chiefs for unpunctuality with the comment '*I notice, Mr Lamb, that you come very late every morning,*' replied, unabashed, '*Yes, but see how early I go.*'

Nevertheless he was regarded with affection and pride by his colleagues and his superiors, and his efficiency in such work as he chose to do is borne out both by the fact that his salary rose from forty pounds a year after his three unpaid years as a probationer to seven hundred and thirty in 1824.

His love of companionship compensated for some of the dullness of his office routine, and it was this companionship that he missed most in his retirement, but for many years before his retirement became a fact he made of it the gateway to happiness.

In 1825 he offered his resignation, and when, after weeks of delay, it was accepted on March 29th, he scribbled a note to Crabb Robinson that is the shortest in all his correspondence – and yet full of feeling:

'I have left the d — d India House for Ever! Give me great joy.'

Work

Who first invented work, and bound the free
And Holiday-rejoicing spirit down
To the ever-haunting importunity
Of business in the green fields, and the town –
To plough, loom, anvil, spade – and (oh most sad!)
To that dry drudgery at the desk's dead wood?
Who but the Being unblest, alien from good,
Sabbathless Satan! he who his unglad
Task ever plies 'mid rotatory burnings,
That round and round incalculably reel –
For wrath Divine hath made him like a wheel –

In that red realm from which are no returnings:
Where toiling and turmoiling ever and aye
He, and his thoughts, keep pensive working-day.

The Examiner, June 1819.

To William Wordsworth

April 7th, 1815.

Dear Wordsworth, – You have made me very proud with
your successive book presents. I have been carefully through
the two volumes, to see that nothing was omitted which
used to be there. I think I miss nothing but a character in
the antithetic manner, which I do not know why you left
out, – the moral to the boys building the giant, the omission
whereof leaves it, in my mind, less complete – and one
admirable line gone (or something come instead of it),
'the stone-chat, and the glancing sand-piper', which was a
line quite alive. I demand these at your hand. I am glad
that you have not sacrificed a verse to those scoundrels. I
would not have had you offer up the poorest rag that lingered upon the stript shoulders of little Alice Fell, to have
atones all their malice; I would not have given 'em a red
cloak to save their souls. I am afraid lest that substitution of
a shell (a flat falsification of the history) for the household
implement, as it stood at first, was a kind of tub thrown out
to the beast, or rather thrown out for him. The tub was a
good honest tub in its place, and nothing could fairly be
said against it. You say you made the alteration for the
'friendly reader', but the 'malicious' will take it to himself.
Damn 'em, if you give 'em an inch, &c. The Preface is noble,
and such as you should write. I wish I could set my name to
it, *Imprimatur*, – but you have set it there yourself, and I
thank you. I would rather be a door-keeper in your margin,
than have their proudest text swelling with my eulogies.
The poems in the volumes which are new to me are so much
in the old tone that I hardly received them as novelties. Of
those of which I had no previous knowledge, the 'Four
Yew Trees', and the mysterious company which you have

assembled there, most struck me – 'Death the Skeleton and
Time the Shadow'. It is a sight not for every youthful poet
to dream of, it is one of the last results he must have gone
thinking on for years for. 'Laodamia' is a very original
poem; I mean original with reference to your own manner.
You have nothing like it. I should have seen it in a strange
place, and greatly admired it, but not suspected its deriva-
tion.

Let me in this place, for I have writ you several letters
naming it, mention that my brother, who is a picture-col-
lector, has picked up an undoubtable picture of Milton.
He gave a few shillings for it, and could get no history with
it, but that some old lady had had it for a great many
years. Its age is ascertainable from the state of the canvas,
and you need only see it to be sure that it is the original of
the heads in the Tonson editions, with which we are all so
familiar. Since I saw you I have had a treat in the reading
way, which comes not every day, the Latin Poems of V.
Bourne, which were quite new to me. What a heart that
man had! all laid out upon town schemes, a proper counter-
poise to *some people*'s rural extravaganzas. Why I mention
him is, that your 'Power of Music' reminded me of his
poem of 'The Ballad Singer in the Seven Dials'. Do you
remember his epigram on the old woman who taught Newton the A B C? which, after all, he says, he hesitates not to
call Newton's 'Principia'. I was lately fatiguing myself
with going through a volume of fine words by Lord Thur-
low, excellent words, and if the heart could live by words
alone, it could desire no better regales; but what an aching
vacuum of matter! I don't stick at the madness of it, for
that is only a consequence of shutting his eyes and thinking
he is in the age of the old Elizabeth poets. From thence I
turned to Bourne. What a sweet, unpretending, pretty-
mannered, *matter-ful* creature! sucking from every flower,
making a flower of every thing, his diction all Latin, and
his thoughts all English. Bless him! Latin wasn't good
enough for him. Why wasn't he content with the language
which Bay and Prior wrote in?

I am almost sorry that you printed extracts from those

c

first poems,[1] or that you did not print them at length. They
do not read to me as they do altogether. Besides, they have
diminished the value of the original, which I possess as a
curiosity. I have hitherto kept them distinct in my mind as
referring to a particular period of your life. All the rest of
your poems are so much of a piece, they might have been
written in the same week, these decidedly speak of an earlier
period. They tell more of what you had been reading. We
were glad to see the poems 'by a female friend'.[2] The one
of the Wind is masterly, but not new to us. Being only three,
perhaps you might have clapt a D. at the corner, and let
it have past as a printer's mark to the uninitiated, as a
delightful hint to the better instructed. As it is, expect a
formal criticism on the poems of your female friend, and
she must expect it. I should have written before, but I am
cruelly engaged, and like to be. On Friday I was at office
from ten in the morning (two hours dinner except) to
eleven at night; last night till nine. My business and office
business in general have increased so; I don't mean I am.
there every night, but I must expect a great deal of it. I
never leave till four, and do not keep a holiday now once in
ten times, where I used to keep all red-letter days, and some
five days besides, which I used to dub Nature's holidays. I
have had my day. I had formerly little to do. So of the little
that is left of life, I may reckon two-thirds as dead, for time
that a man may call his own is his life; and hard work and
thinking about it taints even the leisure hours, – stains
Sunday with work-day contemplation. This is Sunday:
and the headache I have is part late hours at work the two
preceding nights, and part later hours over a consoling
pipe afterwards. But I find stupid acquiescence coming
over me. I bend to the yoke, and it is almost with me and
my household as with the man and his consort –

'To them each evening had its glittering star,
And every Sabbath Day its golden sun' –

[1 The 'Evening Walk', and 'Descriptive Sketches among the
Alps' – Wordsworth's earliest poems.]

[2 Dorothy Wordsworth.]

to such straits am I driven for the life of life, Time! O that
from that superfluity of holiday leisure my youth wasted,
'Age might but take some hours youth wanted not!' N.B.
– I have left off spirituous liquors for four or more months,
with a moral certainty of its lasting. Farewell, dear
Wordsworth!

O happy Paris, seat of idleness and pleasure! from some
returned English I hear that not such a thing as a counting-
house is to be seen in her streets, – scarce a desk. Earth-
quakes swallow up this mercantile city and its 'gripple
merchants', as Drayton hath it – 'born to be the curse of
this brave isle!' I invoke this, not on account of any
parsimonious habits the mercantile interest may have, but,
to confess truth, because I am not fit for office.

Farewell, in haste, from a head that is too ill to methodize,
a stomach too weak to digest, and all out of tune. Better
harmonies await you!

C. LAMB.

Excuse this maddish letter: I am too tired to write *in
formâ*.

To William Wordsworth

Colebrook Cottage,
6 April, 1825.

Dear Wordsworth, I have been several times meditating a
letter to you concerning the good thing which has befallen
me, but the thought of poor Monkhouse came across me.
He was one that I had exulted in the prospect of congratu-
lating me. He and you were to have been the first participa-
tors, for indeed it has been ten weeks since the first motion
of it.

Here I am then after 33 years slavery, sitting in my own
room at 11 o'Clock this finest of all April mornings a freed
man, with £441 a year for the remainder of my life, live
I as long as John Dennis, who outlived his annuity and
starved at 90. £441, i.e. £450, with a deduction of £9 for

a provision secured to my sister, she being survivor, the
Pension guaranteed by Act Georgii Tertii, &c.

I came home for ever on Tuesday in last week. The in-
comprehensibleness of my condition overwhelm'd me. It
was like passing from life into Eternity. Every year to be as
long as three, i.e. to have three times as much real time,
time that is my own, in it! I wandered about thinking I was
happy, but feeling I was not. But that tumultuousness is
passing off, and I begin to understand the nature of the gift.
Holydays, even the annual month, were always uneasy
joys: their conscious fugitiveness – the craving after making
the most of them. Now, when all is holyday, there are no
holydays. I can sit at home in rain or shine without a restless
impulse for walkings. I am daily steadying, and shall soon
find it as natural to me to be my own master, as it has been
irksome to have had a master. Mary wakes every morning
with an obscure feeling that some good has happened to us.

Leigh Hunt and Montgomery after their releasements
describe the shock of their emancipation much as I feel
mine. But it hurt their frames. I eat, drink, and sleep sound
as ever. I lay no anxious schemes for going hither and thither, but take things as they occur. Yesterday I excursioned
20 miles, to day I write a few letters. Pleasuring was for
fugitive play days, mine are fugitive only in the sense that
life is fugitive. Freedom and life co-existent.

At the foot of such a call upon you for gratulation, I am
ashamed to advert to that melancholy event. Monkhouse
was a character I learned to love slowly, but it grew upon
me, yearly, monthly, daily. What a chasm has it made in
our pleasant parties! His noble friendly face was always
coming before me, till this hurrying event in my life came,
and for the time has absorpt all interests. In fact it has shaken
me a little. My old desk companions with whom I have
had such merry hours seem to reproach me for removing
my lot from among them. They were pleasant creatures, but
to the anxieties of business, and a weight of possible worse
ever impending, I was not equal. Tuthill and Gilman gave
me my certificates. I laughed at the friendly lie implied in
them, but my sister shook her head and said it was all true.

Indeed this last winter I was jaded out, winters were always worse than other parts of the year, because the spirits are worse, and I had no daylight. In summer I had daylight evenings. The relief was hinted to me from a superior power, when I poor slave had not a hope but that I must wait another 7 years with Jacob – and lo! the Rachel which I coveted is bro^t. to me –

Have you read the noble dedication of Irving's 'Missionary Orations' to S. T. C. Who shall call this man a Quack hereafter? What the Kirk will think of it neither I nor Irving care. When somebody suggested to him that it would not be likely to do him good, videlicet among his own people, 'That is a reason for doing it' was his noble answer.

That Irving thinks he has profited mainly by S. T. C., I have no doubt. The very style of the Ded. shows it.

Communicate my news to Southey, and beg his pardon for my being so long acknowledging his kind present of the 'Church', which circumstances I do not wish to explain, but having no reference to himself, prevented at the time. Assure him of my deep respect and friendliest feelings.

Divide the same, or rather each take the whole to you, I mean you and all yours. To Miss Hutchinson I must write separate. What's her address? I want to know about Mrs M[onkhouse].

Farewell! and end at last, long selfish Letter!

C. LAMB.

The Superannuated Man

Sera tamen respexit
Libertas.   VIRGIL.
A Clerk I was in London gay. – O'KEEFE.[1]

If peradventure, Reader, it has been thy lot to waste the golden years of thy life – thy shining youth – in the irksome

[1 This quotation is not, in fact, from John O'Keefe but from *Inkle and Yarico* by another late Eighteenth Century farce-writer – George Colman.]

confinement of an office; to have thy prison days prolonged
through middle age down to decrepitude and silver hairs,
without hope of release or respite; to have lived to forget
that there are such things as holidays, or to remember
them but as the prerogatives of childhood; then, and then
only, will you be able to appreciate my deliverance.

It is now six-and-thirty years since I took my seat at the
desk in Mincing Lane. Melancholy was the transition at
fourteen from the abundant playtime, and the frequently-
intervening vacations of schooldays, to the eight, nine, and
sometimes ten hours' a day attendance at the counting-
house. But time partially reconciles us to anything. I
gradually became content – doggedly contented, as wild
animals in cages.

It is true I had my Sundays to myself; but Sundays, admirable as the institution of them is for purposes of worship,
are for that very reason the very worst adapted for days of
unbending and recreation. In particular, there is a gloom
for me attendant upon a city Sunday, a weight in the air.
I miss the cheerful cries of London, the music, and the ballad-
singers – the buzz and stirring murmur of the streets. Those
eternal bells depress me. The closed shops repel me.
Prints, pictures, all the glittering and endless succession of
knacks and gewgaws, and ostentatiously displayed wares of
tradesmen, which make a week-day saunter through the
less busy parts of the metropolis so delightful – are shut out.
No book-stalls deliciously to idle over – no busy faces to
re-create the idle man who contemplates them ever passing
by – the very face of business a charm by contrast to his
temporary relaxation from it. Nothing to be seen but unhappy countenances – or half-happy at best – of emancipated 'prentices and little tradesfolks, with here and there
a servant-maid that has got leave to go out, who, slaving all
the week, with the habit has lost almost the capacity of
enjoying a free hour; and livelily expressing the hollowness
of a day's pleasuring. The very strollers in the fields on that
day look anything but comfortable.

But besides Sundays, I had a day at Easter, and a day at
Christmas, with a full week in the summer to go and air

myself in my native fields of Hertfordshire. This last was a
great indulgence; and the prospect of its recurrence, I
believe, alone kept me up through the year, and made my
durance tolerable. But when the week came round, did the
glittering phantom of the distance keep touch with me, or
rather was it not a series of seven uneasy days, spent in restless pursuit of pleasure, and a wearisome anxiety to find
out how to make the most of them? Where was the quiet,
where the promised rest? Before I had a taste of it, it was
vanished. I was at the desk again, counting upon the fifty-
one tedious weeks that must intervene before such another
snatch would come. Still the prospect of its coming threw
something of an illumination upon the darker side of my
captivity. Without it, as I have said, I could scarcely have
sustained my thraldom.

Independently of the rigours of attendance, I have ever
been haunted with a sense (perhaps a mere caprice) of incapacity for business. This, during my latter years, had increased to such a degree, that it was visible in all the lines
of my countenance. My health and my good spirits flagged.
I had perpetually a dread of some crisis, to which I should
be found unequal. Besides my daylight servitude, I served
over again all night in my sleep, and would awake with
terrors of imaginary false entries, errors in my accounts, and
the like. I was fifty years of age, and no prospect of emancipation presented itself. I had grown to my desk, as it were;
and the wood had entered into my soul.

My fellows in the office would sometimes rally me upon
the trouble legible in my countenance; but I did not know
that it had raised the suspicions of any of my employers,
when, on the fifth of last month, a day ever to be remembered by me, L —, the junior partner in the firm, calling
me on one side, directly taxed me with my bad looks, and
frankly inquired the cause of them. So taxed, I honestly
made confession of my infirmity, and added that I was
afraid I should eventually be obliged to resign his service.
He spoke some words of course to hearten me, and there
the matter rested. A whole week I remained labouring
under the impression that I had acted imprudently in my

disclosure; that I had foolishly given a handle against myself, and had been anticipating my own dismissal. A week
passed in this manner – the most anxious one, I verily believe, in my whole life – when on the evening of the 12th of
April, just as I was about quitting my desk to go home (it
might be about eight o'clock), I received an awful sum-
mons to attend the presence of the whole assembled firm
in the formidable back parlour. I thought now my time is
surely come, I have done for myself, I am going to be told
that they have no longer occasion for me. L—, I could see,
smiled at the terror I was in, which was a little relief to me,
– when to my utter astonishment B—, the eldest partner,
began a formal harangue to me on the length of my services,
my very meritorious conduct during the whole of the time
(the deuce, thought I, how did he find out that? I protest
I never had the confidence to think as much). He went on
to descant on the expediency of retiring at a certain time of
life (how my heart panted!), and asking me a few questions
as to the amount of my own property, of which I have a
little, ended with a proposal, to which his three partners
nodded a grave assent, that I should accept from the house,
which I had served so well, a pension for life to the amount
of two-thirds of my accustomed salary – a magnificent offer!
I do not know what I answered between surprise and gratitude, but it was understood that I accepted their proposal,
and I was told that I was free from that hour to leave their
service. I stammered out a bow, and at just ten minutes
after eight I went home – for ever. This noble benefit –
gratitude forbids me to conceal their names – I owe to the
kindness of the most munificent firm in the world – the
house of Boldero, Merryweather, Bosanquet, and Lacy.[1]

Esto perpetua!

For the first day or two I felt stunned – overwhelmed. I
could only apprehend my felicity; I was too confused to
taste it sincerely. I wandered about, thinking I was happy,

[1 A fictitious firm. Elsewhere, in *A Chapter on Ears*, Lamb
asserts, without justification, that Boldero was Leigh Hunt's
real name.]

and knowing that I was not. I was in the condition of a
prisoner in the old Bastile suddenly let loose after a forty
years' confinement. I could scarce trust myself with myself.
It was like passing out of Time into Eternity – for it is a
sort of Eternity for a man to have all his Time to himself.
It seemed to me that I had more time on my hands than I
could ever manage. From a poor man, poor in Time, I
was suddenly lifted up into a vast revenue; I could see no
end of my possessions; I wanted some steward, or judicious
bailiff, to manage my estates in Time for me. And here let
me caution persons grown old in active business, not lightly,
nor without weighing their own resources, to forego their
customary employment all at once, for there may be danger
in it. I feel it by myself, but I know that my resources are
sufficient; and now that those first giddy raptures have
subsided, I have a quiet home-feeling of the blessedness of
my condition. I am in no hurry. Having all holidays, I am
as though I had none. If Time hung heavy upon me, I could
walk it away; but I do *not* walk all day long, as I used to do
in those old transient holidays, thirty miles a day, to make
the most of them. If Time were troublesome, I could read it
away; but I do *not* read in that violent measure, with which,
having no Time my own but candlelight Time, I used to
weary out my head and eyesight in bygone winters. I walk,
read, or scribble (as now) just when the fit seizes me. I no
longer hunt after pleasure; I let it come to me. I am like
the man

      ————that's born, and has his years come to him,
  In some green desert.

'Years!' you will say; 'what is this superannuated simple-
ton calculating upon? He has already told us he is past
fifty.'

I have indeed lived nominally fifty years, but deduct out
of them the hours which I have lived to other people, and
not to myself, and you will find me still a young fellow. For
that is the only true Time, which a man can properly call
his own – that which he has all to himself; the rest, though

in some sense he may be said to live it, is other people's Time, not his. The remnant of my poor days, long or short, is at least multiplied for me threefold. My ten next years, if I stretch so far, will be as long as any preceding thirty. 'Tis a fair rule-of-three sum.

Among the strange fantasies which beset me at the commencement of my freedom, and of which all traces are not yet gone, one was, that a vast tract of time had intervened since I quitted the Counting House. I could not conceive of it as an affair of yesterday. The partners, and the clerks with whom I had for so many years, and for so many hours in each day of the year, been closely associated — being suddenly removed from them — they seemed as dead to me. There is a fine passage, which may serve to illustrate this fancy, in a Tragedy by Sir Robert Howard, speaking of a friend's death : —

> ——'Twas but just now he went away;
> I have not since had time to shed a tear;
> And yet the distance does the same appear
> As if he had been a thousand years from me.
> Time takes no measure in Eternity.

To dissipate this awkward feeling, I have been fain to go among them once or twice since; to visit my old desk-fellows — my co-brethren of the quill — that I had left below in the state militant. Not all the kindness with which they received me could quite restore to me that pleasant familiarity, which I had heretofore enjoyed among them. We cracked some of our old jokes, but methought they went off but faintly. My old desk; the peg where I hung my hat, were appropriated to another. I knew it must be, but I could not take it kindly. D—l take me, if I did not feel some remorse — beast, if I had not — at quitting my old compeers, the faithful partners of my toils for six-and-thirty years, that soothed for me with their jokes and conundrums the ruggedness of my professional road. Had it been so rugged then, after all? or was I a coward simply? Well, it is too late to repent; and I also know that these suggestions are a

common fallacy of the mind on such occasions. But my
heart smote me. I had violently broken the bands betwixt
us. It was at least not courteous. I shall be some time before
I get quite reconciled to the separation. Farewell, old
cronies, yet not for long, for again and again I will come
among ye, if I shall have your leave. Farewell, Ch[ambers],
dry, sarcastic, and friendly! Do[dwell], mild, slow to move,
and gentlemanly! Pl[umley], officious to do, and to volun-
teer, good services! – and thou, thou dreary pile, fit mansion
for a Gresham or a Whittington of old, stately house of
Merchants; with thy labyrinthine passages, and light-
excluding, pent-up offices, where candles for one-half the
year supplied the place of the sun's light; unhealthy contributor to my weal, stern fosterer of my living, farewell!
In thee remain, and not in the obscure collection of some
wandering bookseller, my 'works'! There let them rest, as
I do from my labours, piled on thy massy shelves, more
MSS. in folio than ever Aquinas left, and full as useful! My
mantle I bequeath among ye.

A fortnight has passed since the date of my first communication. At that period I was approaching to tranquillity,
but had not reached it. I boasted of a calm indeed, but it
was comparative only. Something of the first flutter was
left; an unsettling sense of novelty; the dazzle to weak eyes
of unaccustomed light. I missed my old chains, forsooth, as
if they had been some necessary part of my apparel. I was
a poor Carthusian, from strict cellular discipline suddenly
by some revolution returned upon the world. I am now
as if I had never been other than my own master. It is
natural for me to go where I please, to do what I please. I
find myself at 11 o'clock in the day in Bond Street, and it
seems to me that I have been sauntering there at that very
hour for years past. I digress into Soho, to explore a book-
stall. Methinks I have been thirty years a collector. There
is nothing strange nor new in it. I find myself before a fine
picture in the morning. Was it ever otherwise? What is
become of Fish Street Hill? Where is Fenchurch Street?
Stones of old Mincing Lane, which I have worn with my
daily pilgrimage for six-and-thirty years, to the footsteps of

what toil-worn clerk are your everlasting flints now vocal?
I indent the gayer flags of Pall Mall. It is 'Change time, and
I am strangely among the Elgin marbles. It was no hyper-
bole when I ventured to compare the change in my condition to passing into another world. Time stands still in a
manner to me. I have lost all distinction of season. I do not
know the day of the week or of the month. Each day used
to be individually felt by me in its reference to the foreign
post days; in its distance from, or propinquity to, the next
Sunday. I had my Wednesday feelings, my Saturday nights'
sensations. The genius of each day was upon me distinctly
during the whole of it, affecting my appetite, spirits, etc.
The phantom of the next day, with the dreary five to follow,
sate as a load upon my poor Sabbath recreations. What
charm has washed that Ethiop white? What is gone of
Black Monday? All days are the same. Sunday itself – that
unfortunate failure of a holiday, as it too often proved, what
with my sense of its fugitiveness, and over-care to get the
greatest quantity of pleasure out of it – is melted down into
a week-day. I can spare to go to church now, without
grudging the huge cantle which it used to seem to cut out
of the holiday. I have time for everything. I can visit a sick
friend. I can interrupt the man of much occupation when
he is busiest. I can insult over him with an invitation to take
a day's pleasure with me to Windsor this fine May-morning.
It is Lucretian pleasure to behold the poor drudges, whom
I have left behind in the world, carking and caring; like
horses in a mill, drudging on in the same eternal round –
and what is it all for? A man can never have too much
Time to himself, nor too little to do. Had I a little son, I
would christen him 'Nothing-to-do'; he should do nothing.
Man, I verily believe, is out of his element as long as he is
operative. I am altogether for the life contemplative. Will
no kindly earthquake come and swallow up those accursed
cotton-mills? Take me that lumber of a desk there, and
bowl it down

As low as to the fiends.

I am no longer * * * * * *, clerk to the Firm of, etc. I am

Retired Leisure. I am to be met with in trim gardens. I am already come to be known by my vacant face and careless gesture, perambulating at no fixed pace, nor with any settled purpose. I walk about; not to and from. They tell me, a certain *cum dignitate* air, that has been buried so long with my other good parts, has begun to shoot forth in my person. I grow into gentility perceptibly. When I take up a newspaper, it is to read the state of the opera. *Opus operatum est.* I have done all that I came into this world to do. I have worked task-work, and have the rest of the day to myself.

ELIA.

London Magazine, May 1825.

That We Should Rise with the Lark

At what precise minute that little airy musician doffs his night-gear, and prepares to tune up his unseasonable matins, we are not naturalist enough to determine. But for a mere human gentleman – that has no orchestra business to call him from his warm bed to such preposterous exercises – we take ten, or half after ten (eleven, of course, during this Christmas solstice), to be the very earliest hour at which he can begin to think of abandoning his pillow. To think of it, we say; for to do it in earnest requires another half hour's good consideration. Not but there are pretty sun-risings, as we are told, and such like gawds, abroad in the world, in summer-time especially, some hours before what we have assigned; which a gentleman may see, as they say, only for getting up. But having been tempted once or twice, in earlier life, to assist at those ceremonies, we confess our curiosity abated. We are no longer ambitious of being the sun's courtiers, to attend at his morning levees. We hold the good hours of the dawn too sacred to waste them upon such observances; which have in them, besides, something Pagan and Persic. To say truth, we never anticipated our usual hour, or got up with the sun (as 'tis called), to go a journey,

or upon a foolish whole day's pleasuring, but we suffered
for it all the long hours after in listlessness and headaches;
Nature herself sufficiently declaring her sense of our presumption in aspiring to regulate our frail waking courses by
the measures of that celestial and sleepless traveller. We
deny not that there is something sprightly and vigorous, at
the outset especially, in these break-of-day excursions. It
is flattering to get the start of a lazy world; to conquer
Death by proxy in his image. But the seeds of sleep and
mortality are in us; and we pay usually, in strange qualms
before night falls, the penalty of the unnatural inversion.
Therefore, while the busy part of mankind are fast huddling
on their clothes, are already up and about their occupations,
content to have swallowed their sleep by wholesale; we
choose to linger a-bed and digest our dreams. It is the very
time to recombine the wandering images, which night in a
confused mass presented; to snatch them from forgetfulness;
to shape, and mould them. Some people have no good of
their dreams. Like fast feeders, they gulp them too grossly,
to taste them curiously. We love to chew the cud of a fore-
gone vision; to collect the scattered rays of a brighter phantasm, or act over again, with firmer nerves, the sadder noc-
turnal tragedies; to drag into daylight a struggling and half-
vanishing nightmare; to handle and examine the terrors, or
the airy solaces. We have too much respect for these spiritual
communications, to let them go so lightly. We are not so
stupid, or so careless as that Imperial forgetter of his dreams,
that we should need a seer to remind us of the form of them.
They seem to us to have as much significance as our waking
concerns; or rather to import us more nearly, as more
nearly we approach by years to the shadowy world, whither
we are hastening. We have shaken hands with the world's
business; we have done with it, we have discharged ourself
of it. Why should we get up? we have neither suit to solicit,
nor affairs to manage. The drama has shut in upon us at
the fourth act. We have nothing here to expect, but in a
short time a sick-bed, and a dismissal. We delight to antici-
pate death by such shadows as night affords. We are already
half acquainted with ghosts. We were never much in the

world. Disappointment early struck a dark veil between us and its dazzling illusions. Our spirits showed gray before our hairs. The mighty changes of the world already appear as but the vain stuff out of which dramas are composed. We have asked no more of life than what the mimic images in play-houses present us with. Even those types have waxed fainter. Our clock appears to have struck. We are 'super-annuated'. In this dearth of mundane satisfaction, we contract politic alliances with shadows. It is good to have friends at court. The extracted media of dreams seem no ill introduction to that spiritual presence, upon which, in no long time, we expect to be thrown. We are trying to know a little of the usages of that colony; to learn the language and the faces we shall meet with there, that we may be the less awkward at our first coming among them. We willingly call a phantom our fellow, as knowing we shall soon be of their dark companionship. Therefore we cherish dreams. We try to spell in them the alphabet of the invisible world; and think we know already how it shall be with us. Those uncouth shapes which, while we clung to flesh and blood, affrighted us, have become familiar. We feel attenuated into their meagre essences, and have given the hand of half-way approach to incorporeal being. We once thought life to be something; but it has unaccountably fallen from us before its time. Therefore we choose to dally with visions. The sun has no purposes of ours to light us to. Why should we get up?

L.

One of a series of 'Popular Fallacies' contributed to the *New Monthly Magazine* in 1826.

To Bernard Barton

Enfield Chase Side
Saturday 25 July A.D. 1829. – 11 A.M.

There – a fuller plumper juiceier date never dropt from Idumean palm. Am I in the dateive case now? if not, a fig for

dates, which is more than a date is worth. I never stood
much affected to these limitary specialities. Least of all
since the date of my superannuation.

> 'What have I with time to do?'
> Slaves of desks, 'twas meant for you.'

Dear B. B., – Your handwriting has conveyed much pleasure to me in report of Lucy's restoration. Would I could
send you as good news of my poor Lucy. But some wearisome weeks I must remain lonely yet. I have had the loneli-
est time near 10 weeks, broken by a short apparition of
Emma for her holydays, whose departure only deepened the
returning solitude, and by 10 days I have past in Town.
But Town, with all my native hankering after it, is not
what it was. The streets, the shops are left, but all old friends
are gone. And in London I was frightfully convinced of this
as I past houses and places – empty caskets now. I have
ceased to care almost about any body. The bodies I cared
for are in graves, or dispersed. My old Clubs, that lived so
long and flourish'd so steadily, are crumbled away. When I
took leave of our adopted young friend at Charing Cross,
'twas heavy unfeeling rain, and I had no where to go.
Home have I none – and not a sympathising house to turn
to in the great city. Never did the waters of the heaven
pour down on a forlorner head. Yet I tried 10 days at a
sort of friend's house, but it was large and straggling – one
of the individuals of my old long knot of friends, card
players, pleasant companions – that have tumbled to pieces
into dust and other things – and I got home on Thursday,
convinced that I was better to get home to my hole at
Enfield, and hide like a sick cat in my corner. Less than a
month I hope will bring home Mary. She is at Fulham,
looking better in her health than ever, but sadly rambling,
and scarce showing any pleasure in seeing me, or curiosity
when I should come again. But the old feelings will come
back again, and we shall drown all sorrows over a game at
Picquet again. But 'tis a tedious cut out of a life of sixty four,
to lose twelve or thirteen weeks every year or two. And to

make me more alone, our illtemperd maid is gone, who with
all her airs, was yet a home piece of furniture, a record of
better days; the young thing that has succeeded her is good
and attentive, but she is nothing – and I have no one here
to talk over old matters with. Scolding and quarreling have
something of familiarity and a community of interest – they
imply acquaintance – they are of resentment, which is of
the family of dearness. I can neither scold nor quarrel at this
insignificant implement of household services; she is less
than a cat, and just better than a deal Dresser. What I can
do, and do overdo, is to walk, but deadly long are the days –
these summer all-day days, with but a half hour's candlelight and no firelight. I do not write, tell your kind inquisit-
ive Eliza, and can hardly read. In the ensuing Blackwood
will be an old rejected farce of mine, which may be new to
you, if you see that same dull Medley. What things are all
the Magazines now! I contrive studiously not to see them.
The popular New Monthly is perfect trash. Poor Hessey, I
suppose you see, has failed. Hunt and Clarke too. Your
'Vulgar Truths' will be a good name – and I think your
prose must please – me at least – but 'tis useless to write
poetry with no purchasers. 'Tis cold work Authorship without something to puff one into fashion. Could you not write
something on Quakerism – for Quakers to read – but
nominally addrest to Non Quakers? explaining your dogmas – waiting on the Spirit – by the analogy of human
calmness and patient waiting on the judgment? I scarcely
know what I mean, but to make Non Quakers reconciled
to your doctrines, by shewing something like them in mere
human operations – but I hardly understand myself, so let
it pass for nothing. I pity you for over-work, but I assure
you no-work is worse. The mind preys on itself, the most
unwholesome food. I brag'd formerly that I could not have
too much time. I have a surfeit. With few years to come, the
days are wearisome. But weariness is not eternal. Something
will shine out to take the load off, that flags me, which is at
present intolerable. I have killed an hour or two in this poor
scrawl. I am a sanguinary murderer of time, and would kill
him inchmeal just now. But the snake is vital. Well, I shall

write merrier anon. – 'Tis the present copy of my countenance I send – and to complain is a little to alleviate. – May you enjoy yourself as far as the wicked wood will let you – and think that you are not quite alone, as I am. Health to Lucia and to Anna and kind remembce.

Yours forlorn.   C. L.

A GLASS TOO MUCH

To H. F. Cary

Oct. 1834.

I protest I know not in what words to invest my sense of the shameful violation of hospitality, which I was guilty of on that fatal Wednesday. Let it be blotted from the calendar. Had it been committed at a layman's house, say a merchant's or manufacturer's, a cheesemonger's or greengrocer's or, to go higher, a barrister's, a member of Parliament's, a rich banker's, I should have felt alleviation, a drop of self-pity. But to be seen deliberately to go out of the house of a clergyman drunk! a clergyman of the Church of England too! not that alone, but of an expounder of that dark Italian Hierophant, an exposition little short of *his* who dared unfold the Apocalypse: divine riddles both and (without supernal grace vouchsafed) Arks not to be fingered without present blasting to the touchers. And, then, from what house! Not a common glebe or vicarage (which yet had been shameful), but from a kingly repository of sciences, human and divine, with the primate of England for its guardian, arrayed in public majesty, from which the profane vulgar are bid fly. Could all those volumes have taught me nothing better! With feverish eyes on the succeeding dawn I opened upon the faint light, enough to distinguish, in a strange chamber not immediately to be recognized, garters, hose, waistcoat, neckerchief, arranged in dreadful order and proportion, which I knew was not mine own. 'Tis the common symptom, on awaking, I judge my last night's condition from. A tolerable scattering on the floor

I hail as being too probably my own, and if the candlestick
be not removed, I assoil myself. But this finical arrangement,
this finding everything in the morning in exact diametrical
rectitude, torments me. By whom was I divested? Burning
blushes! not by the fair hands of nymphs, the Buffman
Graces? Remote whispers suggested that I *coached* it home
in triumph – far be that from working pride in me, for I was
unconscious of the locomotion; that a young Mentor
accompanied a reprobate old Telemachus; that, the Trojan
like, he bore his charge upon his shoulders, while the wretched incubus, in glimmering sense, hiccuped drunken snatches
of flying on the bats' wings after sunset. An aged servitor was
also hinted at, to make disgrace more complete; one, to
whom my ignominy may offer further occasions of revolt
(to which he was before too fondly inclining) from the true
faith; for, at a sight of my helplessness, what more was
needed to drive him to the advocacy of independency?
Occasion led me through Great Russell Street yesterday. I
gazed at the great knocker. My feeble hands in vain essayed
to lift it. I dreaded that Argus Portitor, who doubtless lan-
terned me out on that prodigious night. I called the Elginian
marbles. They were cold to my suit. I shall never again, I
said, on the wide gates unfolding, say without fear of thrusting back, in a light but a peremptory air, 'I am going to
Mr Cary's'. I passed by the walls of Balclutha. I had imaged
to myself a zodiac of third Wednesdays irradiating by
glimpses the Edmonton dulness. I dreamed of Highmore!
I am de-vited to come on Wednesdays. Villanous old age
that, with second childhood, brings linked hand in hand her
inseparable twin, new inexperience, which knows not effects
of liquor. Where I was to have sate for a sober, middle-aged-
and-a-half gentleman, literary too, the neat-fingered artist
can educe no notions but of a dissolute Silenus, lecturing
natural philosophy to a jeering Chomius or a Mnasilus.
Pudet. From the context gather the lost name of —.

Confessions of a Drunkard

Dehortations from the use of strong liquors have been the

favourite topic of sober declaimers in all ages, and have been received with abundance of applause by water-drinking critics. But with the patient himself, the man that is to be cured, unfortunately their sound has seldom prevailed. Yet the evil is acknowledged, the remedy simple. Abstain. No force can oblige a man to raise the glass to his head against his will. 'Tis as easy as not to steal, not to tell lies.

Alas! the hand to pilfer, and the tongue to bear false witness, have no constitutional tendency. These are actions indifferent to them. At the first instance of the reformed will, they can be brought off without a murmur. The itching finger is but a figure in speech, and the tongue of the liar can with the same natural delight give forth useful truths with which it has been accustomed to scatter their pernicious contraries. But when a man has commenced sot —

O pause, thou sturdy moralist, thou person of stout nerves and a strong head, whose liver is happily untouched, and ere thy gorge riseth at the *name* which I had written, first learn what the *thing* is ; how much of compassion, how much of human allowance, thou mayest virtuously mingle with thy disapprobation. Trample not on the ruins of a man. Exact not, under so terrible a penalty as infamy, a resuscitation from a state of death almost as real as that from which Lazarus rose not but by a miracle.

Begin a reformation, and custom will make it easy. But what if the beginning be dreadful, the first steps not like climbing a mountain but going through fire? what if the whole system must undergo a change violent as that which we conceive of the mutation of form in some insects? what if a process comparable to flaying alive be to be gone through? is the weakness that sinks under such struggles to be confounded with the pertinacity which clings to other vices, which have induced no constitutional necessity, no engagement of the whole victim, body and soul?

I have known one in that state, when he has tried to abstain but for one evening, – though the poisonous potion had long ceased to bring back its first enchantments, though he was sure it would rather deepen his gloom than brighten it, – in the violence of the struggle, and the necessity he had felt of getting rid of the present sensation at any rate, I have known him to scream out, to cry aloud, for the anguish and pain of the strife within him.

Why should I hesitate to declare, that the man of whom I speak is myself? I have no puling apology to make to mankind. I see them all in one way or another deviating from the pure reason. It is to my own nature alone I am accountable for the woe that I have brought upon it.

I believe that there are constitutions, robust heads and iron insides, whom scarce any excesses can hurt; whom brandy (I have seen them drink it like wine), at all events whom wine, taken in ever so plentiful a measure, can do no worse injury to than just to muddle their faculties, perhaps never very pellucid. On them this discourse is wasted. They would but laugh at a weak brother, who, trying his strength with them, and coming off foiled from the contest, would fain persuade them that such agonistic exercises are dangerous. It is to a very different description of persons I speak. It is to the weak – the nervous; to those who feel the want of some artificial aid to raise their spirits in society to what is no more than the ordinary pitch of all around them without it. This is the secret of our drinking. Such must fly the convivial board in the first instance, if they do not mean to sell themselves for term of life.

Twelve years ago I had completed my six-and-twentieth year. I had lived from the period of leaving school to that time pretty much in solitude. My companions were chiefly books, or at most one or two living ones of my own book-loving and sober stamp. I rose early, went to bed betimes, and the faculties which God had given me, I have reason to think, did not rust in me unused.

About that time I fell in with some companions of a different order. They were men of boisterous spirits, sitters up a-nights, disputants, drunken; yet seemed to have something noble about them. We dealt about the wit, or what passes for it after midnight, jovially. Of the quality called fancy I certainly possessed a larger share than my companions. Encouraged by their applause, I set up for a professed joker! I, who of all men am least fitted for such an occupation, having, in addition to the greatest difficulty which I experience at all times of finding words to express my meaning, a natural nervous impediment in my speech!

Reader, if you are gifted with nerves like mine, aspire to any character but that of a wit. When you find a tickling relish upon your tongue disposing you to that sort of conversation, especially if you find a preternatural flow of ideas setting in upon you at the sight of a bottle and fresh glasses, avoid giving way to it as you would fly your greatest destruction. If you cannot crush the power of fancy, or that within you which you mistake for such, divert it, give it some other play. Write an essay, pen a character or description, — but not as I do now, with tears trickling down your cheeks.

To be an object of compassion to friends, of derision to foes; to be suspected by strangers, stared at by fools; to be esteemed dull when you cannot be witty, to be applauded for witty when you know that you have been dull; to be called upon for the extemporaneous exercise of that faculty which no premeditation can give; to be spurred on to efforts which end in contempt; to be set on to provoke mirth which procures the procurer hatred; to give pleasure and be paid with squinting malice; to swallow draughts of life-destroying wine which are to be distilled into airy breath to tickle vain auditors; to mortgage miserable morrows for nights of madness; to waste whole seas of time upon those who pay it back in little inconsiderable drops of grudging applause, — are the wages of buffoonery and death.

Time, which has a sure stroke at dissolving all connections which have no solider fastening than this liquid cement, more kind to me than my own taste or penetration, at length opened my eyes to the supposed qualities of my first friends. No trace of them is left but in the vices which they introduced, and the habits they infixed. In them my friends survive still, and exercise ample retribution for any supposed infidelity that I may have been guilty of towards them.

My next more immediate companions were and are persons of such intrinsic and felt worth, that though accidentally their acquaintance has proved pernicious to me, I do not know that if the thing were to do over again, I should

have the courage to eschew the mischief at the price of for-
feiting the benefit. I came to them reeking from the steams
of my late over-heated notions of companionship; and the
slightest fuel which they unconsciously afforded, was sufficient to feed my own fires into a propensity.

They were no drinkers; but, one from professional habits,
and another from a custom derived from his father, smoked
tobacco. The devil could not have devised a more subtle
trap to re-take a backsliding penitent. The transition, from
gulping down draughts of liquid fire to puffing out innocuous blasts of dry smoke, was so like cheating him. But he is
too hard for us when we hope to commute. He beats us at
barter; and when we think to set off a new failing against
an old infirmity, 'tis odds but he puts the trick upon us of
two for one. That (comparatively) white devil of tobacco
brought with him in the end seven worse than himself.

It were impertinent to carry the reader through all the
processes by which, from smoking at first with malt liquor,
I took my degrees through thin wines, through stronger
wine and water, through small punch, to those juggling
compositions, which, under the name of mixed liquors, slur a
great deal of brandy or other poison under less and less water
continually, until they come next to none, and so to none at
all. But it is hateful to disclose the secrets of my Tartarus.

I should repel my readers, from a mere incapacity of
believing me, were I to tell them what tobacco has been to
me, the drudging service which I have paid, the slavery
which I have vowed to it. How, when I have resolved to
quit it, a feeling as of ingratitude has started up; how it has
put on personal claims and made the demands of a friend
upon me. How the reading of it casually in a book, as where
Adams takes his whiff in the chimney-corner of some inn in
Joseph Andrews, or Piscator in the *Complete Angler* breaks his
fast upon a morning pipe in that delicate room *Piscatoribus
Sacrum*, has in a moment broken down the resistance of
weeks. How a pipe was ever in my midnight path before me,
till the vision forced me to realize it, – how then its ascending
vapours curled, its fragrance lulled, and the thousand
delicious ministerings conversant about it, employing every

faculty, extracted the sense of pain. How from illuminating it came to darken, from a quick solace it turned to a negative relief, thence to a restlessness and dissatisfaction, thence to a positive misery. How, even now, when the whole secret stands confessed in all its dreadful truth before me, I feel myself linked to it beyond the power of revocation. Bone of my bone —

Persons not accustomed to examine the motives of their actions, to reckon up the countless nails that rivet the chains of habit, or perhaps being bound by none so obdurate as those I have confessed to, may recoil from this as from an overcharged picture. But what short of such a bondage is it, which in spite of protesting fiiends, a weeping wife, and a reprobating world, chains down many a poor fellow, of no original indisposition to goodness, to his pipe and his pot?

I have seen a print after Correggio, in which three female figures are ministering to a man who sits fast bound at the root of a tree. Sensuality is soothing him, Evil Habit is nailing him to a branch, and Repugnance at the same instant of time is applying a snake to his side. In his face is feeble delight, the recollection of past rather than perception of present pleasures, languid enjoyment of evil with utter imbecility to good, a Sybaritic effeminacy, a submission to bondage, the springs of the will gone down like a broken clock, the sin and the suffering co-instantaneous, or the latter forerunning the former, remorse preceding action – all this represented in one point of time. – When I saw this, I admired the wonderful skill of the painter. But when I went away, I wept, because I thought of my own condition.

Of *that* there is no hope that it should ever change. The waters have gone over me. But out of the black depths, could I be heard, I would cry out to all those who have but set a foot in the perilous flood. Could the youth, to whom the flavour of his first wine is delicious as the opening scenes of life or the entering upon some newly-discovered paradise, look into my desolation, and be made to understand what a dreary thing it is when a man shall feel himself going down a precipice with open eyes and a passive will, – to see his destruction and have no power to stop it, and yet to feel it

all the way emanating from himself; to perceive all goodness emptied out of him, and yet not to be able to forget a
time when it was otherwise; to bear about the piteous spectacle of his own self-ruins: – could he see my fevered eye,
feverish with last night's drinking, and feverishly looking
for this night's repetition of the folly; could he feel the body
of the death out of which I cry hourly with feebler and
feebler outcry to be delivered, – it were enough to make him
dash the sparkling beverage to the earth in all the pride of
its mantling temptation; to make him clasp his teeth,

> and not undo 'em
> To suffer WET DAMNATION to run thro' 'em.

Yea, but (methinks I hear somebody object) if sobriety
be that fine thing you would have us to understand, if the
comforts of a cool brain are to be preferred to that state of
heated excitement which you describe and deplore, what
hinders in your instance that you do not return to those
habits from which you would induce others never to swerve?
if the blessing be worth preserving, is it not worth recovering?

Recovering! – O if a wish could transport me back to those
days of youth, when a draught from the next clear spring
could slake any heats which summer suns and youthful
exercise had power to stir up in the blood, how gladly
would I return to thee, pure element, the drink of children
and of childlike holy hermit! In my dreams I can sometimes fancy thy cool refreshment purling over my burning
tongue. But my waking stomach rejects it. That which
refreshes innocence only makes me sick and faint.

But is there no middle way betwixt total abstinence and
the excess which kills you? – For your sake, reader, and that
you may never attain to my experience, with pain I must
utter the dreadful truth, that there is none, none that I can
find. In my stage of habit (I speak not of habits less confirmed – for some of them I believe the advice to be most pru-
dential), in the stage which I have reached, to stop short of
that measure which is sufficient to draw on torpor and
sleep, the benumbing apoplectic sleep of the drunkard, is
to have taken none at all. The pain of the self-denial is all

one. And what that is, I had rather the reader should believe
on my credit, than know from his own trial. He will come to
know it, whenever he shall arrive in that state in which,
paradoxical as it may appear, *reason shall only visit him
through intoxication*; for it is a fearful truth, that the intellectual faculties by repeated acts of intemperance may be
driven from their orderly sphere of action, their clear daylight ministeries, until they shall be brought at last to
depend, for the faint manifestation of their departing
energies, upon the returning periods of the fatal madness to
which they owe their devastation. The drinking man is
never less himself than during his sober intervals. Evil is so
far his good.[1]

Behold me then, in the robust period of life, reduced to
imbecility and decay. Hear me count my gains, and the
profits which I have derived from the midnight cup.

Twelve years ago, I was possessed of a healthy frame of
mind and body. I was never strong, but I think my constitution (for a weak one) was as happily exempt from the
tendency to any malady as it was possible to be. I scarce
knew what it was to ail anything. Now, except when I am
losing myself in a sea of drink, I am never free from those
uneasy sensations in head and stomach, which are so much
worse to bear than any definite pains or aches.

At that time I was seldom in bed after six in the morning,
summer and winter. I awoke refreshed, and seldom without some merry thoughts in my head, or some piece of a
song to welcome the new-born day. Now, the first feeling
which besets me, after stretching out the hours of recum-
bence to their last possible extent, is a forecast of the wearisome day that lies before me, with a secret wish that I could
have lain on still, or never awaked.

[1] When poor M — painted his last picture, with a pencil in one
trembling hand, and a glass of brandy and water in the other,
his fingers owed the comparative steadiness with which they
were enabled to go through their task in an imperfect manner,
to a temporary firmness derived from a repetition of practices, the
general effect of which had shaken both them and him so
terribly.

Life itself, my waking life, has much of the confusion, the trouble, and obscure perplexity, of an ill dream. In the daytime I stumble upon dark mountains.

Business, which, though never very particularly adapted to my nature, yet as something of necessity to be gone through, and therefore best undertaken with cheerfulness, I used to enter upon with some degree of alacrity, now wearies, affrights, perplexes me. I fancy all sorts of discouragements, and am ready to give up an occupation which gives me bread, from a harassing conceit of incapacity. The slightest commission given me by a friend, or any small duty which I have to perform for myself, as giving orders to a tradesman, etc., haunts me as a labour impossible to be got through. So much the springs of action are broken.

The same cowardice attends me in all my intercourse with mankind. I dare not promise that a friend's honour, or his cause, would be safe in my keeping, if I were put to the expense of any manly resolution in defending it. So much the springs of moral action are deadened within me.

My favourite occupations in times past now cease to entertain. I can do nothing readily. Application for ever so short a time kills me. This poor abstract of my condition was penned at long intervals, with scarcely an attempt at connection of thought, which is now difficult to me.

The noble passages which formerly delighted me in history or poetic fiction now only draw a few tears, allied to dotage. My broken and dispirited nature seems to sink before anything great and admirable.

I perpetually catch myself in tears, for any cause, or none. It is inexpressible how much this infirmity adds to a sense of shame, and a general feeling of deterioration.

These are some of the instances, concerning which I can say with truth, that it was not always so with me.

Shall I lift up the veil of my weakness any further? – or is this disclosure sufficient?

I am a poor nameless egotist, who have no vanity to consult by these Confessions. I know not whether I shall be laughed at, or heard seriously. Such as they are, I commend them to the reader's attention, if he find his own case any way touched. I have told him what I am come to. Let him stop in time.

First published *Philanthropist*, 1813; included in Basil Montagu's '*Some Enquiries into the Effects of Fermented Liquors*', 1814, and reprinted again, as an Elia essay in the *London Magazine*, August, 1822, with the following note:

Elia on his Confessions of a Drunkard

Many are the sayings of Elia, painful and frequent his lucubrations, set forth, for the most part (such is his modesty!), without a name, scattered about in obscure periodicals and forgotten miscellanies. From the dust of some of these it is our intention occasionally to revive a tract or two that shall seem worthy of a better fate, especially at a time like the present, when the pen of our industrious contributor, engaged in a laborious digest of his recent Continental tour, may haply want the leisure to expatiate in more miscellaneous speculations. We have been induced, in the first instance, to reprint a thing which he put forth in a friend's volume some years since, entitled 'The Confessions of a Drunkard,' seeing that Messieurs the Quarterly Reviewers have chosen to embellish their last dry pages with fruitful quotations therefrom, adding, from their peculiar brains, the gratuitous affirmation that they have reason to believe that the describer (in his delineations of a drunkard, forsooth!) partly sat for his own picture. The truth is, that our friend had been reading among the essays of a contemporary, who has perversely been confounded with him, a paper in which Edax (or the Great Eater) humorously complaineth of an inordinate appetite; and it struck him that a better paper – of deeper interest and wider usefulness – might be made out of the imagined experiences of a Great Drinker. Accordingly he set to work, and, with that mock fervour and counterfeit earnestness with which he is too apt to over-realize his descriptions, has given us a frightful picture indeed, but no more resembling the man Elia than the

fictitious Edax may be supposed to identify itself with Mr
L., its author. It is indeed a compound extracted out of his
long observations of the effects of drinking upon all the
world about him; and this accumulated mass of misery he
hath centred (as the custom is with judicious essayists) in
a single figure. We deny not that a portion of his own
experiences may have passed into the picture (as who,
that is not a washy fellow, but must at some times have felt
the after-operation of a too-generous cup?), but then how
heightened! how exaggerated! how little within the sense
of the Review, where a part, in their slanderous usage,
must be understood to stand for the whole! But it is useless
to expostulate with this Quarterly slime, brood of Nilus,
watery heads with hearts of jelly, spawned under the sign of
Aquarius, incapable of Bacchus, and therefore cold, washy,
spiteful, bloodless. Elia shall string them up one day, and
show their colours, – or rather how colourless and vapid the
whole fry, – when he putteth forth his long-promised, but
unaccountably hitherto delayed, 'Confessions of a Water-
Drinker'.

An Autobiographical Sketch

Charles Lamb born in the Inner Temple 10 Feb. 1775
educated in Christ's Hospital afterwards a clerk in the
Accountants office East India House pensioned off from
that service 1825 after 33 years service, is now a Gentleman
at large, can remember few specialities in his life worth
noting except that he once caught a swallow flying (*teste
sua manu*); below the middle stature, cast of face slightly
Jewish, with no Judaic tinge in his complexional religion;
stammers abominably and is therefore more apt to discharge
his occasional conversation in a quaint aphorism or a poor
quibble than in set and edifying speeches; has consequently
been libelled as a person always aiming at wit, which, as he
told a dull fellow that charged him with it, is at least as
good as aiming at dulness; a small eater but not drinker;

confesses a partiality for the production of the juniper berry, was a fierce smoker of Tobacco, but may be resembled to a volcano burnt out, emitting only now and then a casual puff. Has been guilty of obtruding upon the Public a Tale in Prose, called Rosamund Gray, a Dramatic Sketch named John Woodvil, a Farewell Ode to Tobacco, with sundry other Poems and light prose matter, collected in Two slight crown Octavos and pompously christened his Works, tho' in fact they were his Recreations and his true works may be found on the shelves of Leadenhall Street, filling some hundred Folios. He is also the true Elia whose Essays are extant in a little volume published a year or two since; and rather better known from that name without a meaning, than from anything he has done or can hope to do in his own. He also was the first to draw the Public attention to the old English Dramatists in a work called 'Specimens of English Dramatic Writers who lived about the time of Shakspear', published about 15 years since. In short all his merits and demerits to set forth would take to the end of Mr Upcott's book and then not be told truly. He died†

  18 much lamented.

     Witness his hand, CHARLES LAMB,

       10th Apr. 1827.

† To any Body – Please to fill up these blanks.

THE BLANK FILLED

On 27th December, 1834, Charles Lamb died at Edmonton – much lamented.

PART II

HE SERVES UP HIS FRIENDS

'With what well-disguised humour he
serves up his friends.'
The Spirit of the Age. WILLIAM HAZLITT.

The Old Familiar Faces

[1] Where are they gone, the old familiar faces?

[1] I had a mother, but she died, and left me,
Died prematurely in a day of horrors –
All, all are gone, the old familiar faces.

I have had playmates, I have had companions,
In my days of childhood, in my joyful school-days,
All, all are gone, the old familiar faces.

I have been laughing, I have been carousing,
Drinking late, sitting late, with my bosom cronies,
All, all are gone, the old familiar faces.

I loved a love once, fairest among women;
Closed are her doors on me, I must not see her –
All, all are gone, the old familiar faces.

I have a friend, a kinder friend has no man;
Like an ingrate, I left my friend abruptly;
Left him, to muse on the old familiar faces.

Ghost-like, I paced round the haunts of my childhood.
Earth seemed a desert I was bound to traverse,
Seeking to find the old familiar faces.

Friend of my bosom, thou more than a brother!
Why wert not thou born in my father's dwelling?
So might we talk of the old familiar faces –

How some they have died, and some they have left me,
And some are taken from me; all are departed;
All, all are gone, the old familiar faces.

[1 The first stanza, published when the poem first appeared in
1798, was omitted by Lamb in the edition of his works published
in 1818 – and is now normally omitted.]

D

DOUBLE SINGLENESS

Mackery End, in Hertfordshire

Bridget Elia has been my housekeeper for many a long year. I have obligations to Bridget, extending beyond the period of memory. We house together, old bachelor and maid, in a sort of double singleness; with such tolerable comfort, upon the whole, that I, for one, find in myself no sort of disposition to go out upon the mountains, with the rash king's offspring, to bewail my celibacy. We agree pretty well in our tastes and habits – yet so, as 'with a difference'. We are generally in harmony, with occasional bickerings – as it should be among near relations. Our sympathies are rather understood than expressed; and once, upon my dissembling a tone in my voice more kind than ordinary, my cousin burst into tears, and complained that I was altered. We are both great readers in different directions. While I am hanging over (for the thousandth time) some passage in old Burton, or one of his strange contemporaries, she is abstracted in some modern tale or adventure, whereof our common reading-table is daily fed with assiduously fresh supplies. Narrative teases me. I have little concern in the progress of events. She must have a story – well, ill, or indifferently told – so there be life stirring in it, and plenty of good or evil accidents. The fluctuations of fortune in fiction – and almost in real life – have ceased to interest, or operate but dully upon me. Out-of-the-way humours and opinions – heads with some diverting twist in them – the oddities of authorship, please me most. My cousin has a native disrelish of anything that sounds odd or bizarre. Nothing goes down with her that is quaint, irregular or out of the road of common sympathy. She 'holds Nature more clever'. I can pardon her blindness to the beautiful obliquities of the *Religio Medici*; but she must apologize to me for certain disrespectful insinuations, which she has been pleased to throw out latterly, touching the intellectuals of a dear favourite of mine, of the last century but one – the thrice noble, chaste, and virtuous, but again somewhat fantastical and original brained, generous Margaret Newcastle.

It has been the lot of my cousin, oftener perhaps than I could have wished, to have had for her associates and mine, free-thinkers – leaders, and disciples, of novel philosophies and systems; but she neither wrangles with, nor accepts, their opinions. That which was good and venerable to her, when a child, retains its authority over her mind still. She never juggles or plays tricks with her understanding.

We are both of us inclined to be a little too positive; and I have observed the result of our disputes to be almost uniformly this – that in matters of fact, dates, and circumstances, it turns out that I was in the right, and my cousin in the wrong. But where we have differed upon moral points; upon something proper to be done, or let alone; whatever heat of opposition or steadiness of conviction I set out with, I am sure always, in the long-run, to be brought over to her way of thinking.

I must touch upon the foibles of my kinswoman with a gentle hand, for Bridget does not like to be told of her faults. She hath an awkward trick (to say no worse of it) of reading in company: at which times she will answer *yes* or *no* to a question, without fully understanding its purport – which is provoking, and derogatory in the highest degree to the dignity of the putter of the said questions. Her presence of mind is equal to the most pressing trials of life, but will sometimes desert her upon trifling occasions. When the purpose requires it, and is a thing of moment, she can speak to it greatly; but in matters which are not stuff of the conscience, she hath been known sometimes to let slip a word less seasonably.

Her education in youth was not much attended to; and she happily missed all that train of female garniture which passeth by the name of accomplishments. She was tumbled early, by accident or design, into a spacious closet of good old English reading, without much selection or prohibition, and browsed at will upon that fair and wholesome pasturage. Had I twenty girls, they should be brought up exactly in this fashion. I know not whether their chance in wedlock might not be diminished by it, but I can answer for it that it makes (if the worst come to the worst) most incomparable old maids.

In a season of distress, she is the truest comforter; but in the teasing accidents and minor perplexities, which do not call out the *will* to meet them, she sometimes maketh matters worse by an excess of participation. If she does not always divide your trouble, upon the pleasanter occasions of life she is sure always to treble your satisfaction. She is excellent to be at a play with, or upon a visit; but best, when she goes on a journey with you.

We made an excursion together a few summers since into Hertfordshire, to beat up the quarters of some of our less-known relations in that fine corn country.

The oldest thing I remember is Mackery End, or Mackarel End, as it is spelt, perhaps more properly, in some old maps of Hertfordshire; a farm-house, – delightfully situated within a gentle walk from Wheathampstead. I can just remember having been there, on a visit to a great-aunt, when I was a child, under the care of Bridget; who, as I have said, is older than myself by some ten years. I wish that I could throw into a heap the remainder of our joint existences, that we might share them in equal division. But that is impossible. The house was at that time in the occupation of a substantial yeoman, who had married my grandmother's sister. His name was Gladman. My grandmother was a Bruton, married to a Field. The Gladmans and the Brutons are still flourishing in that part of the country, but the Fields are almost extinct. More than forty years had elapsed since the visit I speak of; and, for the greater portion of that period, we had lost sight of the other two branches also. Who or what sort of persons inherited Mackery End – kindred or strange folk – we were afraid almost to conjecture, but determined some day to explore.

By somewhat a circuitous route, taking the noble park

at Luton in our way from St. Albans, we arrived at the spot of our anxious curiosity about noon. The sight of the old farm-house, though every trace of it was effaced from my recollections, affected me with a pleasure which I had not experienced for many a year. For though *I* had forgotten it, *we* had never forgotten being there together, and we had been talking about Mackery End all our lives, till memory on my part became mocked with a phantom of itself, and I thought I knew the aspect of a place which, when present, O how unlike it was to *that* which I had conjured up so many times instead of it!

Still the air breathed balmily about it; the season was in the 'heart of June', and I could say with the poet,

> But thou, that didst appear so fair
> To fond imagination,
> Dost rival in the light of day
> Her delicate creation!

Bridget's was more a waking bliss than mine, for she easily remembered her old acquaintance again – some altered features, of course, a little grudged at. At first, indeed, she was ready to disbelieve for joy; but the scene soon re-confirmed itself in her affections – and she traversed every outpost of the old mansion, to the wood-house, the orchard, the place where the pigeon-house had stood (house and birds were alike flown) – with a breathless impatience of recognition, which was more pardonable perhaps than decorous at the age of fifty odd. But Bridget in some things is behind her years.

The only thing left was to get into the house – and that was a difficulty which to me singly would have been insurmountable; for I am terribly shy in making myself known to strangers and out-of-date kinsfolk. Love, stronger than scruple, winged my cousin in without me; but she soon returned with a creature that might have sat to a sculptor for the image of Welcome. It was the youngest of the Gladmans; who, by marriage with a Bruton, had become mistress of the old mansion. A comely brood are the Brutons. Six of them, females, were noted as the handsomest

young women in the county. But this adopted Bruton, in
my mind, was better than they all – more comely. She was
born too late to have remembered me. She just recollected
in early life to have had her cousin Bridget once pointed
out to her, climbing a stile. But the name of kindred and of
cousinship was enough. Those slender ties, that prove
slight as gossamer in the rending atmosphere of a metropolis, bind faster, as we found it, in hearty, homely, loving
Hertfordshire. In five minutes we were as thoroughly
acquainted as if we had been born and bred up together;
were familiar, even to the calling each other by our Christian names. So Christians should call one another. To have
seen Bridget and her – it was like the meeting of the two
scriptural cousins! There was a grace and dignity, an ampli-
tude of form and stature, answering to her mind, in this
farmer's wife, which would have shined in a palace – or so
we thought it. We were made welcome by husband and
wife equally – we, and our friend that was with us. – I had
almost forgotten him – but B[arron] F[ield] will not so soon
forget that meeting, if peradventure he shall read this on the
far distant shores where the kangaroo haunts. The fatted
calf was made ready, or rather was already so, as if in
anticipation of our coming; and, after an appropriate glass
of native wine, never let me forget with what honest pride
this hospitable cousin made us proceed to Wheathampstead, to introduce us (as some new-found rarity) to her
mother and sister Gladmans, who did indeed know something more of us, at a time when she almost knew nothing.
– With what corresponding kindness we were received by
them also – how Bridget's memory, exalted by the occasion,
warmed into a thousand half-obliterated recollections of
things and persons, to my utter astonishment, and her
own – and to the astonishment of B. F. who sat by, almost
the only thing that was not a cousin there, – old effaced
images of more than half-forgotten names and circumstances still crowding back upon her, as words written in
lemon come out upon exposure to a friendly warmth, –
when I forget all this, then may my country cousins forget
me; and Bridget no more remember, that in the days of

weakling infancy I was her tender charge – as I have been her care in foolish manhood since – in those pretty pastoral walks, long ago, about Mackery End, in Hertfordshire.

ELIA.

To Sarah Hutchinson

Thurs., 19 Oct., 1815.

Dear Miss H. – I am forced to be the replier to your letter, for Mary has been ill and gone from home these five weeks yesterday. She has left me very lonely and very miserable. I stroll about, but there is no rest but at one's own fireside, and there is no rest for me there now. I look forward to the worse half being past, and keep up as well as I can. She has begun to show some favorable symptoms. The return of her disorder has been frightfully soon this time, with scarce a six month's interval. I am almost afraid my worry of spirits about the E. I. House was partly the cause of her illness, but one always imputes it to the cause next at hand ; more probably it comes from some cause we have no control over or conjecture of. It cuts sad great slices out of the time, the little time we shall have to live together. I don't know but the recurrence of these illnesses might help me to sustain her death better than if we had had no partial separations. But I won't talk of death. I will imagine us immortal, or forget that we are otherwise ; by God's blessing in a few weeks we may be making our meal together, or sitting in the front row of the Pit at Drury Lane, or taking our evening walk past the theatres, to look at the outside of them at least, if not to be tempted in. Then we forget we are assailable, we are strong for the time as rocks, the wind is tempered to the shorn Lambs. Poor C. Lloyd, and poor Priscilla, I feel I hardly feel enough for him, my own calamities press about me and involve me in a thick integument not to be reached at by other folks' misfortunes. But I feel all I can,

and all the kindness I can towards you all. God bless you.
I hear nothing from Coleridge. Yours truly

                                         C. Lamb.

To William Wordsworth

                                 End of May nearly [1833].

Dear Wordsworth, — Your letter, save in what respects
your dear sister's health, cheered me in my new solitude.
Mary is ill again. Her illnesses encroach yearly. The last
was three months, followed by two of depression most
dreadful. I look back upon her earlier attacks with longing:
nice little durations of six weeks or so, followed by complete
restoration, — shocking as they were to me then. In short,
half her life she is dead to me, and the other half is made
anxious with fears and lookings forward to the next shock,
With such prospects, it seemed to me necessary that she
should no longer live with me, and be fluttered with continual removals; so I am come to live with her, at a Mr
Walden's, and his wife, who take in patients, and have
arranged to lodge and board us only. They have had the
care of her before. I see little of her: alas! I too often hear
her. *Sunt lachrymæ rerum!* and you and I must bear it.

To lay a little more load on it, a circumstance has happened, *cujus pars magna fui,* and which, at another crisis, I
should have more rejoiced in. I am about to lose my old
and only walk-companion, whose mirthful spirits were the
'youth of our house', Emma Isola. I have her here now for
a little while, but she is too nervous, properly to be under
such a roof, so she will make short visits, — be no more an
inmate. With my perfect approval, and more than concur-
rence, she is to be wedded to Moxon, at the end of August —
so 'perish the roses and the flowers' — how is it?

Now to the brighter side. I am emancipated from the
Westwoods, and I am with attentive people, and younger.
I am three or four miles nearer the great city; coaches half-
price less, and going always, of which I will avail myself.

I have few friends left there, one or two though, most beloved. But London streets and faces cheer me inexpressibly, though not one known of the latter were remaining.

Thank you for your cordial reception of 'Elia'. Inter nos, the 'Ariadne' is not a darling with me; several incongruous things are in it, but in the composition it served me as illustrative.

I want you in the 'Popular Fallacies' to like the *Home that is no home*, and *Rising with the lark*.

I am feeble, but cheerful in this my genial hot weather. Walked sixteen miles yesterday. I can't read much in summer time.

With my kindest love to all, and prayers for dear Dorothy,
I remain most affectionately yours,

C. LAMB.

Moxon has introduced Emma to Rogers, and he smiles upon the project. I have given E. my 'Milton', (will you pardon me?) in part of a *portion*. It hangs famously in his Murray-like shop.

GOD ALMIGHTY'S GENTLEMAN

To Thomas Manning

[P.M. August 28, 1800].

George Dyer is an Archimedes, and an Archimagus, and a Tycho Brahé, and a Copernicus; and thou art the darling of the Nine, and midwife to their wandering babe also! We take tea with that learned poet and critic on Tuesday night, at half-past five, in his neat library; the repast will be light and Attic, with criticism. If thou couldst contrive to wheel up thy dear carcase on the Monday, and after dining with us on tripe, calves' kidneys, or whatever else the Cornucopia of St Clare may be willing to pour out on

the occasion, might we not adjourn together to the Heathen's – thou with thy Black Backs and I with some innocent
volume of the Bell Letters – Shenstone, or the like? It would
make him wash his old flannel gown (that has not been
washed to my knowledge since it has been *his* – Oh the long
time!) with tears of joy. Thou shouldst settle his scruples
and unravel his cobwebs, and sponge off the sad stuff that
weighs upon his dear wounded pia mater; thou shouldst
restore light to his eyes, and him to his friends and the public;
Parnassus should shower her civic crowns upon thee for
saving the wits of a citizen! I thought I saw a lucid interval
in George the other night – he broke in upon my studies
just at tea-time, and brought with him Dr. Anderson, an
old gentleman who ties his breeches' knees with packthread,
and boasts that he has been disappointed by ministers. The
Doctor wanted to see *me*: for, I being a Poet, he thought I
might furnish him with a copy of verses to suit his 'Agricul-
tural Magazine'. The Doctor, in the course of the conversation, mentioned a poem called 'Epigoniad' by one Wilkie,
an epic poem, in which there is not one tolerable good line
all through, but every incident and speech borrowed from
Homer. George had been sitting inattentive seemingly to
what was going on – hatching of negative quantities – when,
suddenly, the name of his old friend Homer stung his peri-
cranicks, and, jumping up, he begged to know where he
could meet with Wilkie's work. 'It was a curious fact that
there should be such an epic poem and he not know of it;
and he *must* get a copy of it, as he was going to touch pretty
deeply upon the subject of the Epic – and he was sure there
must be some things good in a poem of 1400 lines!' I was
pleased with this transient return of his reason and recurrence to his old ways of thinking: it gave me great hopes
of a recovery, which nothing but your book can completely
insure. Pray come on Monday if you *can*, and stay your own
time. I have a good large room, with two beds in it, in the
handsomest of which thou shalt repose a-nights, and dream
of Spheroides. I hope you will understand by the nonsense
of this letter that I am *not* melancholy at the thoughts of
thy coming: I thought it necessary to add this, because

you love *precision*. Take notice that our stay at Dyer's will not exceed eight o'clock, after which our pursuits will be our own. But indeed I think a little recreation among the Bell Letters and poetry will do you some service in the interval of severer studies. I hope we shall fully discuss with George Dyer what I have never yet heard done to my satisfaction, the reason of Dr Johnson's malevolent strictures on the higher species of the Ode.

C. L.

To Thomas Manning

December 27th, 1800.

At length George Dyer's phrenesis has come to a crisis; he is raging and furiously mad. I waited upon the heathen, Thursday was a se'nnight; the first symptom which struck my eye and gave me incontrovertible proof of the fatal truth was a pair of nankeen pantaloons four times too big for him, which the said Heathen did pertinaciously affirm to be new.

They were absolutely ingrained with the accumulated dirt of ages; but he affirmed them to be clean. He was going to visit a lady that was nice about those things, and that's the reason he wore nankeen that day. And then he danced, and capered, and fidgeted, and pulled up his pantaloons, and hugged his intolerable flannel vestment closer about his poetic loins; anon he gave it loose to the zephyrs which plentifully insinuate their tiny bodies through every crevice, door, window or wainscot, expressly formed for the exclusion of such impertinents. Then he caught at a proof sheet, and catched up a laundress's bill instead -- made a dart at Blomfield's Poems, and threw them in agony aside. I could not bring him to one direct reply; he could not maintain his jumping mind in a right line for the tithe of a moment by Clifford's Inn clock. He must go to the printer's immediately – the most unlucky accident – he had struck off five hundred impressions of his Poems, which were ready for delivery to subscribers, and the Preface must all be expunged. There were eighty pages of Preface, and not till that morning had he discovered that in the very first page of said Preface he had set out with a principle of Criticism fundamentally wrong, which vitiated all his following reasoning. The Preface must be expunged, although it cost him £30 – the lowest calculation, taking in paper and printing! In vain have his real friends remonstrated against this Midsummer madness. George is as obstinate as a Primitive Christian – and wards and parries off all our thrusts with one unanswerable fence; – 'Sir, it's of great consequence that the *world* is not *misled*!'

As for the other Professor, he has actually begun to dive into Tavernier and Chardin's *Persian* Travels for a story, to form a new drama for the sweet tooth of this fastidious age. Hath not Bethlehem College a fair action for non-residence against such professors? Are poets so *few* in *this age*, that He must write poetry? *Is morals* a subject so exhausted, that he must quit that line? Is the metaphysic well (without a bottom) drained dry?

If I can guess at the wicked pride of the Professor's heart, I would take a shrewd wager that he disdains ever again to dip his pen in *Prose*. Adieu, ye splendid theories! Farewell, dreams of political justice! Lawsuits, where I was counsel for Archbishop Fenelon *versus* my own mother, in the famous fire cause!

Vanish from my mind, professors, one and all! I have metal more attractive on foot.

Man of many snipes, – I will sup with thee, Deo volente et diabolo nolente, on Monday night the 5th of January, in the new year, and crush a cup to the infant century.

A word or two of my progress. Embark at six o'clock in the morning, with a fresh gale, on a Cambridge one-decker; very cold till eight at night; land at St Mary's light-house, muffins and coffee upon table (or any other curious production of Turkey or both Indies), snipes exactly at nine, punch to commence at ten, with *argument*; difference of opinion is expected to take place about eleven; perfect unanimity, with some haziness and dimness, before twelve.

– N.B. My single affection is not so singly wedded to snipes; but the curious and epicurean eye would also take a pleasure in beholding a delicate and well-chosen assortment of teals, ortolans, the unctuous and palate-soothing flesh of geese wild and tame, nightingales' brains, the sensorium of a young sucking-pig, or any other Christmas dish, which I leave to the judgment of you and the cook of Gonville.

C. LAMB.

To Mrs Hazlitt

November 1823.

Dear Mrs H. – Sitting down to write a letter is such a painful operation to Mary, that you must accept me as her proxy. You have seen our house. What I now tell you is literally true. Yesterday week George Dyer called upon us, at one o'clock (*bright noonday*), on his way to dine with Mrs Barbauld at Newington. He sat with Mary about half an hour, and took leave. The maid saw him go out, from her kitchen window, but suddenly losing sight of him, ran up in a fright to Mary. G. D., instead of keeping the slip that leads to the gate, had deliberately, staff in hand, in broad open day, marched into the New River. He had not his spectacles on, and you know his absence. Who helped him out they can hardly tell, but between 'em they got him out, drenched thro' and thro'. A mob collected by that time, and accompanied him in. 'Send for the Doctor,' they said: and a one-eyed fellow, dirty and drunk, was fetched from the public house at the end, where it seems he lurks, for the sake of picking up water practice; having formerly had a medal from the Humane Society for some rescue. By his advice the patient was put between blankets; and when I came home at 4 to dinner, I found G. D. a-bed, and raving, light-headed, with the brandy and water which the doctor had administered. He sang, laughed, whimpered, screamed, babbled of guardian angels, would get up and go home; but we kept him there by force; and by next morning he

departed sober, and seems to have received no injury. All
my friends are open-mouth'd about having paling before
the river, but I cannot see, that because a lunatic chooses
to walk into a river with his eyes open at mid day, I am
any the more likely to be drowned in it, coming home at
midnight.

I had the honour of dining at the Mansion House on
Thursday last by special card from the Lord Mayor, who
never saw my face, nor I his; and all from being a writer
in a magazine. The dinner costly, served on massy plate;
champagne, pines, &c.; 47 present, among whom the
Chairman and two other directors of the India Company.

There's for you! and got away pretty sober. Quite saved
my credit.

We continue to like our house prodigiously.

Does Mary Hazlitt go on with her novel? or has she began another? I would not discourage her, though we continue to think it (so far) in its present state not saleable.
Our kind remembrances to her and hers, and you and
yours.

Yours truly,

C. LAMB.

I am pleased that H. liked my letter to the Laureat.

Amicus Redivivus

> Where were ye, Nymphs, when the remorseless deep
> Closed o'er the head of your loved Lycidas ?

I do not know when I have experienced a stranger sensation than on seeing my old friend, G. D., who had been
paying me a morning visit, a few Sundays back, at my cottage at Islington, upon taking leave, instead of turning
down the right-hand path by which he had entered – with
staff in hand, and at noonday, deliberately march right
forwards into the midst of the stream that runs by us, and
totally disappear.

A spectacle like this at dusk would have been appalling enough; but in the broad, open daylight, to witness such an unreserved motion towards self-destruction in a valued friend, took from me all power of speculation.

How I found my feet I know not. Consciousness was quite gone. Some spirit, not my own, whirled me to the spot. I remember nothing but the silvery apparition of a good white head emerging; nigh which a staff (the hand unseen that wielded it) pointed upwards, as feeling for the skies. In a moment (if time was in that time) he was on my shoulders, and I – freighted with a load more precious than his who bore Anchises.

And here I cannot but do justice to the officious zeal of sundry passers-by, who, albeit arriving a little too late to participate in the honours of the rescue, in philanthropic shoals came thronging to communicate their advice as to the recovery; prescribing variously the application, or non-application, of salt, etc., to the person of the patient. Life, meantime, was ebbing fast away, amidst the stifle of conflicting judgments, when one, more sagacious than the rest, by a bright thought, proposed sending for the Doctor. Trite as the counsel was, and impossible, as one should think, to be missed on, – shall I confess? – in this emergency it was to me as if an Angel had spoken. Great previous exertions – and mine had not been inconsiderable – are commonly followed by a debility of purpose. This was a moment of irresolution.

'Monoculus' – for so, in default of catching his true name, I choose to designate the medical gentleman who now appeared – is a grave, middle-aged person, who, without having studied at the college, or truckled to the pedantry of a diploma, hath employed a great portion of his valuable time in experimental processes upon the bodies of unfortunate fellow-creatures, in whom the vital spark, to mere vulgar thinking, would seem extinct and lost for ever. He omitteth no occasion of obtruding his services, from a case of common surfeit suffocation to the ignobler obstructions, sometimes induced by a too wilful application of the plant *cannabis* outwardly. But though he declineth not altogether these drier extinctions, his occupation tendeth, for the most part, to water-practice; for the convenience of which, he hath judiciously fixed his quarters near the grand repository of the stream mentioned, where day and night, from his little watch-tower, at the Middleton's Head, he listeneth to detect the wrecks of drowned mortality – partly, as he said, to be upon the spot – and partly, because the liquids which he useth to prescribe to himself and his patients, on these distressing occasions, are ordinarily more conveniently to be found at these common hostelries than in the shops and phials of the apothecaries. His ear hath arrived to such finesse by practice, that it is reported he can distinguish a plunge, at half a furlong distance; and can tell if it be casual or deliberate. He weareth a medal, suspended over a suit, originally of a sad brown, but which, by time and frequency of nightly divings, has been dinged into a true professional sable. He passeth by the name of Doctor, and is remarkable for wanting his left eye. His remedy – after a sufficient application of warm blankets, friction, etc., is a simple tumbler, or more, of the purest Cognac, with water, made as hot as the convalescent can bear it. Where he findeth, as in the case of my friend, a squeamish subject, he condescendeth to be the taster; and showeth, by his own example, the innocuous nature of the prescription. Nothing can be more kind or encouraging than this procedure. It addeth confidence to the patient, to see his medical adviser go hand in hand with himself in the remedy. When the doctor swalloweth his own draught, what peevish invalid can refuse to pledge him in the potion? In fine, 'Monoculus' is a humane, sensible man, who, for a slender pittance, scarce enough to sustain life, is content to wear it out in the endeavour to save the lives of others – his pretensions so moderate, that with difficulty I could press a crown upon him, for the price of restoring the existence of such an invaluable creature to society as G. D.

It was pleasant to observe the effect of the subsiding alarm upon the nerves of the dear absentee. It seemed to have given a shake to memory, calling up notice after notice, of all the providential deliverances he had experienced in the

course of his long and innocent life. Sitting up on my couch
– my couch which, naked and void of furniture hitherto, for
the salutary repose which it administered, shall be honoured with costly valance, at some price, and henceforth be
a state-bed at Colebrook, – he discoursed of marvellous
escapes – by carelessness of nurses – by pails of gelid, and
kettles of the boiling element, in infancy – by orchard
pranks, and snapping twigs, in schoolboy frolics – by descent of tiles at Trumpington, and of heavier tomes at
Pembroke – by studious watchings, inducing frightful
vigilance – by want, and the fear of want, and all the sore
throbbings of the learned head. – Anon, he would burst
out into little fragments of chanting – of songs long ago –
ends of deliverance hymns, not remembered before since
childhood, but coming up now, when his heart was made
tender as a child's – for the *tremor cordis*, in the retrospect of
a recent deliverance, as in a case of impending danger,
acting upon an innocent heart, will produce a self-tender-
ness, which we should do ill to christen cowardice; and
Shakspeare, in the latter crisis, has made his good Sir Hugh
to remember the sitting by Babylon, and to mutter of
shallow rivers.

Waters of Sir Hugh Middleton – what a spark you were
like to have extinguished for ever! Your salubrious streams to
this City, for now near two centuries, would hardly have
atoned for what you were in a moment washing away.
Mockery of a river – liquid artifice – wretched conduit!
henceforth rank with canals and sluggish aqueducts. Was
it for this that, smit in boyhood with the explorations of that
Abyssinian traveller, I paced the vales of Amwell to explore
your tributary springs, to trace your salutary waters sparkling through green Hertfordshire, and cultured Enfield
parks? – Ye have no swans – no Naïads – no river God – or
did the benevolent hoary aspect of my friend tempt ye to
suck him in, that ye also might have the tutelary genius of
your waters?

Had he been drowned in Cam, there would have been
some consonancy in it; but what willows had ye to wave
and rustle over his moist sepulture? – or, having no *name*,

besides that unmeaning assumption of *eternal novity*, did ye
think to get one by the noble prize, and henceforth to be
termed the 'Stream Dyerian'?

> And could such spacious virtue find a grave
> Beneath the imposthumed bubble of a wave?

I protest, George, you shall not venture out again – no,
not by daylight – without a sufficient pair of spectacles – in
your musing moods especially. Your absence of mind we
have borne, till your presence of body came to be called in
question by it. You shall not go wandering into Euripus
with Aristotle, if we can help it. Fie, man, to turn dipper at
your years, after your many tracts in favour of sprinkling
only!

I have nothing but water in my head o'nights since this
frightful accident. Sometimes I am with Clarence in his
dream. At others, I behold Christian beginning to sink, and
crying out to his good brother Hopeful (that is, to me),
'I sink in deep waters; the billows go over my head, all the
waves go over me. Selah.' Then I have before me Palinurus,
just letting go the steerage. I cry out too late to save. Next
follow – a mournful procession – *suicidal faces*, saved against
their will from drowning; dolefully trailing a length of reluctant gratefulness, with ropy weeds pendent from locks
of watchet hue – constrained Lazari – Pluto's half-subjects
– stolen fees from the grave – bilking Charon of his fare.
At their head Arion – or is it G. D.?– in his singing garments
marcheth singly, with harp in hand, and votive garland,
which Machaon (or Dr Hawes) snatcheth straight, intend-
ing to suspend it to the stern God of Sea. Then follow dismal
streams of Lethe, in which the half-drenched on earth are
constrained to drown downright, by wharfs where Ophelia
twice acts her muddy death.

And doubtless, there is some notice in that invisible world
when one of us approacheth (as my friend did so lately)
to their inexorable precincts. When a soul knocks once,
twice, at Death's door, the sensation aroused within the
palace must be considerable; and the grim Feature, by

modern science so often dispossessed of his prey, must have
learned by this time to pity Tantalus.

A pulse assuredly was felt along the line of the Elysian
shades, when the near arrival of G. D. was announced by
no equivocal indications. From their seats of Asphodel arose
the gentler and the graver ghosts – poet, or historian – of
Grecian or of Roman lore – to crown with unfading chap-
lets the half-finished love-labours of their unwearied scholi-
ast. Him Markland expected – him Tyrwhitt hoped to
encounter – him the sweet lyrist of Peter House, whom he
had barely seen upon earth,[1] with newest airs prepared to
greet —; and patron of the gentle Christ's boy, – who
should have been his patrol through life – the mild Askew,
with longing aspirations leaned foremost from his venerable Æsculapian chair, to welcome into that happy company the matured virtues of the man, whose tender scions
in the boy he himself upon earth had so prophetically fed
and watered.

ELIA.

To George Dyer

Feb. 22nd, 1831.

Dear Dyer, – Mr Rogers, and Mr Rogers's friends, are perfectly assured, that you never intended any harm by an
innocent couplet, and that in the revivification of it by
blundering Barker you had no hand whatever. To imagine
that, at this time of day, Rogers broods over a fantastic
expression of more than thirty years' standing, would be to
suppose him indulging his 'Pleasures of Memory' with a
vengeance. You never penned a line which for its own sake
you need (dying) wish to blot. You mistake your heart if
you think you *can* write a lampoon. Your whips are rods of
roses. Your spleen has ever had for its object vices, not the
vicious – abstract offences, not the concrete sinner. But you

---

[1] *Graium tantum vidit.*

are sensitive, and wince as much at the consciousness of having committed a compliment, as another man would at the perpetration of an affront. But do not lug me into the same soreness of conscience with yourself. I maintain, and will to the last hour, that I never writ of you but *con amore*. That if any allusion was made to your near-sightedness, it was not for the purpose of mocking an infirmity, but of connecting it with scholar-like habits : for is it not erudite and scholarly to be somewhat near of sight, before age naturally brings on the malady? You could not then plead the *obrepens senectus*. Did I not moreover make it an apology for a certain *absence*, which some of your friends may have experienced, when you have not on a sudden made recognition of them in a casual street-meeting, and did I not strengthen your excuse for this slowness of recognition, by further accounting morally for the present engagement of your mind in worthy objects? Did I not, in your person, make the handsomest apology for absent-of-mind people that was ever made? If these things be not so, I never knew what I wrote or meant by my writing, and have been penning libels all my life without being aware of it. Does it follow that I should have exprest myself exactly in the same way of those dear old eyes of yours *now* – now that Father Time has conspired with a hard task-master to put a last extinguisher upon them? I should as soon have insulted the Answerer of Salmasius, when he awoke up from his ended task, and saw no more with mortal vision. But you are many films removed yet from Milton's calamity. You write perfectly intelligibly. Marry, the letters are not all of the same size or tallness; but that only shows your proficiency in the *hands* – text, german-hand, court-hand, sometimes law-hand, and affords variety. You pen better than you did a twelvemonth ago ; and if you continue to improve, you bid fair to win the golden pen which is the prize at your young gentlemen's academy. But you must beware of Valpy, and his printing-house, that hazy cave of Trophonius, out of which it was a mercy that you escaped with a glimmer. Beware of MSS. and Variæ Lectiones. Settle the text for once in your mind, and stick to it. You have some years' good sight in you yet, if you do not tamper with it. It is not for you (for *us* I should say) to go poring into Greek contractions, and star-gazing upon slim Hebrew points. We have yet the sight

Of sun, and moon, and star, throughout the year,
And man and woman.

You have vision enough to discern Mrs Dyer from the other comely gentlewoman who lives up at staircase No. 5; or, if you should make a blunder in the twilight, Mrs Dyer has too much good sense to be jealous for a mere effect of imperfect optics. But don't try to write the Lord's Prayer, Creed, and Ten Commandments, in the compass of a halfpenny; nor run after a midge or a mote to catch it; and leave off hunting for needles in bushels of hay, for all these things strain the eyes. The snow is six feet deep in some parts here. I must put on jack-boots to get at the post-office with this. It is not good for weak eyes to pore upon snow too much. It lies in drifts. I wonder what its drift is; only that it makes good pancakes, remind Mrs Dyer. It turns a pretty green world into a white one. It glares too much for an innocent colour, methinks. I wonder why you think I dislike gilt edges. They set off a letter marvellously. Yours, for instance, looks for all the world like a tablet of curious *hieroglyphics* in a gold frame. But don't go and lay this to your eyes. You always wrote hieroglyphically, yet not to come up to the mystical notations and conjuring characters of Dr Parr. You never wrote what I call a school-master's hand, like Clarke; nor a woman's hand, like Southey; nor a missal hand, like Porson; nor an all-of-the-wrong-side-sloping hand, like Miss Hayes; nor a dogmatic, Mede-and-Persian, peremptory hand, like Rickman; but you ever wrote what I call a Grecian's hand; what the Grecians write (or used) at Christ's Hospital; such as Whalley would have admired, and Boyer have applauded, but Smith or Atwood (writing-masters) would have horsed you for. Your boy-of-genius hand and your mercantile hand are various. By your flourishes, I should think you never learned to make eagles or corkscrews, or flourish the governors' names in the writing-school; and by the tenor and cut of your letters I suspect you were never in it at all. By the length of this scrawl you will think I have a design upon your optics; but I have writ as large as I could out of respect to them – too large, indeed, for beauty. Mine is a sort of deputy Grecian's hand; a little better, and more of a worldly hand, than a Grecian's, but still remote from the mercantile. I don't know how it is, but I keep my rank in fancy still since school-days. I can never forget I was a deputy Grecian! And writing to you, or to Coleridge, besides affection, I feel a reverential deference as to Grecians still. I keep my soaring way above the Great Erasmians, yet far beneath the other. Alas! what am I now? what is a Leadenhall clerk or India pensioner to a deputy Grecian? How art thou fallen, O Lucifer! Just room for our loves to Mrs D., &c.

C. LAMB.

LOGICIAN, METAPHYSICIAN, BARD

To Thomas Manning

[P.M. March 17, 1800.]

Dear Manning, – I am living in a continuous feast. Coleridge has been with me now for nigh three weeks, and the more I see of him in the quotidian undress and relaxation of his mind, the more cause I see to love him, and believe him a *very good man*, and all those foolish impressions to the contrary fly off like morning slumbers. He is engaged in translations, which I hope will keep him this month to come. He is uncommonly kind and friendly to me. He ferrets me day and night to *do something*. He tends me, amidst all his own worrying and heart-oppressing occupations, as a gardener tends his young *tulip*. Marry come up! what a pretty similitude, and how like your humble servant! He has lugged me to the brink of engaging to a newspaper, and has suggested to me for a first plan the forgery of a supposed manuscript of Burton the anatomist of melancholy. I have even written the introductory letter; and, if I can pick up a few guineas this way, I feel they will be most *refreshing*, bread being so dear. If I go on with it, I will apprise you of it, as you may like to see my things! and the *tulip*, of all flowers, loves to be admired most.

Pray pardon me, if my letters do not come very thick. I am so taken up with one thing or other, that I cannot pick out (I will not say time, but) fitting times to write to you. My dear love to Lloyd and Sophia, and pray split this thin letter into three parts, and present them with the *two biggest* in my name.

They are my oldest friends; but ever the new friend driveth out the old, as the ballad sings! God bless you all three! I would hear from Lloyd, if I could.

C. L.

Flour has just fallen nine shillings a sack! we shall be all too rich.

Tell Charles I have seen his Mamma, and am almost fallen in love with *her*, since I mayn't with Olivia. She is so fine and graceful, a complete Matron-Lady-Quaker. She has given me two little books. Olivia grows a charming girl – full of feeling, and thinner than she was.

But I have not time to fall in love.

Mary presents her *general compliments*. She keeps in fine health!

Huzza! boys,
and down with the Atheists.

To S. T. Coleridge

[No date. ? Autumn, 1820.]

Dear C., – Why will you make your visits, which should give pleasure, matter of regret to your friends? You never come but you take away some folio that is part of my exist-

ence. With a great deal of difficulty I was made to comprehend the extent of my loss. My maid Becky brought me a
dirty bit of paper, which contained her description of some
book which Mr Coleridge had taken away. It was 'Luster's
Tables,' which, for some time, I could not make out. 'What!
has he carried away any of the *tables*, Becky?' 'No, it wasn't
any tables, but it was a book that he called Luster's
Tables.' I was obliged to search personally among my
shelves, and a huge fissure suddenly disclosed to me the
true nature of the damage I had sustained. That book, C.,
you should not have taken away, for it is not mine; it is the
property of a friend, who does not know its value, nor indeed have I been very sedulous in explaining to him the
estimate of it; but was rather contented in giving a sort of
corroboration to a hint that he let fall, as to its being suspected to be not genuine, so that in all probability it would
have fallen to me as a deodand; not but I am as sure it is
Luther's as I am sure that Jack Bunyan wrote the " Pilgrim's
Progress;" but it was not for me to pronounce upon the
validity of testimony that had been disputed by learneder
clerks than I. So I quietly let it occupy the place it had
usurped upon my shelves, and should never have thought of
issuing an ejectment against it; for why should I be so
bigoted as to allow rites of hospitality to none but my own
books, children, &c.? – a species of egotism I abhor from
my heart. No; let 'em all snug together, Hebrews and Proselytes of the gate; no selfish partiality of mine shall make
distinction between them; I charge no warehouse-room for
my friends' commodities; they are welcome to come and
stay as long as they like, without paying rent. I have several
such strangers that I treat with more than Arabian courtesy; there's a copy of More's fine poem, which is none of
mine; but I cherish it as my own; I am none of those
churlish landlords that advertise the goods to be taken
away in ten days' time, or then to be sold to pay expenses.
So you see I had no right to lend you that book; I may lend
you my own books, because it is at my own hazard, but it is
not honest to hazard a friend's property; I always make that
distinction. I hope you will bring it with you, or send it by

Hartley; or he can bring that, and you the 'Polemical
Discourses', and come and eat some atoning mutton with
us one of these days shortly. We are engaged two or three
Sundays deep, but always dine at home on week-days at
half-past four. So come all four – men and books I mean –
my third shelf (northern compartment) from the top has
two devilish gaps, where you have knocked out its two eye-
teeth.

Your wronged friend,

C. LAMB.

The Two Races of Men

The human species, according to the best theory I can form
of it, is composed of two distinct races, *the men who borrow,
and the men who lend*. To these two original diversities may be
reduced all those impertinent classifications of Gothic and
Celtic tribes, white men, black men, red men. All the
dwellers upon earth, 'Parthians, and Medes, and Elamites',
flock hither, and do naturally fall in with one or other of
these primary distinctions. The infinite superiority of the
former, which I choose to designate as the *great race*, is
discernible in their figure, port, and a certain instinctive
sovereignty. The latter are born degraded. 'He shall serve
his brethren.' There is something in the air of one of this
cast, lean and suspicious; contrasting with the open, trust-
ing, generous manners of the other.

Observe who have been the greatest borrowers of all
ages – Alcibiades – Falstaff – Sir Richard Steele – our late
incomparable Brinsley – what a family likeness in all four!

What a careless, even deportment hath your borrower!
what rosy gills! what a beautiful reliance on Providence
doth he manifest, – taking no more thought than lilies!
What contempt for money, – accounting it (yours and mine
especially) no better than dross! What a liberal confounding
of those pedantic distinctions of *meum* and *tuum*! or rather,
what a noble simplification of language (beyond Tooke),
resolving these supposed opposites into one clear, intelligible

pronoun adjective! – What near approaches doth he make to the primitive *community*, – to the extent of one half of the principle at least.

He is the true taxer who 'calleth all the world up to be taxed'; and the distance is as vast between him and *one of us*, as subsisted between the Augustan Majesty and the poorest obolary Jew that paid it tribute-pittance at Jerusalem! – His exactions, too, have such a cheerful, voluntary air! So far removed from your sour parochial or state-gatherers, – those ink-horn varlets, who carry their want of welcome in their faces! He cometh to you with a smile, and troubleth you with no receipt; confining himself to no set season. Every day is his Candlemas, or his feast of Holy Michael. He applieth the *lene tormentum* of a pleasant look to your purse, – which to that gentle warmth expands her silken leaves, as naturally as the cloak of the traveller, for which sun and wind contended! He is the true Propontic which never ebbeth! The sea which taketh handsomely at each man's hand. In vain the victim, whom he delighteth to honour, struggles with destiny; he is in the net. Lend therefore cheerfully, O man ordained to lend – that thou lose not in the end, with thy worldly penny, the reversion promised. Combine not preposterously in thine own person the penalties of Lazarus and of Dives! – but, when thou seest the proper authority coming, meet it smilingly, as it were half-way. Come, a handsome sacrifice! See how light *he* makes of it! Strain not courtesies with a noble enemy.

Reflections like the foregoing were forced upon my mind by the death of my old friend, Ralph Bigod, Esq., who parted this life on Wednesday evening; dying, as he had lived, without much trouble. He boasted himself a descendant from mighty ancestors of that name, who heretofore held ducal dignities in this realm. In his actions and sentiments he belied not the stock to which he pretended. Early in life he found himself invested with ample revenues; which, with that noble disinterestedness which I have noticed as inherent in men of the *great race*, he took almost immediate measures entirely to dissipate and bring to nothing: for there is something revolting in the idea of a

king holding a private purse; and the thoughts of Bigod
were all regal. Thus furnished, by the very act of disfurnish-
ment; getting rid of the cumbersome luggage of riches,
more apt (as one sings)

> To slacken virtue, and abate her edge,
> Than prompt her to do aught may merit praise,

he set forth, like some Alexander, upon his great enterprise,
'borrowing and to borrow!'

In his periegesis, or triumphant progress throughout this
island, it has been calculated that he laid a tythe part of
the inhabitants under contribution. I reject this estimate as
greatly exaggerated: – but having had the honour of accompanying my friend, divers times, in his perambulations
about this vast city, I own I was greatly struck at first with
the prodigious number of faces we met, who claimed a
sort of respectful acquaintance with us. He was one day so
obliging as to explain the phenomenon. It seems, these were
his tributaries; feeders of his exchequer; gentlemen, his
good friends (as he was pleased to express himself), to whom
he had occasionally been beholden for a loan. Their multitudes did no way disconcert him. He rather took a pride in
numbering them; and, with Comus, seemed pleased to be
'stocked with so fair a herd'.

With such sources, it was a wonder how he contrived to
keep his treasury always empty. He did it by force of an
aphorism, which he had often in his mouth, that 'money
kept longer than three days stinks'. So he made use of it
while it was fresh. A good part he drank away (for he was
an excellent toss-pot), some he gave away, the rest he threw
away, literally tossing and hurling it violently from him –
as boys to burrs, or as if it had been infectious, – into ponds,
or ditches, or deep holes, inscrutable cavities of the earth;
– or he would bury it (where he would never seek it again)
by a river's side under some bank, which (he would face-
tiously observe) paid no interest – but out away from him
it must go peremptorily, as Hagar's offspring into the wilderness, while it was sweet. He never missed it. The streams

were perennial which fed his fisc. When new supplies became necessary, the first person that had the felicity to fall in with him, friend or stranger, was sure to contribute to the deficiency. For Bigod had an *undeniable* way with him. He had a cheerful, open exterior, a quick jovial eye, a bald forehead, just touched with grey (*cana fides*). He anticipated no excuse, and found none. And, waiving for a while my theory as to the *great race*, I would put it to the most untheorizing reader, who may at times have disposable coin in his pocket, whether it is not more repugnant to the kindliness of his nature to refuse such a one as I am describing, than to say *no* to a poor petitionary rogue (your bastard borrower), who, by his mumping visnomy, tells you that he expects nothing better; and, therefore, whose preconceived notions and expectations you do in reality so much less shock in the refusal.

When I think of this man; his fiery glow of heart; his swell of feeling; how magnificent, how *ideal* he was; how great at the midnight hour; and when I compare with him the companions with whom I have associated since, I grudge the saving of a few idle ducats, and think that I am fallen into the society of *lenders*, and *little* men.

To one like Elia, whose treasures are rather cased in leather covers than closed in iron coffers, there is a class of alienators more formidable than that which I have touched upon; I mean your *borrowers of books* — those mutilators of collections, spoilers of the symmetry of shelves, and creators of odd volumes. There is Comberbatch,[1] matchless in his depredations!

That foul gap in the bottom shelf facing you, like a great eye-tooth knocked out — (you are now with me in my little back study in Bloomsbury, Reader!) — with the huge Switzer-like tomes on each side (like the Guildhall giants, in their reformed posture, guardant of nothing) once held the tallest of my folios, *Opera Bonaventuræ*, choice and massy divinity, to which its two supporters (school divinity also,

[1 In 1793 Coleridge had enlisted in the 15th Light Dragoons under the name of Silas Titus Comberback — '*My habits were so little equestrian that my horse, I doubt not, was of that opinion,*' etc.]

but of a lesser calibre, — Bellarmine, and Holy Thomas),
showed but as dwarfs, — itself an Ascapart! — *that* Comberbatch abstracted upon the faith of a theory he holds, which
is more easy, I confess, for me to suffer by than to refute,
namely, that 'the title to property in a book (my Bonaven-
ture, for instance) is in exact ratio to the claimant's powers
of understanding and appreciating the same'. Should he go
on acting upon this theory, which of our shelves is
safe?

The slight vacuum in the left-hand case — two .shelves
from the ceiling — scarcely distinguishable but by the quick
eye of a loser — was whilom the commodious resting-place
of Browne on Urn Burial. C. will hardly allege that he knows
more about that treatise than I do, who introduced it to
him, and was indeed the first (of the moderns) to discover
its beauties — but so have I known a foolish lover to praise
his mistress in the presence of a rival more qualified to
carry her off than himself. — Just below, Dodsley's dramas
want their fourth volume, where Vittoria Corombona is!
The remainder nine are as distasteful as Priam's refuse
sons, when the Fates *borrowed* Hector. Here stood the
Anatomy of Melancholy, in sober state. — There loitered the
Complete Angler; quiet as in life, by some stream side. In
yonder nook, *John Buncle*, a widower-volume, with 'eyes
closed', mourns his ravished mate.

Onc justice I must do my friend, that if he sometimes,
like the sea, sweeps away a treasure, at another time, sea-
like, he throws up as rich an equivalent to match it. I have
a small under-collection of this nature (my friend's gather-
ings in his various calls), picked up, he has forgotten at
what odd places, and deposited with as little memory at
mine. I take in these orphans, the twice-deserted. These
proselytes of the gate are welcome as the true Hebrews.
There they stand in conjunction; natives, and naturalized.
The latter seem as little disposed to inquire out their true
lineage as I am. — I charge no warehouse-room for these
deodands, nor shall ever put myself to the ungentlemanly
trouble of advertising a sale of them to pay expenses.

To lose a volume to C. carries some sense and meaning

in it. You are sure that he will make one hearty meal on your viands, if he can give no account of the platter after it. But what moved thee, wayward, spiteful K[enney], to be so importunate to carry off with thee, in spite of tears and adjurations to thee to forbear, the Letters of that princely woman, the thrice noble Margaret Newcastle – knowing at the time, and knowing that I knew also, thou most assuredly wouldst never turn over one leaf of the illustrious folio: – what but the mere spirit of contradiction, and childish love of getting the better of thy friend? – Then, worst cut of all! to transport it with thee to the Gallican land –

> Unworthy land to harbour such a sweetness,
> A virtue in which all ennobling thoughts dwelt,
> Pure thoughts, kind thoughts, high thoughts, her sex's
>   wonder!

— hadst thou not thy play-books, and books of jests and fancies, about thee, to keep thee merry, even as thou keepest all companies with thy quips and mirthful tales? Child of the Green-room, it was unkindly done of thee. Thy wife, too, that part-French, better-part-English-woman! – that *she* could fix upon no other treatise to bear away, in kindly token of remembering us, than the works of Fulke Greville, Lord Brook – of which no Frenchman, nor woman of France, Italy, or England, was ever by nature constituted to comprehend a tittle! *Was there not Zimmerman on Solitude?*

   Reader, if haply thou art blessed with a moderate collection, be shy of showing it; or if thy heart overfloweth to lend them, lend thy books; but let it be to such a one as S. T. C. – he will return them (generally anticipating the time appointed) with usury; enriched with annotations, tripling their value. I have had experience. Many are these precious MSS. of his – (in *matter* oftentimes, and almost in *quantity* not unfrequently, vying with the originals) in no very clerkly hand – legible in my Daniel; in old Burton; in Sir Thomas Browne; and those abstruser cogitations of the Greville, now, alas! wandering in Pagan lands. – I counsel thee, shut not thy heart, nor thy library, against S. T. C.

ELIA.

London Magazine, December 1820.

To J. Payne Collier

The Garden of England, Dec. 10, 1829.

Dear J. P. C., – I know how zealously you feel for our friend S. T. Coleridge; and I know that you and your family attended his lectures four or five years ago. He is in bad health, and worse mind: and unless something is done to lighten his mind he will soon be reduced to his extremities; and even these are not in the best condition. I am sure that you will do for him what you can; but at present he seems to be in a mood to do for himself. He projects a new course, not of physic, nor of metaphysic, nor a new course of life, but a new course of lectures on Shakespeare and Poetry. There is no man better qualified (always excepting number one); but I am pre-engaged for a series of dissertations on Indian and Indiapendance, to be completed, at the expense of the Company, in I know not (yet) how many volumes foolscap folio. I am busy getting up my Hindoo mythology; and, for the purpose, I am once more enduring Southey's curse (of 'Kehama'). To be serious, Coleridge's state and affairs make me so, and there are particular reasons just now, and have been any time for the last twenty years, why he should succeed. He will do so with a little encouragement. I have not seen him lately; and he does not know that I am writing.

Yours (for Coleridge's sake) in haste,

C. LAMB.

Death of Coleridge

When I heard of the death of Coleridge, it was without grief. It seemed to me that he long had been on the confines of the next world, – that he had a hunger for eternity. I grieved then that I could not grieve. But since, I feel how great a part he was of me. His great and dear spirit haunts me. I cannot think a thought, I cannot make a criticism on men and books, without an ineffectual turning and reference to him. He was the proof and touchstone of all my cogitations. He was a Grecian (or in the first form) at Christ's Hospital, where I was Deputy-Grecian; and the same subordination and deference to him I have preserved through a life-long acquaintance. Great in his writings, he was greatest in his conversation. In him was disproved that old maxim, that we should allow every one his share of talk. He would talk from morn to dewy eve, nor cease till far midnight; yet who ever would interrupt him – who would obstruct that continuous flow of converse, fetched from Helicon or Zion? He had the tact of making the unintelligible seem plain. Many who read the abstruser parts of his 'Friend' would complain that his works did not answer to his spoken wisdom. They were identical. But he had a tone in oral delivery which seemed to convey sense to those who were otherwise imperfect recipients. He was my fifty-years-old friend without a dissention. Never saw I his likeness, nor probably the world can see again. I seem to love the house he died at more passionately than when he lived. I love the faithful Gilmans more than while they exercised their virtues towards him living. What was his mansion is consecrated to me a chapel.

Chs. Lamb.

[Written, at the request of John Forster, in the album of Mr Keymer, November 1834.]

THREE YOUNG MAIDS IN FRIENDSHIP MET

In a letter to Manning in March, 1803, Lamb writes: '*Dear Manning, – I send you some verses I have made on the death of a young Quaker you may have heard me speak of as being in love with for some years while I lived at Pentonville, though I had never spoken to her in my life. She died about a month since ...*' The verses form one of Lamb's best-known poems.

Hester

When maidens such as Hester die,
Their place ye may not well supply,
Though ye among a thousand try,
   With vain endeavour.

A month or more hath she been dead,
Yet cannot I by force be led
To think upon the wormy bed,
   And her together.

A springy motion in her gait,
A rising step, did indicate
Of pride and joy no common rate,
   That flushed her spirit.

I know not by what name beside
I shall it call: — if 'twas not pride,
It was a joy to that allied
   She did inherit.

Her parents held the Quaker rule,
Which doth the human feeling cool,
But she was trained in Nature's school,
   Nature had blest her.

A waking eye, a prying mind,
A heart that stirs, is hard to bind,
A hawk's keen sight ye cannot blind,
   Ye could not Hester.

My sprightly neighbour, gone before
To that unknown and silent shore,
Shall we not meet, as heretofore,
   Some summer morning,

When from thy cheerful eyes a ray
Hath struck a bliss upon the day,
A bliss that would not go away,
   A sweet forewarning?

E

To Jacob Vale Asbury

April, 1830.

Dear Sir – Some draughts and boluses have been brought here which we conjecture were meant for the young lady whom you saw this morning, though they are labelled for MISS ISOLA LAMB.

No such person is known on the Chase Side, and she is fearful of taking medicines which may have been made up for another patient. She begs me to say that she was born an *Isola* and christened *Emma*. Moreover that she is Italian by birth, and that her ancestors were from Isola Bella (Fair Island) in the kingdom of Naples. She has never changed her name and rather mournfully adds that she has no prospect at present of doing so. She is literally 'I. Sola', or single, at present. Therefore she begs that the obnoxious monosyllable may be omitted on future Phials, – an innocent syllable enough, you'll say, but she has no claim to it. It is the bitterest pill of the seven you have sent her. When a lady loses her good *name*, what is to become of her? Well she must swallow it as well as she can, but begs the dose may not be repeated.

Yours faithfully,

CHARLES LAMB (not Isola.)

To Edward Moxon

July 24th, 1833.

For God's sake give Emma no more watches; *one* has turned her head. She is arrogant and insulting. She said something very unpleasant to our old clock in the passage, as if he did not keep time, and yet he had made her no appointment. She takes it out every instant to look at the moment-hand. She lugs us out into the fields, because there the bird-boys ask you, 'Pray, Sir, can you tell us what's o'clock?' and she answers them punctually. She loses all her time looking to see 'what the time is'. I overheard her whispering, 'Just so many hours, minutes, &c., to Tuesday; I think St George's goes too slow'. This little present of Time! – why, – 'tis Eternity to her!

What can make her so fond of a gingerbread watch?

She has spoiled some of the movements. Between ourselves, she has kissed away 'half-past twelve'. which I suppose to be the canonical hour in Hanover Square.

Well, if 'love me love my watch' answers, she will keep time to you.

It goes right by the Horse Guards.

Dearest M., – Never mind opposite nonsense. She does not love you for the watch, but the watch for you. I will be at the wedding, and keep the 30th July, as long as my poor months last me, as a festival, gloriously.

Yours ever,

ELIA.

We have not heard from Cambridge. I will write the moment we do.

Edmonton, 24th July, twenty minutes past three by Emma's watch.

To Fanny Kelly

20 July, 1819.

Dear Miss Kelly, – We had the pleasure, *pain* I might better call it, of seeing you last night in the new Play. It was a most consummate piece of Acting, but what a task for you to undergo! at a time when your heart is sore from real sorrow! it has given rise to a train of thinking, which I cannot suppress.

Would to God you were released from this way of life; that you could bring your mind to consent to take your lot with us, and throw off for ever the whole burden of your Profession. I neither expect or wish you to take notice of this which I am writing, in your present over occupied & hurried state. – But to think of it at your leisure. I have quite income enough, if that were all, to justify for me making such a proposal with what I may call even a handsome provision for my survivor. What you possess of your own would naturally be appropriated to those, for whose sake chiefly you have made so many hard sacrifices. I am not so foolish as not to know that I am a most unworthy match for such a one as you, but you have for years been a principal object in my mind. In many a sweet assumed character I have learned to love you, but simply as F. M. Kelly I love you better than them all. Can you quite these shadows of existence, & come & be a reality to us? can you leave off harassing yourself to please a thankless multitude, who know nothing of you, and begin at last to live to yourself and your friends?

As plainly and frankly as I have seen you give or refuse assent in some feigned scene, so frankly do me the justice to answer me. It is impossible I should feel injured or aggrieved by your telling me at once, that the proposal does not suit you. It is impossible that I should ever think of molesting you with idle importunity and persecution after your mind [is] once firmly spoken – but happier, far happier, could I have leave to hope a time might come, when our friends might be your friends, our interests yours; our book-knowledge, if in that inconsiderable particular we have any little advantage, might impart something to you, which you would every day have it in your power ten thousand fold to repay by the added cheerfulness and joy which you could not fail to bring as a dowry into whatever family should have the honor and happiness of receiving *you*, the most welcome accession that could be made to it.

In haste, but with entire respect and deepest affection, I subscribe myself

C. LAMB.

From Fanny Kelly

Henrietta Street, July 20th, 1819.

An early and deeply rooted attachment has fixed my heart on one from whom no worldly prospect can well induce me to withdraw it, but while I

*thus frankly and decidedly decline your proposal, believe me, I am not
insensible to the high honour which the preference of such a mind as yours
confers upon me — let me, however, hope that all thought upon this subject will end with this letter, and that you will henceforth encourage no
other sentiment towards me than esteem in my private character and a continuance of that approbation of my humble talents which you have already
expressed so much and so often to my advantage and gratification.*

Believe me I feel proud to acknowledge myself,

Your obliged friend,

F. M. KELLY.

To Fanny Kelly

Dear Miss Kelly, — *Your injunctions shall be obeyed to a tittle.*
I feel myself in a lackadaisical no-how-ish kind of a humour.
I believe it is the rain or something. I had thought to have
written seriously, but I fancy I succeed best in epistles of
mere fun ; puns and *that* nonsense. You will be good friends
with us, will you not? let what has past 'break no bones'
between us. You will not refuse us them next time we send
for them?

C. L.

Do you observe the delicacy of not signing my full name?
N.B. Do not paste that last letter of mine into your Book.

CHARLES LAMB AND CO.

To Mrs William Wordsworth

18 feb. 1818. East India House.

(Mary shall send you all the *news*, which I find I have left
out.)

My dear Mrs Wordsworth, I have repeatedly taken pen
in hand to answer your kind letter. My sister should more

properly have done it, but she having failed, I consider myself answerable for her debts. I am now trying to do it in the midst of Commercial noises, and with a quill which seems more ready to glide into arithmetical figures and names of Goods, Cassia, Cardemoms, Aloes, Ginger, Tea, than into kindly responses and friendly recollections.

The reason why I cannot write letters at home is, that I am never alone. Plato's (I write to *W. W.* now) Plato's double animal parted never longed more to be reciprocally reunited in the system of its first creation, than I sometimes do to be but for a moment single and separate. Except my morning's walk to the office, which is like treading on sands of gold for that reason, I am never so. I cannot walk home from office but some officious friend offers his damn'd unwelcome courtesies to accompany me. All the morning I am pestered. I could sit and gravely cast up sums in great Books, or compare sum with sum, and write 'Paid' against this and 'Unp'd' against t'other, and yet reserve in some 'corner of my mind' some darling thoughts all my own – faint memory of some passage in a Book – or the tone of an absent friend's Voice – a snatch of Miss Burrell's singing – a gleam of Fanny Kelly's divine plain face – The two operations might be going on at the same time without thwarting, as the sun's two motions (earth's I mean), or as I sometimes turn round till I am giddy, in my back parlour, while my sister is walking longitudinally in the front – or as the shoulder of veal twists round with the spit, while the smoke wreathes up the chimney – but there are a set of amateurs of the Belle Lettres – the gay science – who come to me as a sort of rendezvous, putting questions of criticism, of British Institutions, Lalla Rook &c., what Coleridge said at the Lecture last night – who have the form of reading men, but, for any possible use Reading can be to them but to talk of, might as well have been Ante-Cadmeans born, or have lain sucking out the sense of an Egypt^{n}. hieroglyph as long as the Pyramids will last before they should find it. These pests worrit me at business and in all its intervals, perplexing my accounts, poisoning my little salutary warming-time at the fire, puzzling my paragraphs if I take a newspaper, cramming in between my own free thoughts and a column of figures which had come to an amicable compromise but for them. Their noise ended, one of them, as I said, accompanys me home lest I should be solitary for a moment; he at length takes his welcome leave at the door, up I go, mutton on table, hungry as hunter, hope to forget my cares and bury them in the agreeable abstraction of mastication, knock at the door, in comes Mrs Hazlitt, or M. Burney, or Morgan, or Demogorgon, or my brother, or somebody, to prevent my eating alone, a Process absolutely necessary to my poor wretched digestion. O the pleasure of eating alone! – eating my dinner alone! let me think of it. But in they come, and make it absolutely necessary that I should open a bottle of orange – for my meat turns into stone when any one dines with me, if I have not wine – wine can mollify stones. Then *that* wine turns into acidity, acerbity, misanthropy, a hatred of my interrupters (God bless 'em! I love some of 'em dearly), and with the hatred a still greater aversion to their going away. Bad is the dead sea they bring upon me, choaking and death-doing, but worse is the deader dry sand they leave me on if they go before bed time. Come never, I would say to these spoilers of my dinner, but if you come, never go. The fact is, this interruption does not happen very often, but every time it comes by surprise that present bane of my life, orange wine, with all its dreary stifling consequences, follows. Evening Company I should always like had I any mornings, but I am saturated with human faces (*divine* forsooth) and voices all the golden morning, and five evenings in a week would be as much as I should covet to be in company, but I assure you that is a wonderful week in which I can get two, or one, to myself. I am never C. L. but always C. L. and Co.

He, who thought it not good for man to be alone, preserve me from the more prodigious monstrosity of being never by myself. I forget bed time, but even there these sociable frogs clamber up to annoy me. Once a week, generally some singular evening that, being alone, I go to bed at the hour I ought always to be abed, just close to my bedroom window is the club room of a public house, where a set of singers, I take them to be chorus-singers of the two theatres (it must be *both of them*), begin their orgies. They are a set of fellows (as I conceive) who being limited by their talents to the burthen of the song at the play houses, in revenge have got the common popular airs by Bishop or some cheap composer arranged for choruses, that is, to be sung all in chorus. At least I never catch any of the text of the plain song, nothing but the Babylonish choral howl at the tail on't. 'That fury being quenchd' – the howl I mean – a curseder burden succeeds, of shouts and clapping and knocking of the table. At length over tasked nature drops under it and escapes for a few hours into the society of the sweet silent creatures of Dreams, which go away with mocks and mows at cockcrow. And then I think of the words Christobel's father used (bless me, I have dipt in the wrong ink) to say every morning by way of variety when he awoke – 'Every knell, the Baron saith, Wakes us up to a world of death', or something like it. All I mean by this senseless interrupted tale is, that by my central situation I am a little over companied. Not that I have any animosity against the good creatures that are so anxious to drive away the Harpy solitude from me. I like 'em, and cards, and a chearful glass, but I mean merely to give you an idea between office con- finement and after office society, how little time I can call my own. I mean only to draw a picture, not to make an inference. I would not that I know of have it otherwise. I only wish sometimes I could exchange some of my faces and voices for the faces and voices which a late visitation brought most welcome and carried away leaving regret, but more pleasure, even a kind of gratitude, at being so often favored with that kind northern visitation. My Lon- don faces and noises don't hear me – I mean no disrespect – or I should explain myself that instead of their return 220 times a year and the return of W. W. &c. 7 times in 104 weeks, some more equal distribution might be found. I have scarce room to put in Mary's kind love and my poor name.

CH. LAMB.

Many Friends

Unfortunate is the lot of that man, who can look round
about the wide world, and exclaim with truth, *I have no
friend!* Do you know any such lonely sufferer? For mercy
sake send him to me. I can afford him plenty. He shall have
them good, cheap. I have enough and to spare. Truly
society is the balm of human life. But you may take a surfeit
from sweetest odours administered to satiety. Hear my case,
dear 'Variorum', and pity me. I am an elderly gentleman
– not old – a sort of middle-aged-gentleman-and-a-half –
with a tolerable larder, cellar, &c.; and a most unfortunately easy temper for the callous front of impertinence to try
conclusions on. My day times are entirely engrossed by the
business of a public office, where I am any thing but alone
from nine till five. I have forty fellow-clerks about me during
those hours; and, though the human face be divine, I
protest that so many faces seen every day do very much
diminish the homage I am willing to pay to that divinity.
It fares with these divine resemblances as with a Poly-
theism. Multiply the object and you infallibly enfeeble the
adoration. 'What a piece of work is Man! how excellent in
faculty,' &c. But a great many men together – a hot huddle
of rational creatures – Hamlet himself would have lowered
his contemplation a peg or two in my situation. *Tædet me
harum quotidianarum formarum.* I go home every day to my
late dinner, absolutely famished and face-sick. I am sometimes fortunate enough to go off unaccompanied. The relief
is restorative like sleep; but far oftener, alas! some one of
my fellows, who lives *my way* (as they call it) does me the
sociality of walking with me. He sees me to the door; and
now I figure to myself a snug fire-side – comfortable meal –
a respiration from the burthen of society – and the blessedness of a single knife and fork. I sit down to my solitary
mutton, happy as Adam when a bachelor. I have not
swallowed a mouthful, before a startling ring announces the
visit of *a friend.* O! for an everlasting muffle upon that
appalling instrument of torture! A knock makes me nervous;
but a ring is a positive fillip to all the sour passions of my

E*

nature: – and yet such is my effeminacy of temperament,
I neither tie up the one nor dumbfound the other: But these
accursed friends, or fiends, that torture me thus! They come
in with a full consciousness of their being unwelcome – with
a sort of grin of triumph over your weakness. My soul sickens
within when they enter. I can scarcely articulate a 'how
d'ye'. My digestive powers fail. I have enough to do to
maintain them in any healthiness when alone. Eating is a
solitary function; you may drink in company. Accordingly
the bottle soon succeeds; and such is my infirmity, that the
reluctance soon subsides before it. The visitor becomes
agreeable. I find a great deal that is good in him; wonder
I should have felt such aversion on his first entrance; we
get chatty, conversible; insensibly comes midnight; and I
am dismissed to the cold bed of celibacy (the only place,
alas! where I am suffered to be alone) with the reflection
that another day has gone over my head without the
possibility of enjoying my own free thoughts in solitude even
for a solitary moment. O for a Lodge in some vast wilderness! the den of those Seven Sleepers (conditionally the
other six were away) – a *Crusoe* solitude!

What most disturbs me is, that my chief annoyers are
mostly young men. Young men, let them think as they
please, are no company *singly* for a gentleman of my years.
They do mighty well in a mixed society, and where there
are females to take them off, as it were. But to have the load
of one of them to one's own self for successive hours conversation is unendurable.

There was my old friend Captain Beacham – he died some
six years since, bequeathing to my friendship three stout
young men, his sons, and seven girls, the tallest in the land.
Pleasant, excellent young women they were, and for their
sakes I did, and could endure much. But they were too tall.
I am superstitious in that respect, and think that to a just
friendship, something like proportion in stature as well as
mind is desirable. Now I am five feet and a trifle more.
Each of these young women rose to six, and one exceeded
by two inches. The brothers are proportionably taller. I
have sometimes taken the altitude of this friendship; and

on a modest computation I may be said to have known at one time a whole furlong of Beachams. But the young women are married off, and dispersed among the provinces. The brothers are left. Nothing is more distasteful than these relics and parings of past friendships – unmeaning records of agreeable hours flown. There are three of them. If they hunted in triples, or even couples, it were something; but by a refinement of persecution, they contrive to come singly; and so spread themselves out into three evenings molestation in a week. Nothing is so distasteful as the sight of their long legs, couched for continuance upon my fender. They have been mates of India-men; and one of them in particular has a story of a shark swallowing a boy in the bay of Calcutta. I wish the shark had swallowed *him*. Nothing can be more useless than their conversation to me, unless it is mine to them. We have no ideas (save of eating and drinking) in common. The shark story has been told till it cannot elicit a spark of attention; but it goes on just as usual. When I try to introduce a point of literature, or common life, the mates gape at me. When I fill a glass, they fill one too. Here is sympathy. And for this poor correspondency of having a gift of swallowing and retaining liquor in common with my fellow-creatures, I am to be tied up to an ungenial intimacy, abhorrent from every sentiment, and every sympathy besides. But I cannot break the bond. They are sons of my old friend.

LEPUS.

The New Times, January 1825.

PART III

MORE HOUSE LAMB
THAN
GRASS LAMB

'Elia — much more of house Lamb than of grass Lamb — avowedly caring little or nothing for pastoral.' Thomas Hood, in a description of a *London Magazine* dinner.

To Thomas Manning

[P.M. Nov. 28, 1800.]

Dear Manning, – I have received a very kind invitation from Lloyd and Sophia to go and spend a month with them at the Lakes. Now it fortunately happens (which is so seldom the case!) that I have spare cash by me, enough to answer the expenses of so long a journey; and I am determined to get away from the office by some means. The purpose of this letter is to request of you (my dear friend) that you will not take it unkind if I decline my proposed visit to Cambridge *for the present*. Perhaps I shall be able to take Cambridge *in my way*, going or coming. I need not describe to you the expectations which such an one as myself, pent up all my life in a dirty city, have formed of a tour to the Lakes. Consider Grasmere! Ambleside! Wordsworth! Coleridge! I hope you will. Hills, woods, lakes, and mountains, to the eternal devil. I will eat snipes with thee, Thomas Manning. Only confess, confess, a *bite*.

P.S. I think you named the 16th; but was it not modest of Lloyd to send such an invitation! It shows his knowledge of *money* and *time*. I would be loth to think he meant

> ' Ironic satire sidelong sklented
>   On my poor pursie.' – BURNS.

For my part, with reference to my friends northward, I must confess that I am not romance-bit about *Nature*. The earth, and sea, and sky (when all is said) is but as a house to dwell in. If the inmates be courteous, and good liquors flow like the conduits at an old coronation; if they can talk sensibly and feel properly; I have no need to stand staring upon the gilded looking-glass (that strained my friend's purse-strings in the purchase), nor his five-shilling print over the mantelpiece of old Nabbs the carrier (which only betrays his false taste). Just as important to me (in a sense) is all the

furniture of my world – eye-pampering, but satisfies no
heart. Streets, streets, streets, markets, theatres, churches,
Covent Gardens, shops sparkling with pretty faces of industrious milliners, neat sempstresses, ladies cheapening,
gentlemen behind counters lying, authors in the street with
spectacles, George Dyers (you may know them by their gait),
lamps lit at night, pastry-cooks' and silver-smiths' shops,
beautiful Quakers of Pentonville, noise of coaches, drowsy
cry of mechanic watchman at night, with bucks reeling
home drunk; if you happen to wake at midnight, cries of
Fire and Stop thief; inns of court, with their learned air,
and halls, and butteries, just like Cambridge colleges; old
book-stalls, Jeremy Taylors, Burtons on Melancholy, and
Religio Medicis on every stall. These are thy pleasures, O
London with-the-many-sins. For these may Keswick and
her giant brood go hang!

C. L.

To William Wordsworth

[P.M. January 30, 1801.]

Thanks for your Letter and Present. I had already borrowed
your second volume. What most please me are, the Song of
Lucy. ... *Simon's sickly daughter* in the Sexton made me *cry*.
Next to these are the description of the continuous Echoes
in the story of Joanna's laugh, where the mountains and all
the scenery absolutely seem alive – and that fine Shake-
sperian character of the Happy Man, in the Brothers,

> ——that creeps about the fields,
> Following his fancies by the hour, to bring
> Tears down his cheek, or solitary smiles
> Into his face, *until the Setting Sun*
> *Write Fool upon his forehead.*

I will mention one more: the delicate and curious feeling
in the wish for the Cumberland Beggar, that he may have
about him the melody of Birds, altho' he hear them not.
Here the mind knowingly passes a fiction upon herself, first
substituting her own feelings for the Beggar's, and, in the

same breath detecting the fallacy, will not part with the
wish. – The Poet's Epitaph is disfigured, to my taste by the
vulgar satire upon parsons and lawyers in the beginning,
and the coarse epithet of pin point in the 6th stanza. All
the rest is eminently good, and your own. I will just add that
it appears to me a fault in the Beggar, that the instructions
conveyed in it are too direct and like a lecture : they don't
slide into the mind of the reader, while he is imagining no
such matter. An intelligent reader finds a sort of insult in
being told, I will teach you how to think upon this subject.
This fault, if I am right, is in a ten-thousandth worse degree
to be found in Sterne and many many novelists and modern
poets, who continually put a sign post up to shew where
you are to feel. They set out with assuming their readers to
be stupid. Very different from Robinson Crusoe, the Vicar
of Wakefield, Roderick Random, and other beautiful bare
narratives. There is implied an unwritten compact between
Author and reader ; I will tell you a story, and I suppose
you will understand it. Modern novels 'St Leons' and the
like are full of such flowers as these 'Let not my reader
suppose', 'Imagine, *if you can*' – modest ! – &c. – I will here
have done with praise and blame. I have written so much,
only that you may not think I have passed over your book
without observation. – I am sorry that Coleridge has
christened his Ancient Marinere 'a poet's Reverie' – it is as
bad as Bottom the Weaver's declaration that he is not a
Lion but only the scenical representation of a Lion. What
new idea is gained by this Title, but one subversive of all
credit, which the tale should force upon us, of its truth?
For me, I was never so affected with any human Tale. After
first reading it, I was totally possessed with it for many days
– I dislike all the miraculous part of it, but the feelings of
the man under the operation of such scenery dragged me
along like Tom Piper's magic whistle. I totally differ from
your idea that the Marinere should have had a character
and profession. This is a Beauty in Gulliver's Travels, where
the mind is kept in a placid state of little wonderments ;
but the Ancient Marinere undergoes such trials, as overwhelm and bury all individuality or memory of what he

was, like the state of a man in a Bad dream, one terrible peculiarity of which is : that all consciousness of personality is gone. Your other observation is I think as well a little unfounded : the Marinere from being conversant in supernatural events *has* acquired a supernatural and strange cast of *phrase*, eye, appearance, &c. which frighten the wedding guest. You will excuse my remarks, because I am hurt and vexed that you should think it necessary, with a prose apology, to open the eyes of dead men that cannot see. To sum up a general opinion of the second vol. – I do not feel any one poem in it so forcibly as the Ancient Marinere, the Mad Mother, and the Lines at Tintern Abbey in the first. – I could, too, have wished the Critical preface had appeared in a separate treatise. All its dogmas are true and just, and most of them new, *as* criticism. But they associate a *diminishing* idea with the Poems which follow, as having been written for *Experiment* on the public taste, more than having sprung (as they must have done) from living and daily circumstances. – I am prolix, because I am gratified in the opportunity of writing to you, and I don't well know when to leave off. I ought before this to have reply'd to your very kind invitation into Cumberland. With you and your Sister I could gang any where. But I am afraid whether I shall ever be able to afford so desperate a Journey. Separate from the pleasure of your company, I don't much care if I never see a mountain in my life. I have passed all my days in London, u ntil I have formed as many and intense local attachments, as any of you mountaineers can have done with dead nature.

The Lighted shops of the Strand and Fleet Street, the innumerable trades, tradesmen and customers, coaches, waggons, playhouses, all the bustle and wickedness round about Covent Garden, the very women of the Town, the Watchmen, drunken scenes, rattles, – life awake, if you awake, at all hours of the night, the impossibility of being dull in Fleet Street, the crowds, the very dirt & mud, the Sun shining upon houses and pavements, the print shops, the old book stalls, parsons cheap'ning books, coffee houses, steams of soups from kitchens, the pantomimes, London itself a pantomime and a masquerade, – all these things work themselves into my mind and feed me, without a power of satiating me. The wonder of these sights impells me into night-walks about her crowded streets, and I often shed tears in the motley Strand from fulness of joy at so much Life. – All these emotions must be strange to you. So are your rural emotions to me. But consider, what must I have been doing all my life, not to have lent great portions of my heart with usury to such scenes?—

My attachments are all local, purely local. I have no passion (or have had none since I was in love, and then it was the spurious engendering of poetry & books) to groves and vallies. The rooms where I was born, the furniture which has been before my eyes all my life, a book case which has followed me about (like a faithful dog, only exceeding him in knowledge) wherever I have moved – old chairs, old tables, streets, squares, where I have sunned myself, my old school, – these are my mistresses. Have I not enough, without your mountains? I do not envy you. I should pity you, did I not know, that the Mind will make friends of any thing. Your sun & moon and skys and hills & lakes affect me no more, or scarcely come to me in more venerable characters, than as a gilded room with tapestry and tapers, where I might live with handsome visible objects. I consider the clouds above me but as a roof, beautifully painted but unable to satisfy the mind, and at last, like the pictures of the apartment of a connoisseur, unable to afford him any longer a pleasure. So fading upon me, from disuse, have been the Beauties of Nature, as they have been confinedly called ; so ever fresh & green and warm are all the inventions of men and assemblies of men in this great city. I should certainly have laughed with dear Joanna.

Give my kindest love, *and my sister's*, to D[orothy] & your*self* and a kiss from me to little Barbara Lewthwaite.

C. LAMB.

Thank you for Liking my Play!!

The Londoner

I was born under the shadow of St Dunstan's steeple, just where the conflux of the eastern and western inhabitants of this twofold city meet and jostle in friendly opposition at Temple Bar. The same day which gave me to the world saw London happy in the celebration of her great annual feast. This I cannot help looking upon as a lively omen of the future great good-will which I was destined to bear toward the city, resembling in kind that solicitude which every chief magistrate is supposed to feel for whatever concerns her interests and well-being. Indeed, I consider myself in some sort a speculative Lord Mayor of London; for though circumstances unhappily preclude me from the hope of ever arriving at the dignity of a gold chain and Spital sermon, yet thus much will I say of myself in truth, that Whittington with his cat (just emblem of vigilance and a furred gown) never went beyond me in affection which I bear to the citizens.

I was born, as you have heard, in a crowd. This has begot in me an entire affection for that way of life, amounting to an almost insurmountable aversion from solitude and rural scenes. This aversion was never interrupted or suspended except for a few years in the younger part of my life, during a period in which I had set my affections upon a charming young woman. Every man, while the passion is upon him, is for a time at least addicted to groves and meadows and purling streams. During this short period of my existence, I contracted just familiarity enough with rural *objects* to understand tolerably well ever after the *poets* when they declaim in such passionate terms in favour of a country life.

For my own part, now the fit is past, I have no hesitation in declaring that a mob of happy faces crowding up at the pit-door of Drury Lane Theatre, just at the hour of six, gives me ten thousand sincerer pleasures than I could ever receive from all the flocks of silly sheep that ever whitened the plains of Arcadia or Epsom Downs.

This passion for crowds is nowhere feasted so full as in London. The man must have a rare recipe for melancholy who can be dull in Fleet Street. I am naturally inclined to Hypochondria, but in London it vanishes, like all other ills. Often, when I have felt a weariness or distaste at home, have I rushed out into her crowded Strand and fed my humour, till tears have wetted my cheek for unutterable sympathies with the multitudinous moving picture, which she never fails to present at all hours, like the scenes of a shifting panto-mime.

The very deformities of London, which give distaste to others, from habit do not displease me. The endless suc-cession of shops, where *fancy, miscalled folly,* is supplied with perpetual gauds and toys, excite in me no puritanical aversion. I gladly behold every appetite supplied with its proper food. The obliging customer and the obliged trades-man – things which live by bowing and things which exist but for homage – do not affect me with disgust; from habit I perceive nothing but urbanity, where other men, more refined, discover meanness. I love the very smoke of London because it has been the medium most familiar to my vision. I see grand principles of honour at work in the dirty ring which encompasses two combatants with fists, and prin-ciples of no less eternal justice in the detection of a pick-pocket. The salutary astonishment with which an execution is surveyed convinces me, more forcibly than a hundred volumes of abstract polity, that the universal instinct of man in all ages has leaned to order and good government.

Thus an art of extracting morality from the commonest incidents of a town life is attained by the same well-natured alchemy with which the foresters of Arden, in a beautiful country –

> Found tongues in trees, books in the running brooks,
> Sermons in stones, and good in everything.

Where has Spleen her food but in London? Humour, Interest, Curiosity, suck at her measureless breasts without a possibility of being satiated. Nursed amid her noise, her

crowds, her beloved smoke, what have I been doing all my
life, if I have not lent out my heart with usury to such
scenes!

This essay was collected in the 1818 edition of Lamb's works
as addressed to the Editor of the *Reflector*. In fact it had been
published in the *Morning Post*, eight years before the birth of
Leigh Hunt's short-lived quarterly, in February 1802, and did
not appear in the pages of the *Reflector*.

To Thomas Manning

24th Sept., 1802, London.

My dear Manning, – Since the date of my last letter, I have
been a traveller. A strong desire seized me of visiting remote
regions. My first impulse was to go and see Paris. It was a
trivial objection to my aspiring mind, that I did not understand a word of the language, since I certainly intend some
time in my life to see Paris, and equally certainly never intend to learn the language; therefore that could be no
objection. However, I am very glad I did not go, because
you had left Paris (I see) before I could have set out. I
believe, Stoddart promising to go with me another year
prevented that plan. My next scheme, (for to my restless,
ambitious mind London was become a bed of thorns) was
to visit the far-famed Peak in Derbyshire, where the Devil
sits, they say, without breeches. *This* my purer mind rejected as indelicate. And my final resolve was a tour to the
Lakes. I set out with Mary to Keswick, without giving
Coleridge any notice; for my time being precious did not
admit of it. He received us with all the hospitality in the
world, and gave up his time to show us all the wonders of
the country. He dwells upon a small hill by the side of
Keswick, in a comfortable house, quite enveloped on all
sides by a net of mountains: great floundering bears and
monsters they seemed, all couchant and asleep. We got in
in the evening, travelling in a post-chaise from Penrith, in
the midst of a gorgeous sunshine, which transmuted all the

mountains into colours, purple, &c., &c. We thought we
had got into fairyland. But that went off (as it never came
again – while we stayed we had no more fine sunsets);
and we entered Coleridge's comfortable study just in the
dusk, when the mountains were all dark with clouds upon
their heads. Such an impression I never received from
objects of sight before, nor do I suppose I can ever again.
Glorious creatures, fine old fellows, Skiddaw, &c. I never
shall forget ye, how ye lay about that night, like an in-
trenchment; gone to bed, as it seemed for the night, but
promising that ye were to be seen in the morning. Coleridge
had got a blazing fire in his study; which is a large, antique,
ill-shaped room, with an old-fashioned organ, never played
upon, big enough for a church, shelves of scattered folios, an
Æolian harp, and an old sofa, half-bed, &c. And all looking
out upon the last fading view of Skiddaw and his broad-
breasted brethren: what a night! Here we stayed three full
weeks, in which time I visited Wordsworth's cottage, where
we stayed a day or two with the Clarksons (good people
and most hospitable, at whose house we tarried one day
and night), and saw Lloyd. The Wordsworths were gone
to Calais. They have since been in London and past much
time with us: he is now gone into Yorkshire to be married
to a girl of small fortune, but he is in expectation of aug-
menting his own in consequence of the death of Lord Lons-
dale, who kept him out of his own in conformity with a plan
my lord had taken up in early life of making everybody
unhappy. So we have seen Keswick, Grasmere, Ambleside,
Ulswater (where the Clarksons live), and a place at the
other end of Ulswater – I forget the name – to which we
travelled on a very sultry day, over the middle of Helvellyn.
We have clambered up to the top of Skiddaw, and I have
waded up the bed of Lodore. In fine, I have satisfied myself,
that there is such a thing as that which tourists call *romantic*,
which I very much suspected before: they make such a
spluttering about it, and toss their splendid epithets around
them, till they give as dim a light as at four o'clock next
morning the lamps do after an illumination. Mary was ex-
cessively tired, when she got about half-way up Skiddaw,

but we came to a cold rill (than which nothing can be
imagined more cold, running over cold stones), and with
the reinforcement of a draught of cold water she surmounted
it most manfully. Oh, its fine black head, and the bleak air
atop of it, with a prospect of mountains all about, and about,
making you giddy; and then Scotland afar off, and the
border countries so famous in song and ballad! It was a day
that will stand out, like a mountain, I am sure, in my life.
But I am returned (I have now been come home near three
weeks – I was a month out), and you cannot conceive the
degradation I felt at first, from being accustomed to wander
free as air among mountains, and bathe in rivers without
being controlled by any one, to come home and *work*. I
felt very *little*. I had been dreaming I was a very great man.
But that is going off, and I find I shall conform in time to
that state of life to which it has pleased God to call me.
Besides, after all, Fleet-Street and the Strand are better
places to live in for good and all than among Skiddaw.
Still, I turn back to those great places where I wandered
about, participating in their greatness. After all, I could
not *live* in Skiddaw. I could spend a year – two, three years
– among them, but I must have a prospect of seeing Fleet-
Street at the end of that time, or I should mope and pine
away, I know. Still, Skiddaw is a fine creature. My habits
are changing, I think: *i.e.* from drunk to sober. Whether I
shall be happier or not remains to be proved. I shall certainly be more happy in a morning; but whether I shall not
sacrifice the fat, and the marrow, and the kidneys, *i.e.* the
night, the glorious care-drowning night, that heals all our
wrongs, pours wine into our mortifications, changes the
scene from indifferent and flat to bright and brilliant! – O
Manning, if I should have formed a diabolical resolution,
by the time you come to England, of not admitting any
spirituous liquors into my house, will you be my guest on
such shame-worthy terms? Is life, with such limitations,
worth trying? The truth is, that my liquors bring a nest of
friendly harpies about my house, who consume me. This is
a pitiful tale to be read at St Gothard; but it is just now
nearest my heart. Fenwick is a ruined man. He is hiding

himself from his creditors, and has sent his wife and children into the country. Fell, my other drunken companion (that has been: nam hic cæstus artemque repono), is turned editor of a 'Naval Chronicle'. Godwin (with a pitiful artificial wife) continues a steady friend, though the same facility does not remain of visiting him often. That Bitch has detached Marshall from his house, Marshall the man who went to sleep when the 'Ancient Mariner' was reading; the old, steady, unalterable friend of the Professor. Holcroft is not yet come to town. I expect to see him, and will deliver your message. How I hate *this part* of a letter. Things come crowding in to say, and no room for 'em. Some things are too little to be told, *i.e.* to have a preference; some are too big and circumstantial. Thanks for yours, which was most delicious. Would I had been with you, benighted &c. I fear my head is turned with wandering. I shall never be the same acquiescent being. Farewell; write again quickly, for I shall not like to hazard a letter, not knowing where the fates have carried you. Farewell, my dear fellow.

C. LAMB.

To William Wordsworth

[Dated at end: August 9, 1814.]

Dear Wordsworth, I cannot tell you how pleased I was at the receit of the great Armful of Poetry which you have sent me, and to get it before the rest of the world too! I have gone quite through with it, and was thinking to have accomplished that pleasure a second time before I wrote to thank you, but M. Burney came in the night (while we were out) and made holy theft of it, but we expect restitution in a day or two. It is the noblest conversational poem I ever read. A day in heaven. The part (or rather main body) which has left the sweetest odour on my memory (a bad term for the remains of an impression so recent) is the Tales of the Churchyard. The only girl among seven brethren, born out of due time and not duly taken away again –

the deaf man and the blind man – the Jacobite and the Hanoverian whom antipathies reconcile – the Scarron-entry of the rusticating parson upon his solitude – these were all new to me too. My having known the story of Margaret (at the beginning), a very old acquaintance, even as long back as I saw you first at Stowey, did not make her reappearance less fresh. I don't know what to pick out of this Best of Books upon the best subjects for partial naming.

That gorgeous Sunset is famous, I think it must have been the identical one we saw on Salisbury plain five years ago, that drew Phillips from the card table where he had sat from rise of that luminary to its unequall'd set, but neither he nor I had gifted eyes to see those symbols of common things glorified such as the prophets saw them, in that sunset – the wheel – the potter's clay – the wash pot – the wine press – the almond tree rod – the baskets of figs – the four-fold visaged head, the throne and him that sat thereon.

One feeling I was particularly struck with as what I recognized so very lately at Harrow Church on entering in it after a hot and secular day's pleasure, – the instantaneous coolness and calming, almost transforming, properties of a country church just entered – a certain fragrance which it has – either from its holiness, or being kept shut all the week, or the air that is let in being pure country – exactly what you have reduced into words but I am feeling I cannot. The reading your lines about it fixed me for a time, a monument, in Harrow Church, (do you know it?) with its fine long Spire white as washd marble, to be seen by vantage of its high site as far as Salisbury spire itself almost.

I shall select a day or two very shortly when I am coolest in brain to have a steady second reading, which I feel will lead to many more, for it will be a stock book with me while eyes or spectacles shall be lent me.

There is a deal of noble matter about mountain scenery, yet not so much as to overpower and discountenance a poor Londoner or South country man entirely, though Mary seems to have felt it occasionally a little too powerfully, for it was her remark during reading it that by your system it was doubtful whether a Liver in Towns had a Soul to be

Saved. She almost trembled for that invisible part of us in her.

Save for a late excursion to Harrow and a day or two on the banks of the Thames this Summer, rural images were fast fading from my mind, and by the wise provision of the Regent all that was countryfy'd in the Parks is all but obliterated. The very colour of green is vanishd, the whole surface of Hyde Park is dry crumbling sand (Arabia Arenosa), not a vestige or hint of grass ever having grown there, booths and drinking places go all round it for a mile and half I am confident — I might say two miles in circuit — the stench of liquors, *bad* tobacco, dirty people and provisions, conquers the air and we are stifled and suffocated in Hyde Park.

Order after Order has been issued by L^d. Sidmouth in the name of the Regent (acting in behalf of his Royal father) for the dispersion of the varlets, but in vain. The vis unita of all the Publicans in London, Westm^r., Marybone, and miles round is too powerful a force to put down. The Regent has rais'd a phantom which he cannot lay. There they'll stay probably for ever. The whole beauty of the Place is gone — that lake-look of the Serpentine — it has got foolish ships upon it — but something whispers to have confidence in nature and its revival —

> at the coming of the *milder day*
> These monuments shall all be overgrown.

Meantime I confess to have smoked one delicious Pipe in one of the cleanliest and goodliest of the booths — a tent rather, 'O call it not a booth!' — erected by the public Spirit of Watson, who keeps the Adam and Eve at Pancras (the ale houses have all emigrated with their train of bottles, mugs, corkscrews, waiters, into Hyde Park — whole Ale houses with all their Ale!) in company with some of the guards that had been in France and a fine French girl (habited like a Princess of Banditti) which one of the dogs had transported from the Garonne to the Serpentine. The unusual scene in H. Park, by Candlelight in open air, good tobacco, bottled stout, made it look like an interval in a campaign, a repose after battle, I almost fancied scars smarting and was ready to club a story with my comrades of some of my lying deeds.

After all, the fireworks were splendid – the Rockets in clusters, in trees and all shapes, spreading about like young stars in the making, floundering about in Space (like un-broke horses) till some of Newton's calculations should fix them, but then they went out. Any one who could see 'em and the still finer showers of gloomy rain fire that fell sulkily and angrily from 'em, and could go to bed without dream-ing of the Last Day, must be as hardened an Atheist as * * * * * *.

Again let me thank you for your present and assure you that fireworks and triumphs have not distracted me from receiving a calm and noble enjoyment from it (which I trust I shall often), and I sincerely congratulate you on its appearance.

With kindest remembrances to you & household, we remain – yours sincerely

C. LAMB and sister.

9 Aug., 1814.

Written at Cambridge, August 15, 1819

I was not train'd in Academic bowers
And to those learned streams I nothing owe
Which copious from those twin fair founts do flow;
Mine have been anything but studious hours.
Yet can I fancy, wandering 'mid thy towers,
Myself a nursling, Granta, of thy lap;
My brow seems tightening with the Doctor's cap
And I walk gownéd; feel unusual powers.
Strange forms of logic clothe my admiring speech,
Old Ramus' ghost is busy at my brain;
And my skull teems with notions infinite.
Be still ye reed of Camus, while I teach
Truths, which transcend the searching schoolman's vein
And half had stagger'd that stout Stagirite!

Examiner, 1819.

Oxford in the Vacation

Casting a preparatory glance at the bottom of this article – as the very connoisseur in prints, with cursory eye (which, while it reads, seems as though it read not), never fails to consult the *quis sculpsit* in the corner, before he pronounces some rare piece to be a Vivares, or a Woollet – methinks I hear you exclaim, Reader, *Who is Elia?*

Because in my last I tried to divert thee with some half-forgotten humours of some old clerks defunct, in an old house of business, long since gone to decay, doubtless you have already set me down in your mind as one of the self-same college – a votary of the desk – a notched and cropt scrivener – one that sucks his sustenance, as certain sick people are said to do, through a quill.

Well, I do agnise something of the sort. I confess that it is my humour, my fancy – in the fore-part of the day, when the mind of your man of letters requires some relaxation (and none better than such as at first sight seems most abhorrent from his beloved studies) – to while away some good hours of my time in the contemplation of indigos, cottons, raw silks, piece-goods, flowered or otherwise. In the first place * * * and then it sends you home with such increased appetite to your books * * * not to say, that your outside sheets, and waste wrappers of foolscap, do receive into them, most kindly and naturally, the impression of sonnets, epigrams, *essays* – so that the very parings of a counting-house are, in some sort, the settings up of an author. The enfranchised quill, that has plodded all the morning among the cart-rucks of figures and ciphers, frisks and curvets so at its ease over the flowery carpet-ground of a midnight dissertation. – It feels its promotion. * * * * * * So that you see, upon the whole, the literary dignity of *Elia* is very little, if at all compromised in the condescension.

Not that, in my anxious detail of the many commodities incidental to the life of a public office, I would be thought blind to certain flaws, which a cunning carper might be able to pick in this Joseph's vest. And here I must have leave, in the fulness of my soul, to regret the abolition, and doing-

away-with altogether, of those consolatory interstices, and
sprinklings of freedom, through the four seasons, – the *red-
letter days*, now become, to all intents and purposes, *dead-
letter days*. There was Paul, and Stephen, and Barnabas –

Andrew and John, men famous in old times

– we were used to keep all their days holy, as long back as
when I was at school at Christ's. I remember their effigies,
by the same token, in the old *Baskett* Prayer Book. There
hung Peter in his uneasy posture – holy Bartlemy in the
troublesome act of flaying, after the famous Marsyas by
Spagnoletti. – I honoured them all, and could almost have
wept the defalcation of Iscariot – so much did we love to
keep holy memories sacred : – only methought I a little
grudged at the coalition of the *better Jude* with Simon –
clubbing (as it were) their sanctities together, to make up
one poor gaudy-day between them – as an economy unworthy of the dispensation.

These were bright visitations in a scholar's and a clerk's
life – 'far off their coming shone.' – I was as good as an
almanac in those days. I could have told you such a saint's-
day falls out next week, or the week after. Peradventure the
Epiphany, by some periodical infelicity, would, once in six
years, merge in a Sabbath. Now am I little better than one
of the profane. Let me not be thought to arraign the wisdom of my civil superiors, who have judged the further
observation of these holy tides to be papistical, superstitious.
Only in a custom of such long standing, methinks, if their
Holinesses the Bishops had, in decency, been first sounded –
but I am wading out of my depths. I am not the man to
decide the limits of civil and ecclesiastical authority – I
am plain Elia – no Selden, nor Archbishop Usher – though
at present in the thick of their books, here in the heart of
learning, under the shadow of the mighty Bodley.

I can here play the gentleman, enact the student. To such
a one as myself, who has been defrauded in his young years
of the sweet food of academic institution, nowhere is so
pleasant, to while away a few idle weeks at, as one or other
of the Universities. Their vacation, too, at this time of the

year, falls in so pat with *ours*. Here I can take my walks un-
molested, and fancy myself of what degree or standing I
please. I seem admitted *ad eundem*. I fetch up past oppor-
tunities. I can rise at the chapel-bell, and dream that it
rings for *me*. In moods of humility I can be a Sizar, or a
Servitor. When the peacock vein rises, I strut a Gentleman
Commoner. In graver moments, I proceed Master of Arts.
Indeed I do not think I am much unlike that respectable
character. I have seen your dim-eyed vergers, and bed-
makers in spectacles, drop a bow or a curtsy, as I pass,
wisely mistaking me for something of the sort. I go about
in black, which favours the notion. Only in Christ Church
reverend quadrangle I can be content to pass for nothing
short of a Seraphic Doctor.

The walks at these times are so much one's own, – the
tall trees of Christ's, the groves of Magdalen! The halls
deserted, and with open doors, inviting one to slip in un-
perceived, and pay a devoir to some Founder, or noble or
royal Benefactress (that should have been ours) whose portrait seems to smile upon their over-looked beadsman, and
to adopt me for their own. Then, to take a peep in by the
way at the butteries, and sculleries, redolent of antique
hospitality: the immense caves of kitchens, kitchen fire-
places, cordial recesses; ovens whose first pies were baked
four centuries ago; and spits which have cooked for
Chaucer! Not the meanest minister among the dishes but is
hallowed to me through his imagination, and the Cook
goes forth a Manciple.

Antiquity! thou wondrous charm, what art thou? that,
being nothing, art everything! When thou *wert*, thou wert
not antiquity – then thou wert nothing, but hadst a re-
moter *antiquity*, as thou calledst it, to look back to with blind
veneration; thou thyself being to thyself flat, jejune, *modern*!
What mystery·lurks in this retroversion? or what half
Januses[1] are we, that cannot look forward with the same
idolatry with which we for ever revert! The mighty future
is as nothing, being everything! the past is everything, being
nothing!

[1] Januses of one face.—SIR THOMAS BROWNE.

What were thy *dark ages*? Surely the sun rose as brightly then as now, and man got him to his work in the morning? Why is it we can never hear mention of them without an accompanying feeling, as though a palpable obscure had dimmed the face of things, and that our ancestors wandered to and fro groping!

Above all thy rarities, old Oxenford, what do most arride and solace me, are thy repositories of mouldering learning, thy shelves —

What a place to be in is an old library! It seems as though all the souls of all the writers, that have bequeathed their labours to these Bodleians, were reposing here, as in some dormitory, or middle state. I do not want to handle, to profane the leaves, their winding-sheets. I could as soon dislodge a shade. I seem to inhale learning, walking amid their foliage; and the odour of their old moth-scented coverings is fragrant as the first bloom of those sciential apples which grew amid the happy orchard.

Still less have I curiosity to disturb the elder repose of MSS. Those *variæ lectiones*, so tempting to the more erudite palates, do but disturb and unsettle my faith. I am no Herculanean raker. The credit of the three witnesses might have slept unimpeached for me. I leave these curiosities to Porson, and to G[eorge] D[yer] – whom, by the way, I found busy as a moth over some rotten archive, rummaged out of some seldom-explored press, in a nook at Oriel. With long poring, he is grown almost into a book. He stood as passive as one by the side of the old shelves. I longed to new-coat him in russia, and assign him his place. He might have mustered for a tall Scapula.

D. is assiduous in his visits to these seats of learning. No inconsiderable portion of his moderate fortune, I apprehend, is consumed in journeys between them and Clifford's Inn – where, like a dove on the asp's nest, he has long taken up his unconscious abode, amid an incongruous assembly of attorneys, attorneys' clerks, apparitors, promoters, vermin of the law, among whom he sits, 'in calm and sinless peace'. The fangs of the law pierce him not – the winds of litigation blow over his humble chambers – the hard sheriff's officer

moves his hat as he passes – legal nor illegal discourtesy
touches him – none thinks of offering violence or injustice
to him – you would as soon 'strike an abstract idea'.

D. has been engaged, he tells me, through a course of
laborious years, in an investigation into all curious matter
connected with the two Universities; and has lately lit
upon a MS. collection of charters, relative to C[ambridge],
by which he hopes to settle some disputed points – particularly that long controversy between them as to priority of
foundation. The ardour with which he engages in these
liberal pursuits, I am afraid, has not met with all the
encouragement it deserved, either here or at C —. Your
caputs, and heads of colleges, care less than anybody else
about these questions. – Contented to suck the milky
fountains of their Alma Maters, without inquiring into the
venerable gentlewomen's years, they rather hold such
curiosities to be impertinent – unreverend. They have their
good glebe lands *in manu*, and care not much to rake into
the title-deeds. I gather at least so much from other sources,
for D. is not a man to complain.

D. started like an unbroke heifer, when I interrupted
him. *A priori* it was not very probable that we should have
met in Oriel. But D. would have done the same, had I
accosted him on the sudden in his own walks in Clifford's
Inn, or in the Temple. In addition to a provoking short-
sightedness (the effect of late studies and watchings at the
midnight oil) D. is the most absent of men. He made a call
the other morning at our friend M.'s in Bedford Square; and,
finding nobody at home, was ushered into the hall, where,
asking for pen and ink, with great exactitude of purpose
he enters me his name in the book – which ordinarily lies
about in such places, to record the failures of the untimely
or unfortunate visitor – and takes his leave with many
ceremonies, and professions of regret. Some two or three
hours after, his walking destinies returned him into the
same neighbourhood again, and again the quiet image of the
fireside circle at M[ontagu]'s – Mrs M. presiding at it like
a Queen Lar, with pretty A[nne] S[kepper] at her side –
striking irresistibly on his fancy, he makes another call (for-

F

getting that they were 'certainly not to return from the country before that day week'), and disappointed a second time, inquires for pen and paper as before: again the book is brought, and in the line just above that in which he is about to print his second name (his re-script) — his first name (scarce dry) looks out upon him like another Sosia, or as if a man should suddenly encounter his own duplicate! — The effect may be conceived. D. made many a good resolution against any such lapses in future. I hope he will not keep them too rigorously.

For with G. D. — to be absent from the body, is some-times (not to speak it profanely) to be present with the Lord. At the very time when, personally encountering thee, he passes on with no recognition — or, being stopped, starts like a thing surprised — at that moment, Reader, he is on Mount Tabor — or Parnassus — or co-sphered with Plato — or, with Harrington, framing 'immortal commonwealths' — devising some plan of amelioration to thy country, or thy species — peradventure meditating some individual kind-ness or courtesy, to be done to *thee thyself*, the returning consciousness of which made him to start so guiltily at thy obtruded personal presence.

[D. commenced life, after a course of hard study in the house of 'pure Emanuel', as usher to a knavish fanatic schoolmaster at * * *, at a salary of eight pounds per annum, with board and lodging. Of this poor stipend, he never received above half in all the laborious years he served this man. He tells a pleasant anecdote, that when poverty, staring out at his ragged knees, has sometimes compelled him, against the modesty of his nature, to hint at arrears, Dr * * * would take no immediate notice, but after supper, when the school was called together to evensong, he would never fail to introduce some instructive homily against riches, and the corruption of the heart occasioned through the desire of them — ending with 'Lord, keep Thy servants, above all things, from the heinous sin of avarice. Having food and raiment, let us therewithal be content. Give me Agur's wish' — and the like — which, to the little auditory, sounded like a doctrine full of Christian prudence and simplicity, but to poor D. was a receipt in full for that quarter's demand at least.

And D. has been underworking for himself ever since; — drudging at low rates for unappreciating booksellers, — wasting his fine erudition in silent corrections of the classics, and in those unostentatious but solid services to learning which commonly fall to the lot of laborious scholars, who have not the heart to sell themselves to the best advantage. He has published poems, which do not sell, because their character is unobtrusive, like his own, and because he has been too much absorbed in ancient literature to know what the popular mark in poetry is, even if he could have hit it. And, therefore, his verses are properly, what he terms them, *crotchets*; voluntaries; odes to liberty and spring; effusions; little tributes and offerings, left behind him upon tables and window-seats at parting from friends' houses, and from all the inns of hospitality, where he has been courteously (or but tolerably) received in his pilgrimage. If his muse of kindness halt a little behind the strong lines in fashion in this excitement-loving age, his prose is the best of the sort in the world, and exhibits a faithful transcript of his own healthy, natural mind, and cheerful, innocent tone of conversation.]

D. is delightful anywhere, but he is at the best in such places as these. He cares not much for Bath. He is out of his element at Buxton, at Scarborough, or Harrowgate. The Cam and the Isis are to him 'better than all the waters of Damascus'. On the Muses' hill he is happy, and good, as one of the Shepherds on the Delectable Mountains; and when he goes about with you to show you the halls and colleges, you think you have with you the Interpreter at the House Beautiful.

ELIA.

London Magazine, October 1820.

The Old Margate Hoy

I am fond of passing my vacations (I believe I have said so before) at one or other of the Universities. Next to these my choice would fix me at some woody spot, such as the neighbourhood of Henley affords in abundance, on the banks of my beloved Thames. But somehow or other my cousin contrives to wheedle me, once in three or four seasons, to a watering-place. Old attachments cling to her in spite of experience. We have been dull at Worthing one summer, duller at Brighton another, dullest at Eastbourn a third, and are at this moment doing dreary penance at – Hastings! – and all because we were happy many years ago for a brief week at Margate. That was our first seaside experiment, and many circumstances combined to make it the most agreeable holiday of my life. We had neither of us seen the sea, and we had never been from home so long together in company.

Can I forget thee, thou old Margate Hoy, with thy weather-beaten, sun-burnt captain, and his rough accommodations – ill exchanged for the foppery and fresh-water niceness of the modern steam-packet? To the winds and waves thou committedst thy goodly freightage, and didst ask no aid of magic fumes, and spells, and boiling caldrons. With the gales of heaven thou wentest swimmingly; or, when it was their pleasure, stoodest still with sailor-like patience. Thy course was natural, not forced, as in a hotbed; nor didst thou go poisoning the breath of ocean with sulphureous smoke – a great sea chimera, chimneying and furnacing the deep; or liker to that fire-god parching up Scamander.

Can I forget thy honest, yet slender crew, with their coy reluctant responses (yet to the suppression of anything like contempt) to the raw questions, which we of the great city would be ever and anon putting to them, as to the uses of this or that strange naval implement? 'Specially can I forget thee, thou happy medium, thou shade of refuge between us and them, conciliating interpreter of their skill to our

simplicity, comfortable ambassador between sea and land!
– whose sailor-trousers did not more convincingly assure
thee to be an adopted denizen of the former, than thy white
cap, and whiter apron over them, with thy neat-fingered
practice in thy culinary vocation, bespoke thee to have
been of inland nurture heretofore – a master cook of East-
cheap? How busily didst thou ply thy multifarious occupation, cook, mariner, attendant, chamberlain; here, there,
like another Ariel, flaming at once about all parts of the
desk, yet with kindlier ministrations – not to assist the tempest, but, as if touched with a kindred sense of our infirmities,
to soothe the qualms which that untried motion might
haply raise in our crude land-fancies. And when the o'er-
washing billows drove us below deck (for it was far gone in
October, and we had stiff and blowing weather), how did
thy officious ministerings, still catering for our comfort,
with cards, and cordials, and thy more cordial conversation,
alleviate the closeness and the confinement of thy else (truth
to say) not very savoury, nor very inviting, little cabin!

With these additaments to boot, we had on board a
fellow-passenger, whose discourse in verity might have be-
guiled a longer voyage than we meditated, and have made
mirth and wonder abound as far as the Azores. He was a
dark, Spanish-complexioned young man, remarkably handsome, with an officer-like assurance, and an insuppressible
volubility of assertion. He was, in fact, the greatest liar I
had met with then, or since. He was none of your hesitating,
half story-tellers (a most painful description of mortals)
who go on sounding your belief, and only giving you as
much as they see you can swallow at a time – the nibbling
pickpockets of your patience – but one who committed
downright, daylight depredations upon his neighbour's
faith. He did not stand shivering upon the brink, but was
a hearty, thorough-paced liar, and plunged at once into
the depths of your credulity. I partly believe, he made
pretty sure of his company. Not many rich, not many wise,
or learned, composed at that time the common stowage of a
Margate packet. We were, I am afraid, a set of as unseasoned
Londoners (let our enemies give it a worse name) as Alder-

manbury, or Watling Street, at that time of day could have
supplied. There might be an exception or two among us,
but I scorn to make any invidious distinctions among such
a jolly, companionable ship's company as those were whom
I sailed with. Something too must be conceded to the
Genius Loci. Had the confident fellow told us half the legends
on land which he favoured us with on the other element, I
flatter myself the good sense of most of us would have
revolted. But we were in a new world, with everything
unfamiliar about us, and the time and place disposed us to
the reception of any prodigious marvel whatsoever. Time
has obliterated from my memory much of his wild fablings;
and the rest would appear but dull, as written, and to be
read on shore. He had been Aide-de-camp (among other
rare accidents and fortunes) to a Persian Prince, and at
one blow had stricken off the head of the King of Carimania
on horseback. He, of course, married the Prince's daughter.
I forget what unlucky turn in the politics of that court,
combining with the loss of his consort, was the reason of his
quitting Persia; but, with the rapidity of a magician, he
transported himself, along with his hearers, back to England, where we still found him in the confidence of great
ladies. There was some story of a princess — Elizabeth, if I
remember — having intrusted to his care an extraordinary
casket of jewels, upon some extraordinary occasion — but,
as I am not certain of the name or circumstance at this
distance of time, I must leave it to the Royal daughters of
England to settle the honour among themselves in
private.

I cannot call to mind half his pleasant wonders; but I perfectly remember that, in the course of his travels, he had
seen a phœnix; and he obligingly undeceived us of the vulgar error, that there is but one of that species at a time,
assuring us that they were not uncommon in some parts of
Upper Egypt. Hitherto he had found the most implicit
listeners. His dreaming fancies had transported us beyond
the 'ignorant present'. But when (still hardying more and
more in his triumphs over our simplicity) he went on to
affirm that he had actually sailed through the legs of the

Colossus at Rhodes, it really became necessary to make a stand. And here I must do justice to the good sense and intrepidity of one of our party, a youth, that had hitherto been one of his most deferential auditors, who, from his recent reading, made bold to assure the gentleman, that there must be some mistake, as 'the Colossus in question had been destroyed long since'; to whose opinion, delivered with all modesty, our hero was obliging enough to concede thus much, that 'the figure was indeed a little damaged'. This was the only opposition he met with, and it did not at all seem to stagger him, for he proceeded with his fables, which the same youth appeared to swallow with still more complacency than ever – confirmed, as it were, by the extreme candour of that concession. With these prodigies he wheedled us on till we came in sight of the Reculvers, which one of our own company (having been the voyage before) immediately recognizing, and pointing out to us, was considered by us as no ordinary seaman.

All this time sat upon the edge of the deck quite a different character. It was a lad, apparently very poor, very infirm, and very patient. His eye was ever on the sea, with a smile; and, if he caught now and then some snatches of these wild legends, it was by accident, and they seemed not to concern him. The waves to him whispered more pleasant stories. He was as one being with us, but not of us. He heard the bell of dinner ring without stirring; and when some of us pulled out our private stores – our cold meat and our salads – he produced none, and seemed to want none. Only a solitary biscuit he had laid in; provision for the one or two days and nights, to which these vessels then were oftentimes obliged to prolong their voyage. Upon a nearer acquaintance with him, which he seemed neither to court nor decline, we learned that he was going to Margate, with the hope of being admitted into the Infirmary there for sea-bathing. His disease was a scrofula, which appeared to have eaten all over him. He expressed great hopes of a cure; and when we asked him whether he had any friends where he was going, he replied, 'he *had* no friends'.

These pleasant, and some mournful passages, with the

first sight of the sea, co-operating with youth, and a sense
of holidays, and out-of-door adventure, to me that had been
pent up in populous cities for many months before, – have
left upon my mind the fragrance as of summer days gone
by, bequeathing nothing but their remembrance for cold
and wintry hours to chew upon.

Will it be thought a digression (it may spare some unwelcome comparisons) if I endeavour to account for the *dissatisfaction* which I have heard so many persons confess to
have felt (as I did myself feel in part on this occasion), *at
the sight of the sea for the first time*? I think the reason usually
given – referring to the incapacity of actual objects for
satisfying our preconceptions of them – scarcely goes deep
enough into the question. Let the same person see a lion,
an elephant, a mountain for the first time in his life, and he
shall perhaps feel himself a little mortified. The things do
not fill up that space which the idea of them seemed to take
up in his mind. But they have still a correspondency to his
first notion, and in time grow up to it, so as to produce a
very similar impression: enlarging themselves (if I may
say so) upon familiarity. But the sea remains a disappointment. Is it not, that in *the latter* we had expected to behold
(absurdly, I grant, but, I am afraid, by the law of imagination, unavoidably) not a definite object, as those wild
beasts, or that mountain compassable by the eye, but *all the
sea at once*, 'the commensurate antagonist of the earth'?
I do not say we tell ourselves so much, but the craving of
the mind is to be satisfied with nothing less. I will suppose
the case of a young person of fifteen (as I then was) knowing nothing of the sea, but from description. He comes to
it for the first time – all that he has been reading of it all
his life, and *that* the most enthusiastic part of life, – all he
has gathered from narratives of wandering seamen, – what
he has gained from true voyages, and what he cherishes as
credulously from romance and poetry, – crowding their
images, and exacting strange tributes from expectation.
– He thinks of the great deep, and of those who go down
unto it; of its thousand isles, and of the vast continents it
washes; of its receiving the mighty Plata, or Orellana, into

its bosom, without disturbance, or sense of augmentation;
of Biscay swells, and the mariner

> For many a day, and many a dreadful night,
> Incessant labouring round the stormy Cape;

of fatal rocks, and the 'still-vexed Bermoothes'; of great
whirlpools, and the water-spout; of sunken ships, and sum-
less treasures swallowed up in the unrestoring depths; of
fishes and quaint monsters, to which all that is terrible on
earth –

> Be but as buggs to frighten babes withal,
> Compared with the creatures in the sea's entral;

of naked savages, and Juan Fernandez; of pearls, and shells;
of coral beds, and of enchanted isles; of mermaids' grots –
I do not assert that in sober earnest he expects to be shown
all these wonders at once, but he is under the tyranny of a
mighty faculty, which haunts him with confused hints and
shadows of all these; and when the actual object opens
first upon him, seen (in tame weather, too, most likely)
from our unromantic coasts – a speck, a slip of sea-water, as
it shows to him – what can it prove but a very unsatisfying
and even diminutive entertainment? Or if he has come to it
from the mouth of a river, was it much more than the river
widening? and, even out of sight of land, what had he but
a flat watery horizon about him, nothing comparable to
the vast o'er-curtaining sky, his familiar object, seen daily
without dread or amazement? – Who, in similar circumstances, has not been tempted to exclaim with Charoba, in
the poem of Gebir,

> Is this the mighty ocean? is this *all*?

I love town or country; but this detestable Cinque Port
is neither. I hate these scrubbed shoots, thrusting out their
starved foliage from between the horrid fissures of dusty
innutritious rocks; which the amateur calls 'verdure to the
edge of the sea'. I require woods, and they show me stunted

coppices. I cry out for the water-brooks, and pant for fresh streams, and inland murmurs. I cannot stand all day on the naked beach, watching the capricious hues of the sea, shifting like the colours of a dying mullet. I am tired of looking out at the windows of this island-prison. I would fain retire into the interior of my cage. While I gaze upon the sea, I want to be on it, over it, across it. It binds me in with chains, as of iron. My thoughts are abroad. I should not so feel in Staffordshire. There is no home for me here. There is no sense of home at Hastings. It is a place of fugitive resort, an heterogeneous assemblage of sea-mews and stock-brokers, Amphitrites of the town, and misses that coquet with the Ocean. If it were what it was in its primitive shape, and what it ought to have remained, a fair, honest fishing-town, and no more, it were something — with a few straggling fishermen's huts scattered about, artless as its cliffs, and with their materials filched from them, it were something. I could abide to dwell with Meshek; to assort with fisher-swains, and smugglers. There are, or I dream there are, many of this latter occupation here. Their faces become the place. I like a smuggler. He is the only honest thief. He robs nothing but the revenue — an abstraction I never greatly cared about. I could go out with them in their mackerel boats, or about their less ostensible business, with some satisfaction. I can even tolerate those poor victims to monotony, who from day to day pace along the beach, in endless progress and recurrence, to watch their illicit countrymen — townsfolk or brethren, perchance — whistling to the sheathing and unsheathing of their cutlasses (their only solace), who, under the mild name of preventive service, keep up a legitimated civil warfare in the deplorable absence of a foreign one, to show their detestation of run hollands, and zeal for Old England. But it is the visitants from town, that come here to *say* that they have been here, with no more relish of the sea than a pond-perch or a dace might be supposed to have, that are my aversion. I feel like a foolish dace in these regions, and have as little toleration for myself here as for them. What can they want here? If they had a true relish of the ocean, why have they brought all this land luggage with them? or why pitch their civilized tents in the desert? What mean these scanty book-rooms — marine libraries as they entitle them — if the sea were, as they would have us believe, a book 'to read strange matter in'? what are their foolish concert-rooms, if they come, as they would fain be thought to do, to listen to the music of the waves? All is false and hollow pretension. They come because it is the fashion, and to spoil the nature of the place. They are, mostly, as I have said, stock-brokers; but I have watched the better sort of them — now and then, an honest citizen (of the old stamp), in the simplicity of his heart, shall bring down his wife and daughters to taste the sea breezes. I always know the date of their arrival. It is easy to see it in their countenance. A day or two they go wandering on the shingles, picking up cockle-shells, and thinking them great things; but, in a poor week, imagination slackens: they begin to discover that cockles produce no pearls, and then — O then! — if I could interpret for the pretty creatures (I know they have not the courage to confess it themselves), how gladly would they exchange their seaside rambles for a Sunday walk on the green sward of their accustomed Twickenham meadows!

I would ask one of these sea-charmed emigrants, who think they truly love the sea, with its wild usages, what would their feelings be if some of the unsophisticated aborigines of this place, encouraged by their courteous questionings here, should venture, on the faith of such assured sympathy between them, to return the visit, and come up to see — London. I must imagine them with their fishing-tackle on their back, as we carry our town necessaries. What a sensation would it cause in Lothbury! What vehement laughter would it not excite among

The daughters of Cheapside, and wives of Lombard-street!

I am sure that no town-bred or inland-born subjects can feel their true and natural nourishment at these sea-places. Nature, where she does not mean us for mariners and vagabonds, bids us stay at home. The salt foam seems to nourish a spleen. I am not half so good-natured as by the milder waters of my natural river. I would exchange these sea-gulls for swans, and scud a swallow for ever about the banks of Thamesis.

ELIA.

London Magazine, July 1823.

To Barron Field

Sept. 22nd., 1822.

My dear F., – I scribble hastily at office. Frank wants my letter presently. I and sister are just returned from Paris!! We have eaten frogs. It has been such a treat! You know our monotonous tenor. Frogs are the nicest little delicate things – rabbity-flavoured. Imagine a Lilliputian rabbit! They fricassee them; but in my mind, drest, seethed, plain, with parsley and butter, would have the decision of Apicius. Shelley the great Atheist has gone down by Water to Eternal fire. Hunt and his young fry are left stranded at Pisa, to be adopted by the remaining duumvir Lord Bryon, he, wife and six children and their maid. What a cargo of Jonases, if they had founder'd too. The only use I can find of friends, is that they do borrow money of you – Henceforth I will consort with none but rich rogues. Paris is a glorious picturesque old city. London looks mean and new to it, as the town of Washington would, seen after it. But they have no St. Paul's, or Westminster Abbey. The Seine, so much despised by Cockneys, is exactly the size to run through a magnificent street; palaces a mile long on one side, lofty Edinboro' stone (O the glorious antiques!) houses on the other. The Thames disunites London and Southwark. I had Talma to supper with me. He has picked up, as I believe, an authentic portrait of Shakespeare. He paid a broker about 40L. English for it. It is painted on the one half of a pair of bellows, – a lovely picture, corresponding with the folio head. The bellows has old carved *wings* round it, and

round the visnomy is inscribed, as near as I remember, not
divided into rhyme – I found out the rhyme

> Whom have we here
> Stuck on the bellows,
> But the Prince of good fellows,
>   Willy Shakespeare?

At top –

> O base and coward luck
> To be here stuck! – *Poins.*

At bottom –

> Nay! rather a glorious lot is to him assign'd,
> Who, like the Almighty, rides upon the *wind.* – *Pistol.*

This is all in old carved wooden letters. The countenance
smiling, sweet, and intellectual beyond measure, even as he
was immeasurable. It may be a forgery. They laugh at me
and tell me Ireland is in Paris, and has been putting off a
portrait of the Black Prince. How far old wood may be
imitated I cannot say. Ireland was not found out by his
parchments, but by his poetry. I am confident no painter
on either side the Channel could have painted anything
near like the face I saw. Again, would such a painter and
forger have taken 40L. for a thing, if authentic, worth
4000L.? Talma is not in the secret, for he had not even found
out the rhymes in the first inscription. He is coming over
with it, and, my life to Southey's 'Thalaba', it will gain
universal faith.

The letter is wanted, and I am wanted. Imagine the
blank filled up with all kind things.

Our joint hearty remembrances to both of you.

Yours, as ever,

C. LAMB.

PART IV

JUICES OF MEATS
INNOCENT VANITIES
AND JESTS

'Sun, and sky, and breeze and solitary walks, and summer holidays, and
the greenness of fields, and the delicious juices of meats and fishes, and
society, and the cheerful glass, and
candlelight, and fireside conversa-
tions, and innocent vanities and jests,
and *irony itself* — do these things go out
with life?' 'New Year's Eve,' *London Magazine*, January 1821.

Grace Before Meat

The custom of saying grace at meals had, probably, its origin in the early times of the world, and the hunter-state of man, when dinners were precarious things, and a full meal was something more than a common blessing! when a belly-full was a wind-fall, and looked like a special provi-dence. In the shouts and triumphal songs with which, after a season of sharp abstinence, a lucky booty of deer's or goat's flesh would naturally be ushered home, existed, perhaps, the germ of the modern grace. It is not otherwise easy to be understood, why the blessing of food – the act of eating – should have had a particular expression of thanksgiving annexed to it, distinct from that implied and silent grati-tude with which we are expected to enter upon the enjoy-ment of the many other various gifts and good things of existence.

I own that I am disposed to say grace upon twenty other occasions in the course of the day besides my dinner. I want a form for setting out upon a pleasant walk, for a moonlight ramble, for a friendly meeting, or a solved problem. Why have we none for books, those spiritual re-pasts – a grace before Milton – a grace before Shakspeare – a devotional exercise proper to be said before reading the *Fairy Queen*? – but the received ritual having prescribed these forms to the solitary ceremony of manducation, I shall confine my observations to the experience which I have had of the grace, properly so called; commending my new scheme for extension to a niche in the grand philosophical, poetical, and perchance in part heretical, liturgy, now com-piling by my friend Homo Humanus, for the use of a certain snug congregation of Utopian Rabelæsian Christians, no matter where assembled.

The form, then, of the benediction before eating has its beauty at a poor man's table, or at the simple and un-provocative repast of children. It is here that the grace becomes exceedingly graceful. The indigent man, who hardly knows whether he shall have a meal the next day or not, sits down to his fare with a present sense of the bless-ing, which can be but feebly acted by the rich, into whose minds the conception of wanting a dinner could never, but by some extreme theory, have entered. The proper end of food – the animal sustenance – is barely contemplated by them. The poor man's bread is his daily bread, literally his bread for the day. Their courses are perennial.

Again, the plainest diet seems the fittest to be preceded by the grace. That which is least stimulative to appetite, leaves the mind most free for foreign considerations. A man may feel thankful, heartily thankful, over a dish of plain mutton with turnips, and have leisure to reflect upon the ordinance and institution of eating; when he shall con-fess a perturbation of mind, inconsistent with the purposes of the grace, at the presence of venison or turtle. When I have sate (a *rarus hospes*) at rich men's tables, with the savoury soup and messes steaming up the nostrils, and moistening the lips of the guests with desire and a distracted choice, I have felt the introduction of that ceremony to be unseasonable. With the ravenous orgasm upon you, it seems impertinent to interpose a religious sentiment. It is a confusion of purpose to mutter out praises from a mouth that waters. The heats of epicurism put out the gentle flame of devotion. The incense which rises round is pagan, and the belly-god intercepts it for its own. The very excess of the provision beyond the needs, takes away all sense of proportion between the end and means. The giver is veiled by his gifts. You are startled at the injustice of returning thanks – for what? – for having too much while so many starve. It is to praise the Gods amiss.

I have observed this awkwardness felt, scarce consciously perhaps, by the good man who says the grace. I have seen it in clergymen and others – a sort of shame – a sense of the co-presence of circumstances which unhallow the blessing.

After a devotional tone put on for a few seconds, how rapidly the speaker will fall into his common voice! helping himself or his neighbour, as if to get rid of some uneasy sensation of hypocrisy. Not that the good man was a hypocrite, or was not most conscientious in the discharge of the duty; but he felt in his inmost mind the incompatibility of the scene and the viands before him with the exercise of a calm and rational gratitude.

I hear somebody exclaim, – Would you have Christians sit down at table like hogs to their troughs, without remembering the Giver? – no – I would have them sit down as Christians, remembering the Giver, and less like hogs. Or, if their appetites must run riot, and they must pamper themselves with delicacies for which east and west are ransacked, I would have them postpone their benediction to a fitter season, when appetite is laid; when the still small voice can be heard, and the reason of the grace returns – with temperate diet and restricted dishes. Gluttony and surfeiting are no proper occasions for thanksgiving. When Jeshurun waxed fat, we read that he kicked. Virgil knew the harpy-nature better, when he put into the mouth of Celæno anything but a blessing. We may be gratefully sensible of the deliciousness of some kinds of food beyond others, though that is a meaner and inferior gratitude: but the proper object of the grace is sustenance, not relishes; daily bread, not delicacies; the means of life, and not the means of pampering the carcass. With what frame or composure, I wonder, can a city chaplain pronounce his benediction at some great Hall-feast, when he knows that his last concluding pious word – and that in all probability, the sacred name which he preaches – is but the signal for so many impatient harpies to commence their foul orgies, with as little sense of true thankfulness (which is temperance) as those Virgilian fowl! It is well if the good man himself does not feel his devotions a little clouded, those foggy sensuous steams mingling with and polluting the pure altar sacrifice.

The severest satire upon full tables and surfeits is the banquet which Satan, in the *Paradise Regained*, provides for a temptation in the wilderness:

> A table richly spread in regal mode
> With dishes piled, and meats of noblest sort
> And savour; beasts of chase, or fowl of game,
> In pastry built, or from the spit, or boiled,
> Gris-amber-steamed; all fish from sea or shore,
> Freshet or purling brook, for which was drained
> Pontus, and Lucrine bay, and Afric coast.

The Tempter, I warrant you, thought these cates would go down without the recommendatory preface of a bene-diction. They are like to be short graces where the devil plays the host. I am afraid the poet wants his usual decorum in this place. Was he thinking of the old Roman luxury, or of a gaudy day at Cambridge? This was a temptation fitter for a Heliogabalus. The whole banquet is too civic and culinary, and the accompaniments altogether a profanation of that deep, abstracted, holy scene. The mighty artillery of sauces, which the cook-fiend conjures up, is out of propor-tion to the simple wants and plain hunger of the guest. He that disturbed him in his dreams, from his dreams might have been taught better. To the temperate fantasies of the famished Son of God, what sort of feasts presented them-selves? – He dreamed indeed,

> ——As appetite is wont to dream,
> Of meats and drinks, nature's refreshment sweet.

But what meats? –

> Him thought he by the brook of Cherith stood,
> And saw the ravens with their horny beaks
> Food to Elijah bringing even and morn;
> Though ravenous, taught to abstain from what they brought.
> He saw the prophet also how he fled
> Into the desert, and how there he slept
> Under a juniper; then how awaked
> He found his supper on the coals prepared,
> And by the angel was bid rise and eat,
> And ate the second time after repose,
> The strength whereof sufficed him forty days:
> Sometimes, that with Elijah he partook,
> Or as a guest with Daniel at his pulse.

Nothing in Milton is finelier fancied than these temperate dreams of the divine Hungerer. To which of these two visionary banquets, think you, would the introduction of what is called the grace have been the most fitting and pertinent?

Theoretically I am no enemy to graces; but practically I own that (before meat especially) they seem to involve something awkward and unseasonable. Our appetites, of one or another kind, are excellent spurs to our reason, which might otherwise but feebly set about the great ends of preserving and continuing the species. They are fit blessings to be contemplated at a distance with a becoming gratitude; but the moment of appetite (the judicious reader will apprehend me) is, perhaps, the least fit season for that exercise. The Quakers, who go about their business of every description with more calmness than we, have more title to the use of these benedictory prefaces. I have always admired their silent grace, and the more because I have observed their applications to the meat and drink following to be less passionate and sensual than ours. They are neither gluttons nor wine-bibbers as a people. They eat, as a horse bolts his chopped hay, with indifference, calmness, and cleanly circumstances. They neither grease nor slop themselves. When I see a citizen in his bib and tucker, I cannot imagine it a surplice.

I am no Quaker at my food. I confess I am not indifferent to the kinds of it. Those unctuous morsels of deer's flesh were not made to be received with dispassionate services. I hate a man who swallows it, affecting not to know what he is eating. I suspect his taste in higher matters. I shrink instinctively from one who professes to like minced veal. There is a physiognomical character in the tastes for food. C[oleridge] holds that a man cannot have a pure mind who refuses apple-dumplings. I am not certain but he is right. With the decay of my first innocence, I confess a less and less relish daily for those innocuous cates. The whole vegetable tribe have lost their gust with me. Only I stick to asparagus, which still seems to inspire gentle thoughts. I am impatient and querulous under culinary disappoint-

ments, as to come home at the dinner hour, for instance,
expecting some savoury mess, and to find one quite taste-
less and sapidless. Butter ill melted – that commonest of
kitchen failures – puts me beside my tenor. – The author of
the *Rambler* used to make inarticulate animal noises over a
favourite food. Was this the music quite proper to be preceded by the grace? or would the pious man have done
better to postpone his devotions to a season when the blessing
might be contemplated with less perturbation? I quarrel
with no man's tastes, nor would set my thin face against
those excellent things, in their way, jollity and feasting. But
as these exercises, however laudable, have little in them of
grace or gracefulness, a man should be sure, before he ven-
tures so to grace them, that while he is pretending his
devotions otherwhere, he is not secretly kissing his hand to
some great fish – his Dagon – with a special consecration of
no art but the fat tureen before him. Graces are the sweet
preluding strains to the banquets of angels and children;
to the roots and severer repasts of the Chartreuse; to the
slender, but not slenderly acknowledged, refection of the
poor and humble man : but at the heaped-up boards of the
pampered and the luxurious they become of dissonant
mood, less timed and tuned to the occasion, methinks, than
the noise of those better befitting organs would be which
children hear tales of, at Hog's Norton. We sit too long at
our meals, or are too curious in the study of them, or too
disordered in our application to them, or engross too great
a portion of those good things (which should be common)
to our share, to be able with any grace to say grace. To
be thankful for what we grasp exceeding our proportion, is
to add hypocrisy to injustice. A lurking sense of this truth
is what makes the performance of this duty so cold and
spiritless a service at most tables. In houses where the grace
is as indispensable as the napkin, who has not seen that
never-settled question arise, as to *who shall say it?* while the
good man of the house and the visitor clergyman, or
some other guest belike of next authority, from years or
gravity, shall be bandying about the office between them
as a matter of compliment, each of them not unwilling to

shift the awkward burthen of an equivocal duty from his own shoulders?

I once drank tea in company with two Methodist divines of different persuasions, whom it was my fortune to introduce to each other for the first time that evening. Before the first cup was handed round, one of these reverend gentlemen put it to the other, with all due solemnity, whether he chose to *say anything*. It seems it is the custom with some sectaries to put up a short prayer before this meal also. His reverend brother did not at first quite apprehend him, but upon an explanation, with little less importance he made answer that it was not a custom known in his church: in which courteous evasion the other acquiescing for good manners' sake, or in compliance with a weak brother, the supplementary or tea grace was waived altogether. With what spirit might not Lucian have painted two priests, of *his* religion, playing into each other's hands the compliment of performing or omitting a sacrifice, – the hungry God meantime, doubtful of his incense, with expectant nostrils hovering over the two flamens, and (as between two stools) going away in the end without his supper.

A short form upon these occasions is felt to want reverence; a long one, I am afraid, cannot escape the charge of impertinence. I do not quite approve of the epigrammatic conciseness with which that equivocal wag (but my pleasant school-fellow) C. V. L[e Grice], when importuned for a grace, used to inquire, first slyly leering down the table, 'Is there no clergyman here?' – significantly adding, 'thank G – .' Nor do I think our old form at school quite pertinent, where we were used to preface our bald bread-and-cheese-suppers with a preamble, connecting with that humble blessing a recognition of benefits the most awful and overwhelming to the imagination which religion has to offer. *Non tunc illis erat locus.* I remember we were put to it to reconcile the phrase 'good creatures', upon which the blessing rested, with the fare set before us, wilfully understanding that expression in a low and animal sense, – till some one recalled a legend, which told how, in the golden days of Christ's, the young Hospitallers were wont to have smoking joints of roast meat upon their nightly boards, till some pious benefactor, commiserating the decencies, rather than the palates, of the children, commuted our flesh for garments, and gave us – *horresco referens* – trousers instead of mutton.

To S. T. Coleridge

March 9th, 1822.

Dear C., – It gives me great satisfaction to hear that the pig turned out so well – they are interesting creatures at a certain age – what a pity such buds should blow out into the maturity of rank bacon! You had all some of the crackling – and brain sauce – did you remember to rub it with butter, and gently dredge it a little, just before the crisis? Did the eyes come away kindly with no Œdipean avulsion? Was the crackling the colour of the ripe pomegranate? Had you no complement of boiled neck of mutton before it, to blunt the edge of delicate desire? Did you flesh maiden teeth in it? Not that I sent the pig, or can form the remotest guess what part Owen could play in the business. I never knew him give anything away in my life. He would not begin with strangers. I suspect the pig, after all, was meant for me; but at the unlucky juncture of time being absent, the present somehow went round to Highgate. To confess an honest truth, a pig is one of those things I could never think of sending away. Teals, wigeons, snipes, barn-door fowl, ducks, geese – your tame villatic things – Welsh mutton, collars of brawn, sturgeon, fresh or pickled, your potted char, Swiss cheeses, French pies, early grapes, muscadines, I impart as freely unto my friends as to myself. They are but self-extended; but pardon me if I stop somewhere – where the fine feeling of benevolence giveth a higher smack than the sensual rarity – there my friends (or any good man) may command me; but pigs are pigs, and I myself therein am nearest to myself. Nay, I should think it an affront, an undervaluing done to Nature who bestowed such a boon upon me, if in a churlish mood I parted with the precious gift.

One of the bitterest pangs of remorse I ever felt was when a child – when my kind old aunt had strained her pocket-strings to bestow a sixpenny whole plum-cake upon me. In my way home through the Borough, I met a venerable old man, not a mendicant, but thereabouts – a look-beggar, not a verbal petitionist; and in the coxcombry of taught-charity I gave away the cake to him. I walked on a little in all the pride of an Evangelical peacock, when of a sudden my old aunt's kindness crossed me – the sum it was to her – the pleasure she had a right to expect that I – not the old im-postor – should take in eating her cake – the cursed ingrati-tude by which, under the colour of a Christian virtue, I had frustrated her cherished purpose. I sobbed, wept, and took it to heart so grievously, that I think I never suffered the like – and I was right. It was a piece of unfeeling hypocrisy, and proved a lesson to me ever after. The cake has long been masticated, consigned to dunghill with the ashes of that unseasonable pauper.

But when Providence, who is better to us all than our aunts, gives me a pig, remembering my temptation and my fall, I shall endeavour to act towards it more in the spirit of the donor's purpose.

Yours (short of pig) to command in everything.

C. L.

A Dissertation Upon Roast Pig

Mankind, says a Chinese manuscript, which my friend M[anning] was obliging enough to read and explain to me, for the first seventy thousand ages ate their meat raw, claw-ing or biting it from the living animal, just as they do in Abyssinia to this day. This period is not obscurely hinted at by their great Confucius in the second chapter of his Mun-dane Mutations, where he designates a kind of golden age by the term Cho-fang, literally the Cooks' holiday. The manuscript goes on to say, that the art of roasting, or rather broiling (which I take to be the elder brother) was acci-dentally discovered in the manner following. The swineherd, Ho-ti, having gone out into the woods one morning, as his manner was, to collect mast for his hogs, left his cottage in the care of his eldest son Bo-bo, a great lubberly boy, who being fond of playing with fire, as younkers of his age commonly are, let some sparks escape into a bundle of straw, which kindling quickly, spread the conflagration over every part of their poor mansion, till it was reduced to ashes. Together with the cottage (a sorry antediluvian makeshift of a building, you may think it), what was of much more importance, a fine litter of new-farrowed pigs, no less than nine in number, perished. China pigs have been esteemed a luxury all over the East, from the remotest periods that we read of. Bo-bo was in the utmost consternation, as you may think, not so much for the sake of the tenement, which his father and he could easily build up again with a few dry branches, and the labour of an hour or two, at any time, as for the loss of the pigs. While he was thinking what he should say to his father, and wringing his hands over the smoking remnants of one of those untimely sufferers, an odour assailed his nostrils, unlike any scent which he had before experienced. What could it proceed from? – not from the burnt cottage – he had smelt that smell before – indeed, this was by no means the first accident of the kind which had occurred through the negligence of this unlucky young firebrand. Much less did it resemble that of any known herb, weed, or flower. A premonitory moistening at the same time overflowed his nether lip. He knew not what to think. He next stooped down to feel the pig, if there were any signs of life in it. He burnt his fingers, and to cool them he applied them in his booby fashion to his mouth. Some of the crumbs of the scorched skin had come away with his fingers, and for the first time in his life (in the world's life indeed, for before him no man had known it) he tasted – *crackling!* Again he felt and fumbled at the pig. It did not burn him so much now, still he licked his fingers from a sort of habit. The truth at length broke into his slow understanding, that it was the pig that smelt so, and the pig that tasted so delicious; and surrendering himself up to the new-born pleasure, he fell to tearing up whole handfuls of the scorched skin with the flesh next it, and was cramming it down his throat in his beastly fashion, when his sire entered amid the smoking rafters, armed with retributory cudgel, and finding how affairs stood, began to rain blows upon the young rogue's shoulders, as thick as hail-stones, which Bo-bo heeded not any more than if they had been flies. The tickling pleasure, which he experienced in his lower regions, had rendered him quite callous to any inconveniences he might feel in those remote quarters. His father might lay on, but he could not beat him from his pig, till he had fairly made an end of it, when, becoming a little more sensible of his situation, something like the following dialogue ensued.

'You graceless whelp, what have you got there devouring? Is it not enough that you have burnt me down three houses with your dog's tricks, and be hanged to you! but you must be eating fire, and I know not what — what have you got there, I say?'

'O father, the pig, the pig, do come and taste how nice the burnt pig eats.'

The ears of Ho-ti tingled with horror. He cursed his son, and he cursed himself that ever he should beget a son that should eat burnt pig.

Bo-bo, whose scent was wonderfully sharpened since morning, soon raked out another pig, and fairly rending it asunder, thrust the lesser half by main force into the fists of Ho-ti, still shouting out, 'Eat, eat, eat the burnt pig, father, only taste — O Lord!' — with such-like barbarous ejaculations, cramming all the while as if he would choke.

Ho-ti trembled in every joint while he grasped the abominable thing, wavering whether he should not put his son to death for an unnatural young monster, when the crackling scorching his fingers, as it had done his son's, and applying the same remedy to them, he in his turn tasted some of its flavour, which, make what sour mouths he would for a pretence, proved not altogether displeasing to him. In conclusion (for the manuscript here is a little tedious), both father and son fairly set down to the mess, and never left off till they had despatched all that remained of the litter.

Bo-bo was strictly enjoined not to let the secret escape,

for the neighbours would certainly have stoned them for a
couple of abominable wretches, who could think of improv-
ing upon the good meat which God had sent them. Nevertheless, strange stories got about. It was observed that Ho-
ti's cottage was burnt down now more frequently than
ever. Nothing but fires from this time forward. Some would
break out in broad day, others in the night-time. As often
as the sow farrowed, so sure was the house of Ho-ti to be in
a blaze; and Ho-ti himself, which was the more remarkable,
instead of chastising his son, seemed to grow more indulgent
to him than ever. At length they were watched, the terrible
mystery discovered, and father and son summoned to take
their trial at Pekin, then an inconsiderable assize town.
Evidence was given, the obnoxious food itself produced in
court, and verdict about to be pronounced, when the fore-
man of the jury begged that some of the burnt pig, of which
the culprits stood accused, might be handed into the box.
He handled it, and they all handled it; and burning their
fingers, as Bo-bo and his father had done before them, and
nature prompting to each of them the same remedy, against
the face of all the facts, and the clearest charge which judge
had ever given, – to the surprise of the whole court, townsfolk, strangers, reporters, and all present – without leaving
the box, or any manner of consultation whatever, they
brought in a simultaneous verdict of Not Guilty.

The judge, who was a shrewd fellow, winked at the manifest iniquity of the decision: and when the court was dismissed, went privily and bought up all the pigs that could
be had for love or money. In a few days his lordship's town-
house was observed to be on fire. The thing took wing, and
now there was nothing to be seen but fires in every direction.
Fuel and pigs grew enormously dear all over the district.
The insurance-offices one and all shut up shop. People
built slighter and slighter every day, until it was feared that
the very science of architecture would in no long time be
lost to the world. Thus this custom of firing houses continued, till in process of time, says mȳ manuscript, a sage
arose, like our Locke, who made a discovery that the flesh
of swine, or indeed of any other animal, might be cooked

(*burnt*, as they called it) without the necessity of consuming a whole house to dress it. Then first began the rude form of a gridiron. Roasting by the string or spit came in a century or two later, I forget in whose dynasty. By such slow degrees, concludes the manuscript, do the most useful, and seemingly the most obvious, arts make their way among mankind—

Without placing too implicit faith in the account above given, it must be agreed that if a worthy pretext for so dangerous an experiment as setting houses on fire (especially in these days) could be assigned in favour of any culinary object, that pretext and excuse might be found in ROAST PIG.

Of all the delicacies in the whole *mundus edibilis*, I will maintain it to be the most delicate – *princeps obsoniorum*.

I speak not of your grown porkers – things between pig and pork – those hobbledehoys – but a young and tender suckling – under a moon old – guiltless as yet of the sty – with no original speck of the *amor immunditiæ*, the hereditary failing of the first parent, yet manifest – his voice as yet not broken, but something between a childish treble and a grumble – the mild forerunner or *præludium* of a grunt.

He must be roasted. I am not ignorant that our ancestors ate them seethed, or boiled – but what a sacrifice of the exterior tegument!

There is no flavour comparable, I will contend, to that of the crisp, tawny, well-watched, not over-roasted, *crackling*, as it is well called – the very teeth are invited to their share of the pleasure at this banquet in overcoming the coy, brittle resistance – with the adhesive oleaginous – O call it not fat! but an indefinable sweetness growing up to it – the tender blossoming of fat – fat cropped in the bud – taken in the shoot – in the first innocence – the cream and quintessence of the child-pig's yet pure food – the lean, no lean, but a kind of animal manna – or, rather, fat and lean (if it must be so) so blended and running into each other, that both together make but one ambrosian result or common substance.

Behold him while he is 'doing' – it seemeth rather a refreshing warmth, than a scorching heat, that he is so

passive to. How equally he twirleth round the string!
Now he is just done. To see the extreme sensibility of that
tender age! he hath wept out his pretty eyes – radiant jellies
– shooting stars. –

See him in the dish, his second cradle, how meek he lieth!
– wouldst thou have had this innocent grow up to the gross-
ness and indocility which too often accompany maturer
swinehood? Ten to one he would have proved a glutton, a
sloven, an obstinate, disagreeable animal – wallowing in all
manner of filthy conversation – from these sins he is happily
snatched away –

> Ere sin could blight or sorrow fade,
> Death came with timely care —

his memory is odoriferous – no clown curseth, while his
stomach half rejecteth, the rank bacon – no coal-heaver
bolteth him in reeking sausages – he hath a fair sepulchre
in the grateful stomach of the judicious epicure – and for
such a tomb might be content to die.

He is the best of sapors. Pine-apple is great. She is indeed
almost too transcendent – a delight, if not sinful, yet so like
to sinning, that really a tender-conscienced person would do
well to pause – too ravishing for mortal taste, she woundeth
and excoriateth the lips that approach her – like lovers'
kisses, she biteth – she is a pleasure bordering on pain from
the fierceness and insanity of her relish – but she stoppeth
at the palate – she meddleth not with the appetite – and
the coarsest hunger might barter her consistently for a
mutton-chop.

Pig – let me speak his praise – is no less provocative of the
appetite than he is satisfactory to the criticalness of the
censorious palate. The strong man may batten on him, and
the weakling refuseth not his mild juices.

Unlike to mankind's mixed characters, a bundle of virtues
and vices, inexplicably intertwisted, and not to be un-
ravelled without hazard, he is – good throughout. No part
of him is better or worse than another. He helpeth, as far as
his little means extend, all around. He is the least envious
of banquets. He is all neighbours' fare.

I am one of those who freely and ungrudgingly impart a share of the good things of this life which fall to their lot (few as mine are in this kind) to a friend. I protest I take as great an interest in my friend's pleasures, his relishes, and proper satisfactions, as in mine own. 'Presents,' I often say, 'endear Absents.' Hares, pheasants, partridges, snipes, barn-door chickens (those 'tame villatic fowl'), capons, plovers, brawn, barrels of oysters, I dispense as freely as I receive them. I love to taste them, as it were, upon the tongue of my friend. But a stop must be put somewhere. One would not, like Lear, 'give everything'. I make my stand upon pig. Methinks it is an ingratitude to the Giver of all good flavours to extra-domiciliate, or send out of the house slightingly (under pretext of friendship, or I know not what) a blessing so particularly adapted, predestined, I may say, to my individual palate. – It argues an insensibility.

I remember a touch of conscience in this kind at school. My good old aunt, who never parted from me at the end of a holiday without stuffing a sweetmeat, or some nice thing, into my pocket, had dismissed me one evening with a smoking plum-cake, fresh from the oven. In my way to school (it was over London Bridge) a grey-headed old beggar saluted me (I have no doubt, at this time of day, that he was a counterfeit). I had no pence to console him with, and in the vanity of self-denial, and the very coxcombry of charity, schoolboy-like, I made him a present of – the whole cake! I walked on a little, buoyed up, as one is on such occasions, with a sweet soothing of self-satisfaction; but, before I had got to the end of the bridge, my better feelings returned, and I burst into tears, thinking how ungrateful I had been to my good aunt, to go and give her good gift away to a stranger that I had never seen before, and who might be a bad man for aught I knew; and then I thought of the pleasure my aunt would be taking in thinking that I – I myself, and not another – would eat her nice cake – and what should I say to her the next time I saw her – how naughty I was to part with her pretty present! – and the odour of that spicy cake came back upon my recollection, and the pleasure and the curiosity I had taken in seeing her make it, and her joy when she sent it to the oven, and how disappointed she would feel that I had never had a bit of it in my mouth at last – and I blamed my impertinent spirit of alms-giving, and out-of-place hypocrisy of goodness; and above all I wished never to see the face again of that insidious, good-for-nothing, old grey impostor.

Our ancestors were nice in their method of sacrificing these tender victims. We read of pigs whipt to death with something of a shock, as we hear of any other obsolete custom. The age of discipline is gone by, or it would be curious to inquire (in a philosophical light merely) what effect this process might have towards intenerating and dulcifying a substance, naturally so mild and dulcet as the flesh of young pigs. It looks like refining a violet. Yet we should be cautious, while we condemn the inhumanity, how we censure the wisdom of the practice. It might impart a gusto –

I remember an hypothesis, argued upon by the young students, when I was at St Omer's, and maintained with much learning and pleasantry on both sides, 'Whether, supposing that the flavour of a pig who obtained his death by whipping (*per flagellationem extremam*) superadded a pleasure upon the palate of a man more intense than any possible suffering we can conceive in the animal, is man justified in using that method of putting the animal to death?' I forget the decision.

His sauce should be considered. Decidedly, a few bread crumbs, done up with his liver and brains, and a dash of mild sage. But banish, dear Mrs Cook, I beseech you, the whole onion tribe. Barbecue your whole hogs to your palate, steep them in shallots, stuff them out with plantations of the rank and guilty garlic; you cannot poison them, or make them stronger than they are – but consider, he is a weakling – a flower.

To Mr and Mrs Collier

Twelfth Day, '23.

The pig was above my feeble praise. It was a dear pigmy. There was some contention as to who should have the ears; but, in spite of his obstinacy (deaf as these little creatures are to advice,) I contrived to get at one of them.

It came in boots too, which I took as a favour. Generally these pretty toes, pretty toes! are missing; but I suppose he wore them to look taller.

He must have been the least of his race. His little foot would have gone into the silver slipper. I take him to have been a Chinese and a female.

If Evelyn could have seen him, he would never have farrowed two such prodigious volumes; seeing how much good can be contained in – how small a compass!

He crackled delicately.

I left a blank at the top of my letter, not being determined which to address it to: so farmer and farmer's wife will please to divide our thanks. May your granaries be full, and your rats empty, and your chickens plump, and your envious neighbours lean, and your labourers busy, and you as idle and as happy as the day is long!

VIVE L'AGRICULTURE!

How do you make your pigs so little?
They are vastly engaging at the age:
   I was so myself.
Now I am a disagreeable old hog,
A middle-aged gentleman-and-a-half,
  My faculties (thank God!) are not much impaired.

I have my sight, hearing, taste, pretty perfect; and can read the Lord's Prayer in common type, by the help of a candle, without making many mistakes.

Believe me, that while my faculties last, I shall ever cherish a proper appreciation of your many kindnesses in this way, and that the last lingering relish of past favours upon my dying memory will be the smack of that little ear.

G

It was the left ear, which is lucky. Many happy returns, not of the pig, but of the New Year, to both! Mary, for her share of the pig and the memoirs, desires to send the same. – Dr, Mr C. and Mrs C. –

Yours truly,

C. LAMB.

Thoughts on Presents of Game, &c.

'We love to have our friend in the country sitting thus at our table *by proxy*; to apprehend his presence (though a hundred miles may be between us) by a turkey, whose goodly aspect reflects to us his "plump corpusculum"; to taste him in grouse or woodcock; to feel him gliding down in the toast peculiar to the latter; to concorporate him in a slice of Canterbury brawn. This is indeed to have him within ourselves; to know him intimately; such participation is, methinks, *unitive*, as the old theologians phrase it.' – *Last Essays of Elia.*

Elia presents his acknowledgements to his 'Correspondent Unknown' for a basket of prodigiously fine game. He takes for granted that so amiable a character must be a reader of the *Athenaeum*, else he had meditated a notice in *The Times*. Now if this friend had consulted the Delphic oracle for a present suited to the palate of Elia, he could not have hit upon a morsel so acceptable. The birds he is barely thankful for; pheasants are poor *fowls* disguised in fine feathers; but a hare, roasted hard and brown, with gravy and melted butter! Old Mr Chambers, the sensible clergyman in Warwickshire, whose son's acquaintance has made many hours happy in the life of Elia, used to allow a pound of Epping to every hare. Perhaps that was overdoing it. But, in spite of the note of Philomel, who, like some fine poets, that think no scorn to adopt plagiarisms from an humble brother, reiterates every spring her cuckoo cry of 'Jug, jug, jug', Elia pronounces that a hare, to be truly palated, must be roasted. Jugging sophisticates her. In *our* way it eats so 'crips', as Mrs Minikin says. Time was, when Elia was not arrived at his taste, that he preferred to all luxuries a

roasted pig. But he disclaims all such green-sickness appetites in future, though he hath to acknowledge the receipt
of many a delicacy in that kind from correspondents – good
but mistaken men – in consequence of their erroneous sup-
position that he had carried up into mature life the pre-
possessions of childhood. From the worthy Vicar of Enfield
he acknowledges a tithe contribution of extraordinary sapor.
The ancients must have loved hares, else why adopt the
word *lepores* (obviously from *lepus*) but for some subtle
analogy between the delicate flavour of the latter and the
finer relishes of wit in what we most poorly translate *pleasantries*? The fine madnesses of the poet are the very decoc-
tion of his diet. Thence is he hare-brained. Harum-scarum
is a libellous, unfounded phrase, of modern usage. 'Tis true
the hare is the most circumspect of animals, sleeping with
her eye open. Her ears, ever erect, keep them in that wholesome exercise which conduces them to form the very titbit
of the admirers of this noble animal. Noble will I call her
in spite of her detractors, who, from occasional demonstra-
tions of the principle of self-preservation (common to all
animals), infer in her a defect of heroism. Half a hundred
horsemen, with thrice the number of dogs, scour the
country in pursuit of puss across three counties; and because the well-flavoured beast, weighing the odds, is willing
to evade the hue and cry (with her delicate ears shrinking
perchance from discord), comes the grave naturalist,
Linnaeus perchance, or Buffon, and gravely sets down the
hare as a timid animal. Why, Achilles or Bully Dawson
would have declined the preposterous combat.

In fact, how light of digestion we feel after a hare! How
tender its processes after swallowing! What chyle it pro-
motes! How ethereal! as if its living celerity were a type of
its nimble coursing through the animal juices. The notice
might be longer. It is intended less as a natural history of
the hare than a cursory thanks to the country 'good
unknown'. The hare has many friends, but none sincerer
than

ELIA.

Lamb's delight in giving to the days of the year an individuality of their own, was apparent in many of his essays, in the Elia essays, *All Fools Day*, *Valentine's Day* and *New Year's Eve*, in the *Remarkable Correspondent* (February 28th) and the *Fable for Twelfth Day*, but the most pleasant fantasy of all is in the essay that follows in which the feast days and holidays rejoice together. It is interesting to note the genesis of this idea in a letter to Southey written twenty-five years earlier when Southey was at work on a Calendar.

Dear Southey, — I am ashamed that I have not thanked you before this for the *Joan of Arc*, but I did not know your address, and it did not occur to me to write through Cottle. The poem delighted me, and the notes amused me; but methinks she of Neufchatel, in the print, holds her sword too '*like a dancer*'. I sent your *notice* to Phillips, particularly requesting an immediate insertion, but I suppose it came too late. I am sometimes curious to know what progress you make in that same '*Calendar*': whether you insert the nine worthies and Whittington? what you do or how you can manage when two Saints meet and quarrel for precedency? Martlemas, and Candlemas, and Christmas, are glorious themes for a writer like you, antiquity-bitten, smit with the love of boars' heads and rosemary; but how you can ennoble the list of April I know not. By the way, I had a thing to say, but a certain false modesty has hitherto prevented me: perhaps I can best communicate my wish by a hint. My birthday is on the 10th of February, New Style; but if it interferes with any remarkable event, why rather than my country should lose her fame, I care not if I put my nativity back eleven days. Fine family patronage for your '*Calendar*', if that old lady of prolific memory were living, who lies (or lyes) in some church in London, (saints forgive me, but I have forgot *what* church), attesting that enormous legend of as many children as days in the year. I marvel her impudence did not grasp at a leap-year. Three hundred and sixty-five dedications, and all in a family! You might spit in spirit, on the oneness of Maecenas's patronage!

Rejoicings upon the New Year's Coming of Age

The *Old Year* being dead, and the *New Year* coming of age, which he does, by Calendar Law, as soon as the breath is out of the old gentleman's body, nothing would serve the

young spark but he must give a dinner upon the occasion,
to which all the *Days* in the year were invited. The *Festivals*,
whom he deputed as his stewards, were mightily taken with
the notion. They had been engaged time out of mind, they
said, in providing mirth and good cheer for mortals below;
and it was time they should have a taste of their own bounty.
It was stiffly debated among them whether the *Fasts* should
be admitted. Some said the appearance of such lean,
starved guests, with their mortified faces, would pervert
the ends of the meeting. But the objection was overruled by
Christmas Day, who had a design upon *Ash Wednesday* (as
you shall hear), and a mighty desire to see how the old
Domine would behave himself in his cups. Only the *Vigils*
were requested to come with their lanterns, to light the
gentlefolks home at night.

All the *Days* came to their day. Covers were provided for
three hundred and sixty-five guests at the principal table;
with an occasional knife and fork at the side-board for the
Twenty-Ninth of February.

I should have told you that cards of invitation had been
issued. The carriers were the *Hours*; twelve little, merry,
whirligig foot-pages, as you should desire to see, that went
all round, and found out the persons invited well enough,
with the exception of *Easter Day*, *Shrove Tuesday*, and a few
such *Moveables*, who had lately shifted their quarters.

Well, they all met at last – foul *Days*, fine *Days*, all sorts of
Days, and a rare din they made of it. There was nothing but,
Hail! fellow *Day*, well met – brother *Day* – sister *Day* – only
Lady Day kept a little on the aloof, and seemed somewhat
scornful. Yet some said *Twelfth Day* cut her out and out,
for she came in a tiffany suit, white and gold, like a queen
on a frost-cake, all royal, glittering, and *Epiphanous*. The
rest came, some in green, some in white – but old *Lent and
his family* were not yet out of mourning. Rainy *Days* came
in, dripping; and sunshiny *Days* helped them to change
their stockings. *Wedding Day* was there in his marriage
finery, a little the worse for wear. *Pay Day* came late, as he
always does; and *Doomsday* sent word – he might be
expected.

April Fool (as my young lord's jester) took upon himself to marshal the guests, and wild work he made with it. It would have posed old Erra Pater to have found out any given *Day* in the year to erect a scheme upon – good *Days*, bad *Days*, were so shuffled together, to the confounding of all sober horoscopy.

He had stuck the *Twenty-First of June* next to the *Twenty-Second of December*, and the former looked like a Maypole siding a marrow-bone. *Ash Wednesday* got wedged in (as was concerted) betwixt *Christmas* and *Lord Mayor's Days*. Lord! how he laid about him! Nothing but barons of beef and turkeys would go down with him – to the great greasing and detriment of his new sackcloth bib and tucker. And still *Christmas Day* was at his elbow, plying him with the wassail-bowl, till he roared, and hiccupp'd, and protested there was no faith in dried ling, but commended it to the devil for a sour, windy, acrimonious, censorious, hy-po-crit-crit-critical mess, and no dish for a gentleman. Then he dipt his fist into the middle of the great custard that stood before his *left-hand neighbour*, and daubed his hungry beard all over with it, till you would have taken him for the *Last Day in December*, it so hung in icicles.

At another part of the table, *Shrove Tuesday* was helping the *Second of September* to some cock broth, – which courtesy the latter returned with the delicate thigh of a hen pheasant – so that there was no love lost for that matter. The *Last of Lent* was spunging upon *Shrove-tide's* pancakes; which *April Fool* perceiving, told him that he did well, for pancakes were proper to a *good fry-day*.

In another part, a hubbub arose about the *Thirtieth of January*, who, it seems, being a sour, puritanic character, that thought nobody's meat good or sanctified enough for him, had smuggled into the room a calf's head, which he had cooked at home for that purpose, thinking to feast thereon incontinently; but as it lay in the dish, *March Manyweathers*, who is a very fine lady, and subject to the meagrims, screamed out there was a 'human head in the platter', and raved about Herodias' daughter to that degree, that the obnoxious viand was obliged to be re-

moved; nor did she recover her stomach till she had gulped
down a *Restorative*, confected of *Oak Apple*, which the merry
Twenty-Ninth of May always carries about with him for that
purpose.

The King's health being called for after this, a notable
dispute arose between the *Twelfth of August* (a zealous old
Whig gentlewoman) and the *Twenty-Third of April* (a new-
fangled lady of the Tory stamp), as to which of them should
have the honour to propose it. *August* grew hot upon the
matter, affirming, time out of mind, the prescriptive right
to have lain with her, till her rival had basely supplanted
her; whom she represented as little better than a *kept*
mistress, who went about in *fine clothes*, while she (the
legitimate 'Birthday') had scarcely a rag, etc.

April Fool, being made mediator, confirmed the right, in
the strongest form of words, to the appellant, but decided
for peace' sake, that the exercise of it should remain with
the present possessor. At the same time, he slyly rounded
the first lady in the ear, that an action might lie against the
Crown for *bi-geny*.

It beginning to grow a little duskish, *Candlemas* lustily
bawled out for lights, which was opposed by all the *Days*,
who protested against burning daylight. Then fair water
was handed round in silver ewers, and the *same lady* was
observed to take an unusual time in *Washing* herself.

May Day, with that sweetness which is peculiar to her,
in a neat speech proposing the health of the founder, crown-
ed her goblet (and by her example the rest of the company)
with garlands. This being done, the lordly *New Year*, from
the upper end of the table, in a cordial but somewhat lofty
tone, returned thanks. He felt proud on an occasion of
meeting so many of his worthy father's late tenants, promised to improve their farms, and at the same time to abate
(if anything was found unreasonable) in their rents.

At the mention of this, the four *Quarter Days* involuntarily
looked at each other, and smiled; *April Fool* whistled to an
old tune of 'New Brooms'; and a surly old rebel at the
farther end of the table (who was discovered to be no other
than the *Fifth of November*) muttered out, distinctly enough

to be heard by the whole company, words to this effect —
that 'when the old one is gone, he is a fool that looks for a
better'. Which rudeness of his, the guests resenting, unanimously voted his expulsion; and the malcontent was
thrust out neck and heels into the cellar, as the properest
place for such a *boutefeu* and firebrand as he had shown
himself to be.

Order being restored — the young lord (who, to say
truth, had been a little ruffled, and put beside his oratory)
in as few and yet as obliging words as possible, assured them
of entire welcome; and, with a graceful turn, singling out
poor *Twenty-Ninth of February*, that had sate all this while
mumchance at the side-board, begged to couple his health
with that of the good company before him — which he
drank accordingly; observing that he had not seen his
honest face any time these four years — with a number of
endearing expressions besides. At the same time removing
the solitary *Day* from the forlorn seat which had been
assigned him, he stationed him at his own board, somewhere
between the *Greek Calends* and *Latter Lammas*.

Ash Wednesday being now called upon for a song, with his
eyes fast stuck in his head, and as well as the Canary he had
swallowed would give him leave, struck up a Carol, which
Christmas Day had taught him for the nonce; and was followed by the latter, who gave 'Miserere' in fine style, hitting
off the mumping notes and lengthened drawl of *Old Mortification* with infinite humour. *April Fool* swore they had
exchanged conditions; but *Good Friday* was observed to
look extremely grave; and *Sunday* held her fan before her
face that she might not be seen to smile.

Shrove-tide, *Lord Mayor's Day*, and *April Fool*, next joined
in a glee —

Which is the properest day to drink?

in which all the *Days* chiming in, made a merry burden.

They next fell to quibbles and conundrums. The question
being proposed, who had the greatest number of followers —
the *Quarter Days* said, there could be no question as to that;
for they had all the creditors in the world dogging their

heels. But *April Fool* gave it in favour of the *Forty Days before Easter;* because the debtors in all cases outnumbered the creditors, and they kept *Lent* all the year.

All this while *Valentine's Day* kept courting pretty *May,* who sate next him, slipping amorous *billets-doux* under the table, till the *Dog Days* (who are naturally of a warm constitution) began to be jealous, and to bark and rage ex-exceedingly. *April Fool,* who likes a bit of sport above measure, and had some pretensions to the lady besides, as being but a cousin once removed, – clapped and halloo'd them on; and as fast as their indignation cooled, those mad wags, the *Ember Days,* were at it with their bellows, to blow it into a flame; and all was in a ferment, till old Madam *Septuagesima* (who boasts herself the *Mother of the Days*) wisely diverted the conversation with a tedious tale of the lovers which she could reckon when she was young, and of one Master *Rogation Day* in particular, who was for ever putting the *question* to her; but she kept him at a distance, as the chronicle would tell – by which I apprehend she meant the Almanack. Then she rambled on to the *Days that were gone,* the *good old Days,* and so to the *Days before the Flood* – which plainly showed her old head to be little better than crazed and doited.

Day being ended, the *Days* called for their cloaks and greatcoats, and took their leave. *Lord Mayor's Day* went off in a Mist, as usual; *Shortest Day* in a deep black Fog, that wrapt the little gentleman all round like a hedge-hog. Two *Vigils* – so watchmen are called in heaven – saw *Christmas Day* safe home – they had been used to the business before. Another *Vigil* – a stout, sturdy patrole, called the *Eve of St Christopher* – seeing *Ash Wednesday* in a condition little better than he should be – e'en whipt him over his shoulders, pick-a-back fashion, and *Old Mortification* went floating home singing –

> On the bat's back I do fly,

and a number of old snatches besides, between drunk and sober; but very few Aves or Penitentiaries (you may believe me) were among them. *Longest Day* set off westward in beautiful crimson and gold – the rest, some in one fashion, some in another; but *Valentine* and pretty *May* took their departure together in one of the prettiest silvery twilights a Lover's Day could wish to set in.

First published *Morning Chronicle*, January 1, 1823, and reprinted as an Elia essay in the *London Magazine* in the same month.

Dream Children – A Reverie

Children love to listen to stories about their elders, when *they* were children; to stretch their imagination to the conception of a traditionary great-uncle, or grandame, whom they never saw. It was in this spirit that my little ones crept about me the other evening to hear about their great-grandmother Field, who lived in a great house in Norfolk (a hundred times bigger than that in which they and papa lived) which had been the scene – so at least it was generally believed in that part of the country – of the tragic incidents which they had lately become familiar with from the ballad of the 'Children in the Wood'. Certain it is that the whole story of the children and their cruel uncle was to be seen fairly carved out in wood upon the chimney-piece of the great hall, the whole story down to the Robin Redbreasts; till a foolish rich person pulled it down to set up a marble one of modern invention in its stead, with no story upon it. Here Alice put out one of her dear mother's looks, too tender to be called upbraiding. Then I went on to say, how religious and how good their great-grandmother Field was, how beloved and respected by everybody, though she was not indeed the mistress of this great house, but had only the charge of it (and yet in some respects she might be said to be the mistress of it too) committed to her by the owner, who preferred living in a newer and more fashionable mansion which he had purchased somewhere in the adjoining county; but still she lived in it in a manner as if it had been her own, and kept up the dignity of the great house in a sort while she lived, which afterwards came to decay, and

was nearly pulled down, and all its old ornaments stripped
and carried away to the owner's other house, where they
were set up, and looked as awkward as if some one were to
carry away the old tombs they had seen lately at the Abbey,
and stick them up in Lady C.'s tawdry gilt drawing-room.
Here John smiled, as much as to say, 'that would be foolish
indeed'. And then I told how, when she came to die, her
funeral was attended by a concourse of all the poor, and
some of the gentry too, of the neighbourhood for many
miles round, to show their respect for her memory, because
she had been such a good and religious woman; so good
indeed that she knew all the Psaltery by heart, ay, and a
great part of the Testament besides. Here little Alice spread
her hands. Then I told what a tall, upright, graceful person
their great-grandmother Field once was; and how in her
youth she was esteemed the best dancer – here Alice's little
right foot played an involuntary movement, till, upon my
looking grave, it desisted – the best dancer, I was saying, in
the county, till a cruel disease, called a cancer, came, and
bowed her down with pain; but it could never bend her
good spirits, or make them stoop, but they were still upright, because she was so good and religious. Then I told
how she was used to sleep by herself in a lone chamber of the
great lone house; and how she believed that an apparition of
two infants was to be seen at midnight gliding up and down
the great staircase near where she slept, but she said 'those
innocents would do her no harm'; and how frightened I
used to be, though in those days I had my maid to sleep
with me, because I was never half so good or religious as
she – and yet I never saw the infants. Here John expanded
all his eyebrows and tried to look courageous. Then I told
how good she was to all her grandchildren, having us to the
great house in the holydays, where I in particular used to
spend many hours by myself, in gazing upon the old busts
of the twelve Cæsars, that had been Emperors of Rome, till
the old marble heads would seem to live again, or I to be
turned into marble with them; how I never could be tired
with roaming about that huge mansion, with its vast empty
rooms, with their worn-out hangings, fluttering tapestry,

and carved oaken panels, with the gilding almost rubbed
out – sometimes in the spacious old-fashioned gardens
which I had almost to myself, unless when now and then a
solitary gardening man would cross me – and how the
nectarines and peaches hung upon the walls, without my
ever offering to pluck them, because they were forbidden
fruit, unless now and then, – and because I had more pleasure in strolling about among the old melancholy-looking
yew-trees, or the firs, and picking up the red berries, and
the fir-apples, which were good for nothing but to look at
– or in lying about upon the fresh grass with all the fine
garden smells around me – or basking in the orangery, till
I could almost fancy myself ripening too along with the
oranges and the limes in that grateful warmth – or in
watching the dace that darted to and fro in the fish-pond,
at the bottom of the garden, with here and there a great
sulky pike hanging midway down the water in silent state,
as if it mocked at their impertinent friskings, – I had more
pleasure in these busy-idle diversions than in all the sweet
flavours of peaches, nectarines, oranges, and such-like common baits of children. Here John slyly deposited back upon
the plate a bunch of grapes, which, not unobserved by
Alice, he had meditated dividing with her, and both seemed
willing to relinquish them for the present as irrelevant.
Then, in somewhat a more heightened tone, I told how,
though their great-grandmother Field loved all her grandchildren, yet in an especial manner she might be said to
love their uncle, John L[amb], because he was so handsome
and spirited a youth, and a king to the rest of us; and, instead of moping about in solitary corners, like some of us,
he would mount the most mettlesome horse he could get,
when but an imp no bigger than themselves, and make it
carry him half over the county in a morning, and join the
hunters when there were any out – and yet he loved the old
great house and gardens too, but had too much spirit to be
always pent up within their boundaries – and how their
uncle grew up to man's estate as brave as he was handsome,
to the admiration of everybody, but of their great-grandmother Field most especially; and how he used to carry me

upon his back when I was a lame-footed boy – for he was a
good bit older than me – many a mile when I could not
walk for pain ; – and how in after life he became lame-footed
too, and I did not always (I fear) make allowances enough
for him when he was impatient and in pain, nor remember
sufficiently how considerate he had been to me when I was
lame-footed ; and how when he died, though he had not
been dead an hour, it seemed as if he had died a great while
ago, such a distance there is betwixt life and death ; and
how I bore his death as I thought pretty well at first, but
afterwards it haunted and haunted me ; and though I did
not cry or take it to heart as some do, and as I think he would
have done if I had died, yet I missed him all day long,
and knew not till then how much I had loved him. I
missed his kindness, and I missed his crossness, and wished
him to be alive again, to be quarrelling with him (for we
quarrelled sometimes), rather than not have him again,
and was as uneasy without him, as he, their poor uncle,
must have been when the doctor took off his limb. – Here
the children fell a-crying, and asked if their little mourning
which they had on was not for uncle John, and they looked
up, and prayed me not to go on about their uncle, but to
tell them some stories about their pretty dead mother.
Then I told how for seven long years, in hope sometimes,
sometimes in despair, yet persisting ever, I courted the fair
Alice W—n ; and as much as children could understand, I
explained to them what coyness, and difficulty, and denial,
meant in maidens – when suddenly turning to Alice, the
soul of the first Alice looked out at her eyes with such a
reality of re-presentment, that I became in doubt which of
them stood there before me, or whose that bright hair was ;
and while I stood gazing, both the children gradually
grew fainter to my view, receding, and still receding, till
nothing at last but two mournful features were seen in the
uttermost distance, which, without speech, strangely impressed upon me the effects of speech : 'We are not of Alice,
nor of thee, nor are we children at all. The children of Alice
call Bartrum father. We are nothing ; less than nothing,
and dreams. We are only what might have been, and must

wait upon the tedious shores of Lethe millions of ages before we have existence, and a name' – and immediately awaking, I found myself quietly seated in my bachelor armchair, where I had fallen asleep, with the faithful Bridget unchanged by my side – but John L. (or James Elia) was gone for ever.

London Magazine, March 1822.

PART V

CRITICAL AND ANTI-CRITICAL

'There is a spirit in Mr Lamb's productions, which is in itself so *anti-critical*, and tends so much to reconcile us to all that is in the world', that the effect is almost neutralizing to everything but complacency and a queer admiration – his very criticisms chiefly tend to overthrow the critical spirit.' Leigh Hunt. *The Examiner*, March 1819 (Reviewing Lamb's *Works*, 1818).

THE FRONT ROW OF THE PIT

My First Play

At the north end of Cross-court there yet stands a portal, of some architectural pretensions, though reduced to humble use, serving at present for an entrance to a printing-office. This old door-way, if you are young, reader, you may not know was the identical pit entrance to old Drury – Garrick's Drury – all of it that is left. I never pass it without shaking some forty years from off my shoulders, recurring to the evening when I passed through it to see *my first play*. The afternoon had been wet, and the condition of our going (the elder folks and myself) was, that the rain should cease. With what a beating heart did I watch from the window the puddles, from the stillness of which I was taught to prognosticate the desired cessation! I seem to remember the last spurt, and the glee with which I ran to announce it.

We went with orders, which my godfather [Francis] F[ielde] had sent us. He kept the oil shop (now Davies's) at the corner of Featherstone-buildings, in Holborn. F. was a tall grave person, lofty in speech, and had pretensions above his rank. He associated in those days with John Palmer, the comedian, whose gait and bearing he seemed to copy; if John (which is quite as likely) did not rather borrow somewhat of his manner from my godfather. He was also known to and visited by Sheridan. It was to his house in Holborn that young Brinsley[1] brought his first wife on her elopement with him from a boarding-school at Bath – the beautiful Maria Linley. My parents were present (over a quadrille table) when he arrived in the evening with his harmonious

[1] Richard Brinsley Sheridan.

charge. From either of these connections it may be inferred that my godfather could command an order for the then Drury-lane theatre at pleasure – and, indeed, a pretty liberal issue of those cheap billets, in Brinsley's easy autograph, I have heard him say, was the sole remuneration which he had received for many years' nightly illumination of the orchestra and various avenues of that theatre – and he was content it should be so. The honour of Sheridan's familiarity – or supposed familiarity – was better to my godfather than money.

F. was the most gentlemanly of oilmen; grandiloquent, yet courteous. His delivery of the commonest matters of fact was Ciceronian. He had two Latin words almost constantly in his mouth (how odd sounds Latin from an oilman's lips!), which my better knowledge since has enabled me to correct. In strict pronunciation they should have been sounded *vice versâ* – but in those young years they impressed me with more awe than they would now do, read aright from Seneca or Varro – in his own peculiar pronunciation, monosyllabically elaborated, or Anglicized, into something like *verse verse*. By an imposing manner, and the help of these distorted syllables, he climbed (but that was little) to the highest parochial honours which St Andrew's has to bestow.

He is dead – and thus much I thought due to his memory, both for my first orders (little wondrous talismans! – slight keys, and insignificant to outward sight, but opening to me more than Arabian paradises!) and, moreover, that by his testamentary beneficence I came into possession of the only landed property which I could ever call my own – situate near the road-way village of pleasant Puckeridge, in Hertfordshire. When I journeyed down to take possession, and planted foot on my own ground, the stately habits of the donor descended upon me, and I strode (shall I confess the vanity?) with larger paces over my allotment of three-quarters of an acre, with its commodious mansion in the midst, with the feeling of an English freeholder that all betwixt sky and centre was my own. The estate has passed into more prudent hands, and nothing but an agrarian can restore it.

In those days were pit orders. Beshrew the uncomfortable manager who abolished them! – with one of these we went. I remember the waiting at the door – not that which is left – but between that and an inner door in shelter – O when shall I be such an expectant again! – with the cry of non-pareils, an indispensable play-house accompaniment in those days. As near as I can recollect, the fashionable pronunciation of the theatrical fruiteresses then was, 'Chase some oranges, chase some numparels, chase a bill of the play'; – chase *pro* chuse. But when we got in, and I beheld the green curtain that veiled a heaven to my imagination, which was soon to be disclosed – the breathless anticipations I endured! I had seen something like it in the plate prefixed to *Troilus and Cressida*, in Rowe's Shakspeare – the tent scene with Diomede – and a sight of that plate can always bring back in a measure the feeling of that evening. – The boxes at that time, full of well-dressed women of quality, projected over the pit; and the pilasters reaching down were adorned with a glistening substance (I know not what) under glass (as it seemed), resembling – a homely fancy – but I judged it to be sugar-candy – yet to my raised imagination, divested of its homelier qualities, it appeared a glorified candy! – The orchestra lights at length rose, those 'fair Auroras!' Once the bell sounded. It was to ring out yet once again – and, incapable of the anticipation, I reposed my shut eyes in a sort of resignation upon the maternal lap. It rang the second time. The curtain drew up – I was not past six years old, and the play was *Artaxerxes*!

I had dabbled a little in the *Universal History* – the ancient part of it – and here was the court of Persia. – It was being admitted to a sight of the past. I took no proper interest in the action going on, for I understood not its import – but I heard the word Darius, and I was in the midst of Daniel. All feeling was absorbed in vision. Gorgeous vests, gardens, palaces, princesses, passed before me. I knew not players. I was in Persepolis for the time, and the burning idol of their devotion almost converted me into a worshipper. I was awe-struck, and believed those significations to be something more than elemental fires. It was all enchantment

and a dream. No such pleasure has since visited me but in
dreams. – Harlequin's invasion followed; where, I remember, the transformation of the magistrates into reverend
beldams seemed to me a piece of grave historic justice, and
the tailor carrying his own head to be as sober a verity as
the legend of St Denys.

The next play to which I was taken was the *Lady of the
Manor*, of which, with the exception of some scenery, very
faint traces are left in my memory. It was followed by a
pantomime, called *Lun's Ghost* – a satiric touch, I apprehend,
upon Rich, not long since dead – but to my apprehension
(too sincere for satire), Lun was as remote a piece of antiquity as Lud – the father of a line of Harlequins – trans-
mitting his dagger of lath (the wooden sceptre) through
countless ages. I saw the primeval Motley come from his
silent tomb in a ghastly vest of white patchwork, like the
apparition of a dead rainbow. So Harlequins (thought I)
look when they are dead.

My third play followed in quick succession. It was the
Way of the World. I think I must have sat at it as grave as a
judge; for I remember the hysteric affectations of good
Lady Wishfort affected me like some solemn tragic passion.
Robinson Crusoe followed; in which Crusoe, man Friday, and
the parrot, were as good and authentic as in the story. –
The clownery and pantaloonery of these pantomimes have
clean passed out of my head. I believe, I no more laughed
at them, than at the same age I should have been disposed
to laugh at the grotesque Gothic heads (seeming to me then
replete with devout meaning) that gape and grin, in stone
around the inside of the old Round Church (my church)
of the Templars.

I saw these plays in the season 1781–2, when I was from
six to seven years old. After the intervention of six or seven
other years (for at school all play-going was inhibited) I
again entered the doors of a theatre. That old *Artaxerxes*
evening had never done ringing in my fancy. I expected
the same feelings to come again with the same occasion.
But we differ from ourselves less at sixty and sixteen, than
the latter does from six. In that interval what had I

not lost! At the first period I knew nothing, understood nothing, discriminated nothing. I felt all, loved all, wondered all –

> Was nourished, I could not tell how—

I had left the temple a devotee, and was returned a rationalist. The same things were there materially; but the emblem, the reference, was gone! – The green curtain was no longer a veil, drawn between two worlds, the unfolding of which was to bring back past ages, to present a 'royal ghost', – but a certain quantity of green baize, which was to separate the audience for a given time from certain of their fellowmen who were to come forward and pretend those parts. The lights – the orchestra lights – came up a clumsy machinery. The first ring, and the second ring, was now but a trick of the prompter's bell – which had been, like the note of the cuckoo, a phantom of a voice, no hand seen or guessed at which ministered to its warning. The actors were men and women painted. I thought the fault was in them; but it was in myself, and the alteration which those many centuries – of six short twelvemonths – had wrought in me. – Perhaps it was fortunate for me that the play of the evening was but an indifferent comedy, as it gave me time to crop some unreasonable expectations, which might have interfered with the genuine emotions with which I was soon after enabled to enter upon the first appearance to me of Mrs Siddons in *Isabella*. Comparison and retrospection soon yielded to the present attraction of the scene; and the theatre became to me, upon a new stock, the most delightful of recreations!

ELIA.

London Magazine, December 1821.

To William Wordsworth

December 11th, 1806.

Mary's love to all of you – I wouldn't let her write.
Dear Wordsworth, – *Mr H*. came out last night, and

failed. I had many fears; the subject was not substantial enough. John Bull must have solider fare than a *letter*. We are pretty stout about it; have had plenty of condoling friends; but, after all, we had rather it should have succeeded. You will see the prologue in most of the morning papers. It was received with such shouts as I never witnessed to a prologue. It was attempted to be encored. How hard! – a thing I did merely as a task, because it was wanted, and set no great store by; and *Mr H.!!* The number of friends we had in the house – my brother and I being in public offices, &c. – was astonishing, but they yielded at length to a few hisses.

A hundred hisses! (Damn the word, I write it like kisses – how different!) – a hundred hisses outweigh a thousand claps. The former come more directly from the heart. Well 'tis withdrawn, and there is an end.

Better luck to us.

C. LAMB.

P.S. Pray, when any of you write to the Clarksons, give our kind loves, and say we shall not be able to come and see them at Christmas, as I shall have but a day or two, and tell them we bear our mortification pretty well.

On the Custom of Hissing at the Theatres

(With some account of a Club of Damned Authors)

Mr. Reflector, – I am one of those persons whom the world has thought proper to designate by the title of Damned Authors. In that memorable season of dramatic failures, 1806–7, in which no fewer, I think, than two tragedies, four comedies, one opera, and three farces suffered at Drury Lane Theatre, I was found guilty of constructing an afterpiece, and was *damned*.

Against the decision of the public in such instances there can be no appeal. The Clerk of Chatham might as well have protested against the decision of Cade and his followers, who

were then *the public*. Like him, I was condemned because I
could write.

Not but it did appear to some of us that the measures of
the popular tribunal at that period savoured a little of
harshness and of the *summum jus*. The public mouth was early
in the season fleshed upon the 'Vindictive Man', and some
pieces of that nature; and it retained, through the remainder of it, a relish of blood. As Dr Johnson would have said,
'Sir, there was a habit of sibilation in the house'.

Still less am I disposed to inquire into the reason of the
comparative lenity, on the other hand, with which some
pieces were treated, which to indifferent judges seemed at
least as much deserving of condemnation as some of those
which met with it. I am willing to put a favourable construction upon the votes that were given against us. I
believe that there was no bribery or designed partiality in
the case: only 'our nonsense did not happen to suit their
nonsense'; that was all.

But against the *manner* in which the public on these
occasions think fit to deliver their disapprobation, I must
and ever will protest.

Sir, imagine – but you have been present at the damning
of a piece (those who never had that felicity, I beg them to
imagine) – a vast theatre, like that which Drury Lane was
before it was a heap of dust and ashes (I insult not over its
fallen greatness, let it recover itself when it can for me; let
it lift up its towering head once more, and take in poor
authors to write for it; *hic caestus artemque repono*), – a theatre
like that, filled with all sorts of disgusting sounds, shrieks,
groans, hisses, but chiefly the last, like the noise of many
waters, or that which Don Quixote heard from the fulling-
mills, or that wilder combination of devilish sounds which
St Anthony listened in to the wilderness.

O Mr Reflector! is it not a pity that the sweet human
voice, which was given man to speak with, to sing with, to
whisper tones of love in, to express compliance, to convey a
favour or to grant a suit, – that voice which in a Siddons or
a Braham rouses us, in a siren Catalani charms and capti-
vates us, – that the musical, expressive human voice should

be converted into a rival of the noises of silly geese and irrational venomous snakes?

I never shall forget the sounds on *my night*. I never before that time fully felt the reception which the Author of all ill, in the 'Paradise Lost', meets with from the critics in the *pit*, at the final close of his 'Tragedy upon the Human Race,' – though that, alas! met with too much success: –

> — From innumerable tongues
> A dismal universal *hiss*, the sound
> Of public scorn. Dreadful was the din
> Of *hissing* through the hall, thick swarming now
> With complicated monsters, head and tail,
> Scorpion and asp, and Amphisbaena dire,
> Cerastes horned, Hydrus, and Elops drear,
> And Dipsas.

For *hall* substitute *theatre*, and you have the very image of what takes place at what is called the *damnation* of a piece, – and properly so called; for here you see its origin plainly, whence the custom was derived, and what the first piece was that so suffered. After this, none can doubt the propriety of the appellation.

But, sir, as to the justice of bestowing such appalling, theart-withering denunciations of the popular obloquy upon he venial mistake of a poor author, who thought to please us in the act of filling his pockets, – for the sum of his demerits amounts to no more than that, – it does, I own, seem to me a species of retributive justice, far too severe for the offence. A culprit in the pillory (bate the eggs) meets with no severer exprobation.

Indeed, I have often wondered that some modest critic has not proposed that there should be a wooden machine to that effect erected in some convenient part of the proscenium, which an unsuccessful author should be required to mount, and stand his hour, exposed to the apples and oranges of the pit. This *amende honorable* would well suit with the meanness of some authors, who, in their prologues, fairly prostrate their skulls to the audience, and seem to invite a pelting.

Or why should they not have their pens publicly broke over their heads, as the swords of recreant knights in old times were, and an oath administered to them that they should never write again?

Seriously, *Messieurs the Public*, this outrageous way which you have got of expressing your displeasure is too much for the occasion. When I was deafening under the effects of it, I could not help asking what crime of great moral turpitude I had committed: for every man about me seemed to feel the offence as personal to himself, as something which public interest and private feelings alike called upon him, in the strongest possible manner, to stigmatize with infamy.

The Romans, it is well known to you, Mr Reflector, took a gentler method of marking their disapprobation of an author's work. They were a humane and equitable nation. They left the *furca* and the *patibulum*, the axe and the rods, to great offenders; for these minor, and (if I may so term them) extra-moral offences, *the bent thumb* was considered as a sufficient sign of disapprobation, – *vertere pollicem*; as *the pressed thumb*, *premere pollicem*, was a mark of approving.

And really there seems to have been a sort of fitness in this method, a correspondency of sign in the punishment to the offence. For as the action of writing is performed by bending the thumb forward, the retroversion or bending back of that joint did not inaptly point to the opposite of that action; implying that it was the will of the audience that the author should *write no more*: a much more significant as well as more humane way of expressing that desire than our custom of hissing, which is altogether senseless and indefensible. Nor do we find that the Roman audiences deprived themselves, by this lenity, of any tittle of that supremacy which audiences in all ages have thought themselves bound to maintain over such as have been candidates for their applause. On the contrary, by this method they seem to have had the author, as we should express it, completely *under finger and thumb*.

The provocations to which a dramatic genius is exposed from the public are so much the more vexatious as they are removed from any possibility of retaliation, which sweetens most other injuries; for the public *never writes itself*. Not but something very like it took place at the time of the O[ld] P[rices] differences.[1] The placards which were nightly exhibited were, properly speaking, the composition of the public. The public wrote them, the public applauded them; and precious *morceaux* of wit and eloquence they were, – except some few, of a better quality, which it is well known were furnished by professed dramatic writers. After this specimen of what the public can do for itself, it should be a little slow in condemning what others do for it.

As the degrees of malignancy vary in people according as they have more or less of the Old Serpent (the father of hisses) in their composition, I have sometimes amused myself with analysing this many-headed hydra, which calls itself the public, into the component parts of which it is 'complicated, head and tail', and seeing how many varieties of the snake kind it can afford.

First, there is the *Common English Snake*. This is that part of the auditory who are always the majority at damnations, but who, having no critical venom in themselves to sting them on, stay till they hear others hiss, and then join in for company.

The Blind Worm is a species very nearly allied to the foregoing. Some naturalists have doubted whether they are not the same.

The Rattlesnake. – These are your obstreperous talking critics, – the impertinent guides of the pit, – who will not give a plain man leave to enjoy an evening's entertainment, but, with their frothy jargon and incessant finding of faults, either drown his pleasure quite, or force him, in his own defence, to join in their clamorous censure. The hiss always originates with these. When this creature springs his *rattle*, you would think from the noise it makes there was something in it; but you have only to examine the instrument

[1 Covent Garden Theatre was burnt down in 1808. On the opening of the new theatre in 1809, the audience rioted for 'Old Prices'.]

from which the noise proceeds, and you will find it typical of a critic's tongue, – a shallow membrane, empty, voluble, and seated in the most contemptible part of the creature's body.

The Whipsnake. – This is he that lashes the poor author the next day in the newspapers.

The Deaf Adder, or *Surda Echidna* of Linnaeus. – Under this head may be classed all that portion of the spectators (for audience they properly are not), who, not finding the first act of a piece answer to their preconceived notions of what a first act should be, like Obstinate in John Bunyan, positively thrust their fingers in their ears, that they may not hear a word of what is coming, though perhaps the very next act may be composed in a style as different as possible, and be written quite to their own tastes. These adders refuse to hear the voice of the charmer, because the tuning of his instrument gave them offence.

I should weary you and myself too, if I were to go through all the classes of the serpent kind. Two qualities are common to them all. They are creatures of remarkably cold digestions, and chiefly haunt *pits* and low grounds.

I proceed with more pleasure to give you an account of a club to which I have the honour to belong. There are fourteen of us, who are all authors that have been once in our lives what is called *damned*. We meet on the anniversary of our respective nights, and make ourselves merry at the expense of the public. The chief tenets which distinguish our society, and which every man among us is bound to hold for gospel, are –

That the public or mob, in all ages, have been a set of blind, deaf, obstinate, senseless, illiterate savages. That no man of genius, in his senses, would be ambitious of pleasing such a capricious, ungrateful rabble. That the only legitimate end of writing for them is to pick their pockets, and that failing, we are at full liberty to vilify and abuse them as much as ever we think fit.

That authors, by their affected pretences to humility, which they make use of as a cloak to insinuate their writings into the callous senses of the multitude, obtuse to everything but the grossest flattery, have by degrees made that great beast their master, as we may act submission to children till we are obliged to practise it in earnest. That authors are and ought to be considered the masters and preceptors of the public, and not *vice versa*. That it was so in the days of Orpheus, Linus, and Musaeus, and would be so again if it were not that writers prove traitors to themselves. That, in particular, in the days of the first of those three great authors just mentioned, audiences appear to have been perfect models of what audiences should be; for though, along with the trees and the rocks and the wild creatures which he drew after him to listen to his strains, some serpents doubtless came to hear his music, it does not appear that any one among them ever lifted up a *dissentient voice*. They knew what was due to authors in those days. Now every stock and stone turns into a serpent and has a voice.

That the terms 'courteous reader' and 'candid auditors' as having given rise to a false notion in those to whom they were applied, as if they conferred upon them some right, *which they cannot have*, of exercising their judgements, ought to be utterly banished and exploded.

These are our distinguishing tenets. To keep up the memory of the cause in which we suffered, as the ancients sacrificed a goat, a supposed unhealthy animal, to Aesculapius on our feast nights we cut up a goose, an animal typical of the *popular voice*, to the deities of Candour and Patient Hearing. A zealous member of the society once proposed that we should revive the obsolete luxury of the viper-broth; but the stomachs of some of the company rising at the proposition, we lost the benefit of that highly salutary and *antidotal dish*.

The privilege of admission to our club is strictly limited to such as have been fairly *damned*. A piece that has met with ever so little applause, that has but languished its night or two and then gone out, will never entitle its author to a seat among us. An exception to our usual readiness in conferring this privilege is in the case of a writer who, having been once condemned, writes again, and becomes candidate for a second martyrdom. Simple damnation we hold to be a merit; but to be twice damned we adjudge infamous. Such a one we utterly reject, and blackball without a hearing: –

'The common damned shun his society.'

Hoping that your publication of our regulations may be a means of inviting some more members into our society, I conclude this long letter. – I am, sir, yours,

SEMEL-DAMNATUS.

The Reflector, 1811

Stage Illusion

A play is said to be well or ill acted, in proportion to the scenical illusion produced. Whether such illusion can in any case be perfect, is not the question. The nearest approach to it, we are told, is when the actor appears wholly unconscious of the presence of spectators. In tragedy – in all which is to affect the feelings – this undivided attention to his stage business seems indispensable. Yet it is, in fact, dispensed with every day by our cleverest tragedians; and while these references to an audience, in the shape of rant or sentiment, are not too frequent or palpable, a sufficient quantity of illusion for the purposes of dramatic interest may be said to be produced in spite of them. But, tragedy apart, it may be inquired whether, in certain characters in comedy, especially those which are a little extravagant, or which involve some notion repugnant to the moral sense, it is not a proof of the highest skill in the comedian when, without absolutely appealing to an audience, he keeps up a tacit understanding with them; and makes them, unconsciously to themselves, a party in the scene. The utmost nicety is required in the mode of doing this; but we speak only of the great artists in the profession.

The most mortifying infirmity in human nature, to feel in ourselves, or to contemplate in another, is, perhaps, cowardice. To see a coward *done to the life* upon a stage would produce anything but mirth. Yet we most of us remember Jack Bannister's cowards. Could anything be more agreeable, more pleasant? We loved the rogues. How was this effected but by the exquisite art of the actor in a perpetual sub-insinuation to us, the spectators, even in the extremity of the shaking fit, that he was not half such a coward as we took him for? We saw all the common symptoms of the malady upon him; the quivering lip, the cowering knees, the teeth chattering; and could have sworn 'that man was frightened'. But we forgot all the while − or kept it almost a secret to ourselves − that he never once lost his self-possession; that he let out, by a thousand droll looks and gestures − meant at *us*, and not at all supposed to be visible to his fellows in the scene, that his confidence in his own resources had never once deserted him. Was this a genuine picture of a coward; or not rather a likeness, which the clever artist contrived to palm upon us instead of an original; while we secretly connived at the delusion for the purpose of greater pleasure, than a more genuine counterfeiting of the imbecility, helplessness, and utter self-desertion, which we know to be concomitants of cowardice in real life, could have given us?

Why are misers so hateful in the world, and so endurable on the stage, but because the skilful actor, by a sort of subreference, rather than direct appeal to us, disarms the character of a great deal of its odiousness, by seeming to engage *our* compassion for the insecure tenure by which he holds his money-bags and parchments? By this subtle vent half of the hatefulness of the character − the self-closeness with which in real life it coils itself up from the sympathies of men − evaporates. The miser becomes sympathetic; *i.e.*, is no genuine miser. Here again a diverting likeness is substituted for a very disagreeable reality.

Spleen, irritability − the pitiable infirmities of old men, which produce only pain to behold in the realities, counterfeited upon a stage, divert not altogether for the comic appendages to them, but in part from an inner conviction that they are *being acted* before us; that a likeness only is going on, and not the thing itself. They please by being done under the life, or beside it; not *to the life*. When Gattie acts an old man, is he angry indeed? or only a pleasant counter-feit, just enough of a likeness to recognize, without pressing upon us the uneasy sense of a reality?

Comedians, paradoxical as it may seem, may be too natural. It was the case with a late actor. Nothing could be more earnest or true than the manner of Mr Emery; this told excellently in his Tyke, and characters of a tragic cast. But when he carried the same rigid exclusiveness of attention to the stage business, and wilful blindness and oblivion of everything before the curtain into his comedy, it produced a harsh and dissonant effect. He was out of keep-ing with the rest of the *dramatis personæ*. There was as little link between him and them, as betwixt himself and the audience. He was a third estate – dry, repulsive, and un-social to all. Individually considered, his execution was masterly. But comedy is not this unbending thing; for this reason, that the same degree of credibility is not required of it as to serious scenes. The degrees of credibility demanded to the two things may be illustrated by the different sort of truth which we expect when a man tells us a mournful or a merry story. If we suspect the former of falsehood in any one tittle, we reject it altogether. Our tears refuse to flow at a suspected imposition. But the teller of a mirthful tale has latitude allowed him. We are content with less than ab-solute truth. 'Tis the same with dramatic illusion. We con-fess we love in comedy to see an audience naturalized be-hind the scenes – taken into the interest of the drama, welcomed as bystanders, however. There is something un-gracious in a comic actor holding himself aloof from all participation or concern with those who are come to be diverted by him. Macbeth must see the dagger, and no ear but his own be told of it; but an old fool in farce may think he *sees something*, and by conscious words and looks express it, as plainly as he can speak, to pit, box, and gallery. When an impertinent in tragedy, an Osric, for instance, breaks in upon the serious passions of the scene, we approve of the contempt with which he is treated. But when the plea-sant impertinent of comedy, in a piece purely meant to give delight, and raise mirth out of whimsical perplexities, worries the studious man with taking up his leisure, or making his house his home, the same sort of contempt expressed (however *natural*) would destroy the balance of delight in the spectators. To make the intrusion comic, the actor who plays the annoyed man must a little desert nature; he must, in short, be thinking of the audience, and express only so much dissatisfaction and peevishness as is consistent with the pleasure of comedy. In other words, his perplexity must seem half put on. If he repel the intruder with the sober set face of a man in earnest, and more especially if he deliver his expostulations in a tone which in the world must necessarily provoke a duel, his real-life manner will destroy the whimsical and purely dramatic existence of the other character (which to render it comic demands an antagonist comicality on the part of the character opposed to it), and convert what was meant for mirth, rather than belief, into a downright piece of impertinence indeed, which would raise no diversion in us, but rather stir pain, to see inflicted in earnest upon any worthy person. A very judicious actor (in most of his parts) seems to have fallen into an error of this sort in his playing with Mr Wrench in the farce of *Free and Easy*.

Many instances would be tedious; these may suffice to show that comic acting at least does not always demand from the performer that strict abstraction from all reference to an audience which is exacted of it; but that in some cases a sort of compromise may take place, and all the purposes of dramatic delight be attained by a judicious understanding, not too openly announced, between the ladies and gentlemen – on both sides of the curtain.

ELIA.

London Magazine, August 1825.

On the Artificial Comedy of the Last Century

The artificial Comedy, or Comedy of manners, is quite extinct on our stage. Congreve and Farquhar show their heads once in seven years only, to be exploded and put down instantly. The times cannot bear them. Is it for a few wild speeches, an occasional licence of dialogue? I think not altogether. The business of their dramatic characters will not stand the moral test. We screw everything up to that. Idle gallantry in a fiction, a dream, the passing pageant of an evening, startles us in the same way as the alarming indications of profligacy in a son or ward in real life should startle a parent or guardian. We have no such middle emotions as dramatic interests left. We see a stage libertine playing his loose pranks of two hours' duration, and of no after consequence, with the severe eyes which inspect real vices with their bearings upon two worlds. We are spectators to a plot or intrigue (not reducible in life to the point of strict morality), and take it all for truth. We substitute a real for a dramatic person, and judge him accordingly. We try him in our courts, from which there is no appeal to the *dramatis personæ*, his peers. We have been spoiled with – not sentimental comedy – but a tyrant far more pernicious to our pleasures which has succeeded to it, the exclusive and all-devouring drama of common life; where the moral point is everything; where, instead of the fictitious half-believed personages of the stage (the phantoms of old comedy), we recognize ourselves, our brothers, aunts, kinsfolk, allies, patrons, enemies, – the same as in life, – with an interest in what is going on so hearty and substantial, that we cannot afford our moral judgment, in its deepest and most vital results, to compromise or slumber for a moment. What is *there* transacting, by no modification is made to affect us in any other manner than the same events or characters would do in our relationships of life. We carry our fireside concerns to the theatre with us. We do not go thither like our ancestors, to escape from the pressure of reality, so much as to confirm our experience of it; to make assurance double, and take a bond of fate. We must live our toilsome lives twice over, as it was the mournful privilege of Ulysses to descend twice to the shades. All that neutral ground of character, which stood between vice and virtue; or which in fact was indifferent to neither, where

H

neither properly was called in question; that happy breath-
ing-place from the burthen of a perpetual moral question-
ing – the sanctuary and quiet Alsatia of hunted casuistry –
is broken up and disfranchised, as injurious to the interests
of society. The privileges of the place are taken away by
law. We dare not dally with images, or names, of wrong.
We bark like foolish dogs at shadows. We dread infection
from the scenic representation of disorder, and fear a painted pustule. In our anxiety that our morality should not take
cold, we wrap it up in a great blanket surtout of precaution
against the breeze and sunshine.

I confess for myself that (with no great delinquencies to
answer for) I am glad for a season to take an airing beyond
the diocese of the strict conscience, – not to live always in
the precincts of the law courts, – but now and then, for a
dream-while or so, to imagine a world with no meddling
restrictions – to get into recesses, whither the hunter cannot
follow me –

> —— Secret shades
> Of woody Ida's inmost grove,
> While yet there was no fear of Jove.

I come back to my cage and my restraint the fresher and
more healthy for it. I wear my shackles more contentedly
for having respired the breath of an imaginary freedom. I
do not know how it is with others, but I feel the better
always for the perusal of one of Congreve's – nay, why
should I not add even of Wycherley's – comedies. I am the
gayer at least for it; and I could never connect those sports
of a witty fancy in any shape with any result to be drawn
from them to imitation in real life. They are a world of
themselves almost as much as fairy land. Take one of their
characters, male or female (with few exceptions they are
alike), and place it in a modern play, and my virtuous
indignation shall rise against the profligate wretch as warm-
ly as the Catos of the pit could desire; because in a modern
play I am to judge of the right and the wrong. The standard
of *police* is the measure of *political justice*. The atmosphere
will blight it; it cannot live here. It has got into a moral

world, where it has no business, from which it must needs fall headlong; as dizzy, and incapable of making a stand, as a Swedenborgian bad spirit that has wandered unawares into the sphere of one of his Good Men, or Angels. But in its own world do we feel the creature is so very bad? – The Fainalls and the Mirabels, the Dorimants and the Lady Touchwoods, in their own sphere, do not offend my moral sense; in fact, they do not appeal to it at all. They seem engaged in their proper element. They break through no laws or conscientious restraints. They know of none. They have got out of Christendom into the land – what shall I call it? – of cuckoldry – the Utopia of gallantry, where pleasure is duty, and the manners perfect freedom. It is altogether a speculative scene of things, which has no reference whatever to the world that is. No good person can be justly offended as a spectator, because no good person suffers on the stage. Judged morally, every character in these plays – the few exceptions only are *mistakes* – is alike essentially vain and worthless. The great art of Congreve is especially shown in this, that he has entirely excluded from his scenes – some little generosities in the part of Angelica perhaps excepted – not only anything like a faultless character, but any pretensions to goodness or good feelings whatsoever. Whether he did this designedly, or instinctively, the effect is as happy as the design (if design) was bold. I used to wonder at the strange power which his *Way of the World* in particular possesses of interesting you all along in the pursuits of characters, for whom you absolutely care nothing – for you neither hate nor love his personages – and I think it is owing to this very indifference for any, that you endure the whole. He has spread a privation of moral light, I will call it, rather than by the ugly name of palpable darkness, over his creations; and his shadows flit before you without distinction or preference. Had he introduced a good character, a single gush of moral feeling, a revulsion of the judgment to actual life and actual duties, the impertinent Goshen would have only lighted to the discovery of deformities, which now are none, because we think them none.

Translated into real life, the characters of his, and his

friend Wycherley's dramas, are profligates and strumpets,
– the business of their brief existence, the undivided pursuit
of lawless gallantry. No other spring of action, or possible
motive of conduct, is recognized; principles which, universally acted upon, must reduce this frame of things to a chaos.
But we do them wrong in so translating them. No such
effects are produced, in *their* world. When we are among
them, we are amongst a chaotic people. We are not to judge
them by our usages. No reverend institutions are insulted
by their proceedings – for they have none among them. No
peace of families is violated – for no family ties exist among
them. No purity of the marriage bed is stained – for none is
supposed to have a being. No deep affections are disquieted,
no holy wedlock bands are snapped asunder – for affection's
depth and wedded faith are not of the growth of that soil.
There is neither right nor wrong, – gratitude or its opposite,
– claim or duty, – paternity or sonship. Of what consequence is it to Virtue, or how is she at all concerned about
it, whether Sir Simon or Dapperwit steal away Miss Martha;
or who is the father of Lord Froth's or Sir Paul Pliant's
children?

The whole is a passing pageant, where we should sit as
unconcerned at the issues, for life or death, as at the battle
of the frogs and mice. But, like Don Quixote, we take part
against the puppets, and quite as impertinently. We dare
not contemplate an Atlantis, a scheme, out of which our
coxcombical moral sense is for a little transitory ease excluded. We have not the courage to imagine a state of
things for which there is neither reward nor punishment.
We cling to the painful necessities of shame and blame.
We would indict our very dreams.

Amidst the mortifying circumstances attendant upon
growing old, it is something to have seen the *School for
Scandal* in its glory. This comedy grew out of Congreve and
Wycherley, but gathered some alloys of the sentimental
comedy which followed theirs. It is impossible that it should
be now *acted*, though it continues, at long intervals, to be
announced in the bills. Its hero, when Palmer played it at
least, was Joseph Surface. When I remember the gay bold-

ness, the graceful solemn plausibility, the measured step, the insinuating voice – to express it in a word – the downright *acted* villany of the part, so different from the pressure of conscious actual wickedness, – the hypocritical assumption of hypocrisy, – which made Jack so deservedly a favourite in that character, I must needs conclude the present generation of playgoers more virtuous than myself, or more dense. I freely confess that he divided the palm with me with his better brother; that, in fact, I liked him quite as well. Not but there are passages, – like that, for instance, where Joseph is made to refuse a pittance to a poor relation, – incongruities which Sheridan was forced upon by the attempt to join the artificial with the sentimental comedy, either of which must destroy the other – but over these obstructions Jack's manner floated him so lightly, that a refusal from him no more shocked you, than the easy compliance of Charles gave you in reality any pleasure; you got over the paltry question as quickly as you could, to get back into the regions of pure comedy, where no cold moral reigns. The highly artificial manner of Palmer in this character counteracted every disagreeable impression which you might have received from the contrast, supposing them real, between the two brothers. You did not believe in Joseph with the same faith with which you believed in Charles. The latter was a pleasant reality, the former a no less pleasant poetical foil to it. The comedy, I have said, is incongruous; a mixture of Congreve with sentimental incompatibilities; the gaiety upon the whole is buoyant; but it required the consummate art of Palmer to reconcile the discordant elements.

A player with Jack's talents, if we had one now, would not dare to do the part in the same manner. He would instinctively avoid every turn which might tend to unrealize, and so to make the character fascinating. He must take his cue from his spectators, who would expect a bad man and a good man as rigidly opposed to each other as the deathbeds of those geniuses are contrasted in the prints, which I am sorry to say have disappeared from the windows of my old friend Carrington Bowles, of St Paul's Churchyard

memory – (an exhibition as venerable as the adjacent
cathedral, and almost coeval) of the bad and good man at
the hour of death; where the ghastly apprehensions of the
former, – and truly the grim phantom with his reality of a
toasting-fork is not to be despised, – so finely contrast with
the meek complacent kissing of the rod, – taking it in like
honey and butter, – with which the latter submits to the
scythe of the gentle bleeder, Time, who wields his lancet
with the apprehensive finger of a popular young ladies'
surgeon. What flesh, like loving grass, would not covet to
meet half-way the stroke of such a delicate mower? – John
Palmer was twice an actor in this exquisite part. He was
playing to you all the while that he was playing upon Sir
Peter and his lady. You had the first intimation of a sentiment before it was on his lips. His altered voice was meant
to you, and you were to suppose that his fictitious co-
flutterers on the stage perceived nothing at all of it. What
was it to you if that half reality, the husband, was over-
reached by the puppetry – or the thin thing (Lady Teazle's
reputation) was persuaded it was dying of a plethory?
The fortunes of Othello and Desdemona were not concerned
in it. Poor Jack has passed from the stage in good time,
that he did not live to this our age of seriousness. The pleasant old Teazle *King*, too, is gone in good time. His manner
would scarce have passed current in our day. We must love
or hate – acquit or condémn – censure or pity – exert our
detestable coxcombry of moral judgment upon everything.
Joseph Surface, to go down now, must be a downright
revolting villain – no compromise – his first appearance must
shock and give horror – his specious plausibilities, which the
pleasurable faculties of our fathers welcomed with such
hearty greetings, knowing that no harm (dramatic harm
even) could come, or was meant to come, of them, must
inspire a cold and killing aversion. Charles (the real canting
person of the scene – for the hypocrisy of Joseph has its
ulterior legitimate ends, but his brother's professions of a
good heart centre in downright self-satisfaction) must be
loved, and Joseph *hated*. To balance one disagreeable reality
with another, Sir Peter Teazle must be no longer the comic

idea of a fretful old bachelor bridegroom, whose teasings (while King acted it) were evidently as much played off at you, as they were meant to concern anybody on the stage, – he must be a real person, capable in law of sustaining an injury – a person towards whom duties are to be acknowledged – the genuine crim. con. antagonist of the villainous seducer Joseph. To realize him more, his sufferings under his unfortunate match must have the downright pungency of life – must (or should) make you not mirthful but uncomfortable, just as the same predicament would move you in a neighbour or old friend. The delicious scenes which give the play its name and zest, must affect you in the same serious manner as if you heard the reputation of a dear female friend attacked in your real presence. Crabtree and Sir Benjamin – those poor snakes that live but in the sunshine of your mirth – must be ripened by this hot-bed process of realization into asps or amphisbænas; and Mrs Candour – O! frightful! – become a hooded serpent. O! who that remembers Parsons and Dodd – the wasp and butterfly of the *School for Scandal* – in those two characters; and charming natural Miss Pope, the perfect gentlewoman as distinguished from the fine lady of comedy, in this latter part – would forego the true scenic delight – the escape from life – the oblivion of consequences – the holiday barring out of the pedant Reflection – those Saturnalia of two or three brief hours, well won from the world – to sit instead at one of our modern plays – to have his coward conscience (that forsooth must not be left for a moment) stimulated with perpetual appeals – dulled rather, and blunted, as a faculty without repose must be – and his moral vanity pampered with images of notional justice, notional beneficence, lives saved without the spectator's risk, and fortunes given away that cost the author nothing?

No piece was, perhaps, ever so completely cast in all its parts as this *manager's comedy*. Miss Farren had succeeded to Mrs Abington in Lady Teazle; and Smith, the original Charles, had retired when I first saw it. The rest of the characters, with very slight exceptions, remained. I remember it was then the fashion to cry down John Kemble, who took the part of Charles after Smith; but, I thought, very unjustly. Smith, I fancy, was more airy, and took the eye with a certain gaiety of person. He brought with him no sombre recollections of tragedy. He had not to expiate the fault of having pleased beforehand in lofty declamation. He had no sins of Hamlet or of Richard to atone for. His failure in these parts was a passport to success in one of so opposite a tendency. But, as far as I could judge, the weighty sense of Kemble made up for more personal incapacity than he had to answer for. His harshest tones in this part came steeped and dulcified in good humour. He made his defects a grace. His exact declamatory manner, as he managed it, only served to convey the points of his dialogue with more precision. It seemed to head the shafts to carry them deeper. Not one of his sparkling sentences was lost. I remember minutely how he delivered each in succession, and cannot by any effort imagine how any of them could be altered for the better. No man could deliver brilliant dialogue – the dialogue of Congreve or of Wycherley – because none understood it – half so well as John Kemble. His Valentine, in *Love for Love*, was, to my recollection, faultless. He flagged sometimes in the intervals of tragic passion. He would slumber over the level parts of an heroic character. His Macbeth has been known to nod. But he always seemed to me to be particularly alive to pointed and witty dialogue. The relaxing levities of tragedy have not been touched by any since him – the playful court-bred spirit in which he condescended to the players in *Hamlet* – the sportive relief which he threw into the darker shades of Richard – disappeared with him. He had his sluggish moods, his torpors – but they were the halting-stones and resting-place of his tragedy – politic savings, and fetches of the breath – husbandry of the lungs, where nature pointed him to be an economist – rather, I think than errors of the judgment. They were, at worst, less painful than the eternal tormenting unappeasable vigilance, – the 'lidless dragon eyes', of present fashionable tragedy.

ELIA.

On the Tragedies of Shakespeare

(Considered with reference to their fitness
for stage representation)

Taking a turn the other day in the Abbey, I was struck
with the affected attitude of a figure, which I do not remember to have seen before, and which upon examination
proved to be a whole-length of the celebrated Mr Garrick.
Though I would not go so far with some good Catholics
abroad as to shut players altogether out of consecrated
ground, yet I own I was not a little scandalized at the
introduction of theatrical airs and gestures into a place set
apart to remind us of the saddest realities. Going nearer, I
found inscribed under the harlequin figure the following
lines : –

> To paint fair Nature, by Divine command,
> Her magic pencil in his glowing hand,
> A Shakespeare rose: then, to expand his fame
> Wide o'er this breathing world, a Garrick came.
> Though, like the bard himself, in night they lay,
> Immortal Garrick called them back to day:
> And till Eternity, with power sublime,
> Shall mark the mortal hour of hoary Time,
> Shakespeare and Garrick like twin-stars shall shine,
> And earth irradiate with a beam divine.

It would be an insult to my readers' understandings to
attempt anything like a criticism on this farrago of false
thoughts and nonsense. But the reflection it led me into was
a kind of wonder how, from the days of the actor here
celebrated to our own, it should have been the fashion to
compliment every performer in his turn, that has had the
luck to please the town in any of the great characters of
Shakespeare, with a notion of possessing a *mind congenial
with the poet's* ; how people should come thus unaccountably
to confound the power of originating poetical images and
conceptions with the faculty of being able to read or recite

the same when put into words;[1] or what connection that
absolute mastery over the heart and soul of man, which a
great dramatic poet possesses, has with those low tricks upon
the eye and ear, which a player, by observing a few general
effects, which some common passion, as grief, anger, &c.,
usually has upon the gestures and exterior, can easily compass. To know the internal workings and movements of a
great mind, of an Othello or a Hamlet, for instance, the
when and the *why* and the *how far* they should be moved;
to what pitch a passion is becoming; to give reins and to
pull in the curb exactly at the moment when the drawing
in or the slacking is most graceful; seems to demand a
reach of intellect of a vastly different extent from that
which is employed upon the bare imitation of the signs of
these passions in the countenance or gesture, which signs
are usually observed to be the most lively and emphatic in
the weaker sort of minds, and which signs can, after all,
but indicate some passion, as I said before, anger or grief,
generally; but of the motives and grounds of the passion
wherein it differs from the same passion in low and vulgar
natures, of these the actor can give no more idea by his face
or gesture than the eye (without a metaphor) can speak, or
the muscles utter intelligible sounds. But such is the instantaneous nature of the impressions which we take in at
the eye and ear at a playhouse, compared with the slow
apprehension often-times of the understanding in reading,
that we are apt not only to sink the play-writer in the consideration which we pay to the actor, but even to identify
in our minds in a perverse manner the actor with the character which he represents. It is difficult for a frequent play-
goer to disembarrass the idea of Hamlet from the person
and voice of Mr K[emble]. We speak of Lady Macbeth,

[1] It is observable that we fall into this confusion only in
dramatic recitations. We never dream that the gentleman who
reads Lucretius in public with great applause is therefore a
great poet and philosopher; nor do we find that Tom Davies,
the bookseller, who is recorded to have recited the *Paradise Lost*
better than any man in England in his day (though I cannot
help thinking there must be some mistake in this tradition) was
therefore by his intimate friends, set upon a level with Milton.

while we are in reality thinking of Mrs S[iddons]. Nor is this confusion incidental alone to unlettered persons, who, not possessing the advantage of reading, are necessarily dependent upon the stage-player for all the pleasure which they can receive from the drama, and to whom the very idea of *what an author is* cannot be made comprehensible without some pain and perplexity of mind: the error is one from which persons otherwise not meanly lettered find it almost impossible to extricate themselves.

Never let me be so ungrateful as to forget the very high degree of satisfaction which I received some years back from seeing for the first time a tragedy of Shakespeare performed in which these two great performers sustained the principal parts. It seemed to embody and realize conceptions which had hitherto assumed no distinct shape. But dearly do we pay all our life afterwards for this juvenile pleasure, this sense of distinctness. When the novelty is past, we find to our cost that, instead of realizing an idea, we have only materialized and brought down a fine vision to the standard of flesh and blood. We have let go a dream, in quest of an unattainable substance.

How cruelly this operates upon the mind, to have its free conceptions thus cramped and pressed down to the measure of a strait-lacing actuality, may be judged from that delightful sensation of freshness with which we turn to those plays of Shakespeare which have escaped being performed, and to those passages in the acting plays of the same writer which have happily been left out in performance. How far the very custom of hearing anything *spouted* withers and blows upon a fine passage, may be seen in those speeches from *Henry the Fifth*, &c., which are current in the mouths of schoolboys from their being found in 'Enfield Speakers', and such kind of books. I confess myself utterly unable to appreciate that celebrated soliloquy in 'Hamlet' beginning 'To be or not to be', or to tell whether it be good, bad, or indifferent; it has been so handled and pawed about by declamatory boys and men, and torn so inhumanly from its living place, and principle of continuity in the play, till it is become to me a perfect dead member.

It may seem a paradox, but I cannot help being of opinion that the plays of Shakespeare are less calculated for performance on a stage than those of almost any other dramatist whatever. Their distinguished excellence is a reason that they should be so. There is so much in them which comes not under the province of acting, with which eye, and tone, and gesture have nothing to do.

The glory of the scenic art is to personate passion and the turns of passion; and the more coarse and palpable the passion is, the more hold upon the eyes and ears of the spectators the performer obviously possesses. For this reason, scolding scenes, scenes where two persons talk themselves into a fit of fury, and then in a surprising manner talk themselves out of it again, have always been the most popular upon our stage. And the reason is plain, because the spectators are here most palpably appealed to, they are the proper judges in this war of words, they are the legitimate ring that should be formed round such 'intellectual prize-fighters'. Talking is the direct object of the imitation here. But in the best dramas, and in Shakespeare above all, how obvious it is that the form of *speaking*, whether it be in soliloquy or dialogue, is only a medium, and often a highly artificial one, for putting the reader or spectator into possession of that knowledge of the inner structure and workings of mind in a character, which he could otherwise never have arrived at *in that form of composition* by any gift short of intuition. We do here as we do with novels written in the *epistolary form*. How many improprieties, perfect solecisms in letter-writing, do we put up with in 'Clarissa' and other books, for the sake of the delight which that form upon the whole gives us.

But the practice of stage representation reduces everything to a controversy of elocution. Every character, from the boisterous blasphemings of Bajazet to the shrinking timidity of womanhood, must play the orator. The love dialogues of 'Romeo and Juliet', those silver-sweet sounds of lovers' tongues by night; the more intimate and sacred sweetness of nuptial colloquy between an Othello or a Posthumus with their married wives, all those delicacies which are so delightful in the reading, as when we read of those youthful dalliances in Paradise –

As beseemed
Fair couple linked in happy nuptial league
Alone:

by the inherent fault of stage representation, how are these things sullied and turned from their very nature by being exposed to a large assembly; when such speeches as Imogen addresses to her lord come drawling out of the mouth of a hired actress, whose courtship, though nominally addressed to the personated Posthumus, is manifestly aimed at the spectators, who are to judge of her endearments and her returns of love.

The character of Hamlet is perhaps that by which, since the days of Betterton, a succession of popular performers have had the greatest ambition to distinguish themselves. The length of the part may be one of their reasons. But for the character itself, we find it in a play, and therefore we judge it a fit subject of dramatic representation. The play itself abounds in maxims and reflections beyond any other, and therefore we consider it a proper vehicle for conveying moral instruction. But Hamlet himself – what does he suffer meanwhile by being dragged forth as a public schoolmaster to give lectures to the crowd! Why, nine parts in ten of what Hamlet does are transactions between himself and his moral sense, they are the effusions of his solitary musings, which he retires to holes and corners and the most sequestered parts of the palace to pour forth, or rather, they are the silent meditations with which his bosom is bursting, reduced to *words* for the sake of the reader, who must else remain ignorant of what is passing there. These profound sorrows, these light-and noise-abhorring ruminations, which the tongue scarce dares utter to deaf walls and chambers, how can they be represented by a gesticulating actor, who comes and mouths them out before an audience, making four hundred people his confidants at once? I say not that it is the fault of the actor so to do; he must pronounce them *ore rotundo*, he must accompany them with

his eye, he must insinuate them into his auditory by some
trick of eye, tone, or gesture, or he fails. *He must be thinking
all the while of his appearance because he knows that all the while
the spectators are judging of it*. And this is the way to represent
the shy, negligent, retiring Hamlet: –

It is true that there is no other mode of conveying a vast
quantity of thought and feeling to a great portion of the
audience, who otherwise would never learn it for themselves
by reading, and the intellectual acquisition gained this way
may, for aught I know, be inestimable; but I am not arguing
that 'Hamlet' should not be acted, but how much 'Hamlet'
is made another thing by being acted. I have heard much
of the wonders which Garrick performed in this part; but
as I never saw him, I must have leave to doubt whether
the representation of such a character came within the
province of his art. Those who tell me of him speak of his
eye, of the magic of his eye, and of his commanding voice:
physical properties, vastly desirable in an actor, and without
which he can never insinuate meaning into an auditory, –
but what have they to do with Hamlet? what have they to
do with intellect? In fact, the things aimed at in theatrical
representation are to arrest the spectator's eye upon the
form and the gesture, and so to gain a more favourable
hearing to what is spoken: it is not what the character is,
but how he looks; not what he says, but how he speaks it.
I see no reason to think that if the play of 'Hamlet' were
written over again by some such writer as Banks or Lillo,
retaining the process of the story, but totally omitting all
the poetry of it, all the divine features of Shakespeare, his
stupendous intellect, and only taking care to give us enough
of passionate dialogue, which Banks or Lillo were never at
a loss to furnish; I see not how the effect could be much
different upon an audience, nor how the actor has it in his
power to represent Shakespeare to us differently from his
representation of Banks or Lillo. Hamlet would still be a
youthful, accomplished prince, and must be gracefully
personated; he might be puzzled in his mind, wavering in
his conduct, seemingly cruel to Ophelia, he might see a
ghost, and start at it, and address it kindly when he found

it to be his father; all this in the poorest and most homely language of the servilest creeper after nature that ever consulted the palate of an audience; without troubling Shakespeare for the matter: and I see not but there would be room for all the power which an actor has to display itself. All the passions and changes of passion might remain; for those are much less difficult to write or act than is thought; it is a trick easy to be attained; it is but rising or falling a note or two in the voice, a whisper with a significant foreboding look to announce its approach, and so contagious the counterfeit appearance of any emotion is, that let the words be what they will, the look and tone shall carry it off and make it pass for deep skill in the passions.

It is common for people to talk of Shakespeare's plays being *so natural* that everybody can understand him. They are natural indeed, they are grounded deep in nature, so deep that the depth of them lies out of the reach of most of us. You shall hear the same person say that 'George Barnwell' is very natural, and 'Othello' is very natural; that they are both very deep; and to them they are the same kind of thing. At the one they sit and shed tears because a good sort of young man is tempted by a naughty woman to commit *a trifling peccadillo*, the murder of an uncle or so,[1] that is all, and so comes to an untimely end, which is *so*

---

[1] If this note could hope to meet the eye of any of the managers, I would entreat and beg of them, in the name of both the galleries, that this insult upon the morality of the common people of London should cease to be eternally repeated in the holiday weeks. Why are the 'Prentices of this famous and well-governed city, instead of an amusement, to be treated over and over again with the nauseous sermon of George Barnwell? Why *at the end of their vistas* are we to place the *gallows*? Were I an uncle, I should not much like a nephew of mine to have such an example placed before his eyes. It is really making uncle-murder too trivial to exhibit it as done upon such slight motives; – it is attributing too much to such characters as Millwood; it is putting things into the heads of good young men, which they would never otherwise have dreamed of. Uncles that think anything of their lives should fairly petition the Chamberlain against it.

moving; and at the other, because a blackamoor in a fit of jealousy kills his innocent white wife : and the odds are that ninety-nine out of a hundred would willingly behold the same catastrophe happen to both the heroes, and have thought the rope more due to Othello than to Barnwell. For of the texture of Othello's mind, the inward construction marvellously laid open, with all its strengths and weaknesses, its heroic confidences and its human misgivings, its agonies of hate springing from the depths of love, they see no more than the spectators at a cheaper rate, who pay their pennies apiece to look through the man's telescope in Leicester Fields see into the inward plot and topography of the moon. Some dim thing or other they see, they see an actor personating a passion, a grief or anger, for instance, and they recognize it as a copy of the usual external effects of such passion; or at least as being true to *that symbol of the emotion which passes current at the theatre for it*, for it is often no more than that : but of the grounds of the passion, its correspondence to a great and heroic nature, which is the only worthy object of tragedy, – that common auditors know anything of this, or can have any such notions dinned into them by the mere strength of an actor's lungs – that apprehension foreign to them should be thus infused into them by storm, I can neither believe, nor understand how it can be possible.

We talk of Shakespeare's admirable observation of life when we should feel that not from a petty inquisition into those cheap and everyday characters which surrounded him, as they surround us, but from his own mind, which was, to borrow a phrase of Ben Jonson's, the very 'sphere of humanity', he fetched those images of virtue and of knowledge, of which every one of us recognizing a part, think we comprehend in our natures the whole, and oftentimes mistake the powers which he positively creates in us, for nothing more than indigenous faculties of our own minds, which only waited the application of corresponding virtues in him to return a full and clear echo of the same.

To return to Hamlet. Among the distinguishing features of that wonderful character, one of the most interesting (yet painful) is that soreness of mind which makes him treat the intrusions of Polonius with harshness, and that asperity which he puts on in his interviews with Ophelia. These tokens of an unhinged mind (if they be not mixed in the latter case with a profound artifice of love, to alienate Ophelia by affected discourtesies, so to prepare her mind for the breaking off of that loving intercourse which can no longer find a place amidst business so serious as that which he has to do) are parts of his character, which to reconcile with our admiration of Hamlet, the most patient consideration of his situation is no more than necessary; they are what we *forgive afterwards*, and explain by the whole of his character, but *at the time* they are harsh and unpleasant. Yet such is the actor's necessity of giving strong blows to the audience, that I have never seen a player in this character who did not exaggerate and strain to the utmost these ambiguous features, – these temporary deformities in the character. They make him express a vulgar scorn at Polonius which utterly degrades his gentility, and which no explanation can render palatable; they make him show contempt, and curl up the nose at Ophelia's father, – contempt in its very grossest and most hateful form; but they get applause by it: it is natural, people say; that is, the words are scornful, and the actor expresses scorn, and that they can judge of: but why so much scorn, and of that sort, they never think of asking.

So to Ophelia. All the Hamlets that I have ever seen rant and rave at her as if she had committed some great crime, and the audience are highly pleased, because the words of the part are satirical, and they are enforced by the strongest expression of satirical indignation of which the face and voice are capable. But then, whether Hamlet is likely to have put on such brutal appearances to a lady whom he loved so dearly is never thought on. The truth is, that in all such deep affections as had subsisted between Hamlet and Ophelia there is a stock of *supererogatory love* (if I may venture to use the expression), which in any great grief of heart, especially where that which preys upon the mind cannot be communicated, confers a kind of indulgence upon the grieved party to express itself, even to its heart's dearest object, in the language of a temporary alienation; but it is not alienation, it is a distraction purely, and so it always makes itself to be felt by that object: it is not anger, but grief assuming the appearance of anger, – love awkwardly counterfeiting hate, as sweet countenances when they try to frown: but such sternness and fierce disgust as Hamlet is made to show is no counterfeit, but the real face of absolute aversion, of irreconcilable alienation. It may be said he puts on the madman; but then he should only so far put on this counterfeit lunacy as his own real distraction will give him leave, that is, incompletely, imperfectly; not in that confirmed, practised way, like a master of his art, or, as Dame Quickly would say, 'like one of those harlotry players'.

I mean no disrespect to any actor, but the sort of pleasure which Shakespeare's plays give in the acting seems to me not at all to differ from that which the audience receive from those of other writers; and *they being in themselves essentially so different from all others*, I must conclude that there is something in the nature of acting which levels all distinctions. And, in fact, who does not speak indifferently of the 'Gamester' and of 'Macbeth' as fine stage performances, and praise the Mrs Beverley in the same way as the Lady Macbeth of Mrs Siddons? Belvidera, and Calista, and Isabella, and Euphrasia, are they less liked than Imogen, or than Juliet, or than Desdemona? Are they not spoken of and remembered in the same way? Is not the female performer as great (as they call it) in one as in the other? Did not Garrick shine, and was he not ambitious of shining in every drawling tragedy that his wretched day produced, the productions of the Hills and the Murphys and the Browns, and shall he have that honour to dwell in our minds for ever as an inseparable concomitant with Shakespeare? A kindred mind! O who can read that affecting sonnet of Shakespeare which alludes to his profession as a player: –

O for my sake do you with Fortune chide,
The guilty goddess of my harmful deeds,

> That did not better for my life provide
> Than public means which public custom breeds –
> Thence comes it that my name receives a brand;
> And almost thence my nature is subdued
> To what it works in, like the dyer's hand; –

Or that other confession –

> Alas! 'tis true, I have gone here and there,
> And made myself a motley to the view,
> Gored mine own thoughts, sold cheap what is most dear; –

who can read these instances of jealous self-watchfulness in
our sweet Shakespeare and dream of any congeniality between him and one that, by every tradition of him, appears
to have been as mere a player as ever existed; to have had
his mind tainted with the lowest player's vices, envy and
jealousy, and miserable cravings after applause; one who in
the exercise of his profession was jealous even of the women
performers that stood in his way; a manager full of mana-
gerial tricks and stratagems and finesse: that any resem-
balance should be dreamed of between him and Shakespeare, – Shakespeare who, in the plenitude and consciousness of his own powers, could with that noble modesty
which we can neither imitate nor appreciate, express
himself thus of his own sense of his own defects: –

> Wishing me like to one more rich in hope,
> Featured like him, like him with friends possessed:
> Desiring *this man's art and that man's scope.*

I am almost disposed to deny to Garrick the merit of
being an admirer of Shakespeare. A true lover of his excel-
lences he certainly was not; for would any true lover of
them have admitted into his matchless scenes such ribald
trash as Tate and Cibber, and the rest of them, that

> With their darkness durst affront his light,

have foisted into the acting plays of Shakespeare? I believe it impossible that he could have had a proper reverence for Shakespeare, and have condescended to go through that interpolated scene in 'Richard the Third', in which Richard tries to break his wife's heart by telling her he loves another woman, and says, 'If she survives this she is immortal.' Yet I doubt not he delivered this vulgar stuff with as much anxiety of emphasis as any of the genuine parts; and for acting, it is as well calculated as any. But we have seen the part of Richard lately produce great fame to an actor by his manner of playing it, and it lets us into the secret of acting, and of popular judgements of Shakespeare derived from acting. Not one of the spectators who have witnessed Mr C's exertions in that part but has come away with a proper conviction that Richard is a very wicked man, and kills little children in their beds with something like the pleasure which the giants and ogres in children's books are represented to have taken in that practice; moreover, that he is very close and shrewd, and devilish cunning, for you could see that by his eye.

But is, in fact, this the impression we have in reading the Richard of Shakespeare? Do we feel anything like disgust, as we do at that butcher-like representation of him that passes for him on the stage? A horror at his crimes blends with the effect which we feel, but how is it qualified, how is it carried off, by the rich intellect which he displays, his resources, his wit, his buoyant spirits, his vast knowledge and insight into characters, the poetry of his part – not an atom of all which is made perceivable in Mr C.'s way of acting it. Nothing but his crimes, his actions, is visible; they are prominent and staring; the murderer stands out, but where is the lofty genius, the man of vast capacity, – the profound, the witty, accomplished Richard?

The truth is, the characters of Shakespeare are so much the objects of meditation rather than of interest or curiosity as to their actions, that while we are reading any of his great criminal characters, Macbeth, Richard, even Iago, we think not so much of the crimes which they commit as the ambition, the aspiring spirit, the intellectual activity which prompts them to overleap those moral fences. Barn-

well is a wretched murderer; there is a certain fitness between his neck and the rope; he is the legitimate heir to the
gallows; nobody who thinks at all can think of any allevi-
ating circumstances in his case to make him a fit object of
mercy. Or, to take an instance from the higher tragedy,
what else but a mere assassin is Glenalvon? Do we think of
anything but of the crime which he commits, and the rack
which he deserves? That is all which we really think about
him. Whereas, in corresponding characters in Shakespeare
so little do the actions comparatively affect us, that while
the impulses, the inner mind in all its perverted greatness,
solely seems real and is exclusively attended to, the crime is
comparatively nothing. But when we see these things represented, the acts which they do are comparatively everything, their impulses nothing. The state of sublime emotion
into which we are elevated by those images of night and
horror which Macbeth is made to utter, that solemn pre-
lude with which he entertains the time till the bell shall
strike which is to call him to murder Duncan, – when we
no longer read it in a book, when we have given up that
vantage-ground of abstraction which reading possesses over
seeing, and come to see a man in his bodily shape before
our eyes actually preparing to commit a murder, if the
acting be true and impressive, as I have witnessed it in Mr
K.'s performance of that part, the painful anxiety about
the act, the natural longing to prevent it while it yet seems
unperpetrated, the too close pressing semblance of reality,
give a pain and an uneasiness which totally destroy all the
delight which the words in the book convey, where the
deed doing never presses upon us with the painful sense of
presence: it rather seems to belong to history, – to something
past and inevitable, if it has anything to do with time at all.
The sublime images, the poetry alone, is that which is
present to our minds in the reading.

So to see Lear acted, to see an old man tottering about
the stage with a walking-stick, turned out of doors by his
daughters in a rainy night, has nothing in it but what is
painful and disgusting. We want to take him into shelter
and relieve him. That is all the feeling which the acting of

Lear ever produced in me. But the Lear of Shakespeare cannot be acted. The contemptible machinery by which they mimic the storm which he goes out in, is not more inadequate to represent the horrors of the real elements than any actor can be to represent Lear: they might more easily propose to personate the Satan of Milton upon a stage, or one of Michael Angelo's terrible figures. The greatness of Lear is not in corporal dimension, but in intellectual: the explosions of his passion are terrible as a volcano: they are storms turning up and disclosing to the bottom that sea his mind, with all its vast riches. It is his mind which is laid bare. The case of flesh and blood seems too insignificant to be thought on, even as he himself neglects it. On the stage we see nothing but corporal infirmities and weakness, the impotence of rage; while we read it, we see not Lear, but we are Lear — we are his mind, we are sustained by a grandeur which baffles the malice of daughters and storms; in the aberrations of his reason we discover a mighty irregular power of reasoning, immethodized from the ordinary purposes of life, but exerting its powers, as the wind blows where it listeth, at will upon the corruption and abuses of mankind.

What have looks, or tones, to do with that sublime identification of his age with that of the *heavens themselves*, when in his reproaches to them for conniving at the injustice of his children, he reminds them that 'they themselves are old'? What gestures shall we appropriate to this? What has the voice or the eye to do with such things? But the play is beyond all art, as the tamperings with it show: it is too hard and stony; it must have love scenes, and a happy ending. It is not enough that Cordelia is a daughter, she must shine as a lover too. Tate has put his hook in the nostrils of this Leviathan, for Garrick and his followers, the showmen of scene, to draw the mighty beast about more easily. A happy ending! — as if the living martyrdom that Lear had gone through, the flaying of his feelings alive, did not make a fair dismissal from the stage of life the only decorous thing for him. If he is to live and be happy after, if he could sustain this world's burden after, why all this

pudder and preparation – why torment us with this unnecessary sympathy? As if the childish pleasure of getting
his gilt robes and sceptre again could tempt him to act over
again his misused station – as if at his years, and with his
experience anything was left but to die.

'Lear' is essentially impossible to be represented on a
stage; but how many dramatic personages are there in
Shakespeare which though more tractable and feasible (if
I may so speak) than Lear, yet from some circumstance,
some adjunct to their character, are improper to be shown
to our bodily eye? 'Othello', for instance. Nothing can be
more soothing, more flattering to the nobler parts of our
natures, than to read of a young Venetian lady of the highest extraction, through the force of love and from a sense
of merit in him whom she loved, laying aside every consideration of kindred, and country, and colour, and wedding
with a *coal-black Moor* – (for such he is represented, in the
imperfect state of knowledge respecting foreign countries
in those days compared with our own, or in compliance
with popular notions, though the Moors are now well
enough known to be by many shades less unworthy of
white woman's fancy) – it is the perfect triumph of virtue
over accidents, of the imagination over the senses. She sees
Othello's colour in his mind. But upon the stage, when the
imagination is no longer the ruling faculty, but we are left
to our poor unassisted senses, I appeal to every one that has
seen 'Othello' played whether he did not, on the contrary,
sink Othello's mind in his colour; whether he did not find
something extremely revolting in the courtship and wedded
caresses of Othello and Desdemona; and whether the actual
sight of the thing did not over-weigh all that beautiful
compromise which we make in reading; – and the reason
it should do so is obvious, because there is just so much
reality presented to our senses as to give a perception of dis-
agreement, with not enough of belief in the internal motives
– all that which is unseen – to overpower and reconcile the

first and obvious prejudices.[1] What we see upon a stage is
body and bodily action; what we are conscious of in reading
is almost exclusively the mind and its movement: and this,
I think, may sufficiently account for the very different sort
of delight with which the same play so often affects us in
the reading and the seeing.

It requires little reflection to perceive that if those characters in Shakespeare which are within the precincts of
nature have yet something in them which appeals too exclusively to the imagination to admit of their being made
objects to the senses without suffering a change and a
diminution, that still stronger the objection must lie against
representing another line of characters, which Shakespeare
has introduced to give a wildness and a supernatural elevation to his scenes, as if to remove them still farther from that
assimilation to common life in which their excellence is
vulgarly supposed to consist. When we read the incantations
of those terrible beings the Witches in 'Macbeth', though
some of the ingredients in their hellish composition savour
of the grotesque, yet is the effect upon us other than the
most serious and appalling that can be imagined? Do we
not feel spell-bound as Macbeth was? Can any mirth accompany a sense of their presence? We might as well laugh
under a consciousness of the principle of Evil himself being
truly and really present with us. But attempt to bring these
beings on to a stage, and you turn them instantly into so
many old women, that men and children are to laugh at.
Contrary to the old saying that 'seeing is believing', the

[1] The error of supposing that because Othello's colour does not
offend us in the reading, it should also not offend us in the seeing,
is just such a fallacy as supposing that an Adam and Eve in a
picture shall affect us just as they do in the poem. But in the
poem we for a while have paradisaical senses given us, which
vanish when we see a man and his wife without clothes in the
picture. The painters themselves feel this, as is apparent by the
awkward shifts they have recourse to to make them look not
quite naked, by a sort of prophetic anachronism antedating the
invention of fig-leaves. So in the reading of the play, we see with
Desdemona's eyes; in the seeing of it, we are forced to look with
our own.

sight actually destroys the faith; and the mirth in which we indulge at their expense when we see these creatures upon a stage, seems to be a sort of indemnification which we make to ourselves for the terror which they put us in when reading made them an object of belief — when we surrendered up our reason to the poet, as children to their nurses and their elders; and we laugh, at our fears, as children who thought they saw something in the dark, triumph when the bringing in of a candle discovers the vanity of their fears. For this exposure of supernatural agents upon a stage is truly bringing in a candle to expose their own delusiveness. It is the solitary taper and the book that generates a faith in these terrors: a ghost by chandelier light, and in good company, deceives no spectators, — a ghost that can be measured by the eye, and his human dimensions made out at leisure. The sight of a well-lighted house and a well-dressed audience shall arm the most nervous child against any apprehensions: as Tom Brown says of the impenetrable skin of Achilles with his impenetrable armour over it, 'Bully Dawson would have fought the devil with such advantages.'

Much has been said, and deservedly, in reprobation of the vile mixture which Dryden has thrown into the 'Tempest': doubtless without some such vicious alloy, the impure ears of that age would never have sat out to hear so much innocence of love as is contained in the sweet courtship of Ferdinand and Miranda. But is the 'Tempest' of Shakespeare at all a subject for stage representation? It is one thing to read of an enchanter, and to believe the wondrous tale while we are reading it; but to have a conjuror brought before us in his conjuring-gown, with his spirits about him, which none but himself and some hundred of favoured spectators before the curtain are supposed to see, involves such a quantity of the *hateful incredible*, that all our reverence for the author cannot hinder us from perceiving such gross attempts upon the senses to be in the highest degree childish and inefficient. Spirits and fairies cannot be represented, they cannot even be painted — they can only be believed. But the elaborate and anxious provision of scenery, which the luxury of the age demands, in these cases works a quite contrary effect to what is intended. That which in comedy or plays of familiar life adds so much to the life of the imitation, in plays which appeal to the higher faculties positively destroys the illusion which it is introduced to aid. A parlour or a drawing-room, a library opening into a garden, a garden with an alcove in it, a street or the piazza of Covent Garden, does well enough in a scene; we are content to give as much credit to it as it demands; or rather, we think little about it, – it is little more than reading at the top of a page, 'Scene, a garden'; we do not imagine ourselves there, but we readily admit the imitation of familiar objects. But to think by the help of painted trees and caverns, which we know to be painted, to transport our minds to Prospero and his island and his lonely cell;[1] or by the aid of a fiddle dexterously thrown in, in an interval of speaking, to make us believe that we hear those supernatural noises of which the isle was full: the Orrery Lecturer at the Haymarket might as well hope, by his musical glasses cleverly stationed out of sight behind his apparatus, to make us believe that we do indeed hear the crystal spheres ring out that chime, which, if it were to en-wrap our fancy long, Milton thinks –

> Time would run back and fetch the age of gold,
> And speckled Vanity
> Would sicken soon and die, ·
> And leprous Sin would melt from earthly mould;
> Yea, Hell itself would pass away,
> And leave its dolorous mansions to the peering day.

The garden of Eden, with our first parents in it, is not more impossible to be shown on a stage, than the Enchanted Isle, with its no less interesting and innocent first settlers.

The subject of scenery is closely connected with that of the dresses, which are so anxiously attended to on our

[1] It will be said these things are done in pictures. But pictures and scenes are very different things. Painting is a word of itself, but in scene-painting there is the attempt to deceive: and there is the discordancy, never to be got over, between painted scenes and real people.

stage. I remember the last time I saw Macbeth played, the discrepancy I felt at the changes of garment which he varied, the shiftings and reshiftings, like a Romish priest at mass. The luxury of stage improvements and the importunity of the public eye require this. The coronation robe of the Scottish monarch was fairly a counterpart to that which our King wears when he goes to the Parliament House, just so full and cumbersome, and set out with ermine and pearls. And if things must be represented, I see not what to find fault with in this. But in reading, what robe are we conscious of? Some dim images of royalty – a crown and sceptre – may float before our eyes; but who shall describe the fashion of it? Do we see in our mind's eye what Webb or any other robe-maker could pattern? This is the inevitable consequence of imitating everything to make all things natural. Whereas the reading of a tragedy is a fine abstraction. It presents to the fancy just so much of external appearances as to make us feel that we are among flesh and blood, while by far the greater and better part of our imagination is employed upon the thoughts and internal machinery of the character. But in acting, – scenery, dress, the most contemptible things, call upon us to judge of their naturalness.

Perhaps it would be no bad similitude, to liken the pleasure which we take in seeing one of these fine plays acted, compared with that quiet delight which we find in the reading of it, to the different feelings with which a reviewer, and a man that is not a reviewer, reads a fine poem. The accursed critical habit, the being called upon to judge and pronounce, must make it quite a different thing to the former. In seeing plays acted we are affected just as judges. When Hamlet compares the two pictures of Gertrude's first and second husband, who wants to see the pictures? But in the acting, a miniature must be lugged out, which we know not to be the picture, but only to show how finely a miniature may be represented. This showing of everything levels all things: it makes tricks, bows and curtseys of importance. Mrs Siddons never got more fame by anything than by the manner in which she dismisses the guests in the banquet scene in Macbeth: it is as much remembered as any of her thrilling tones or impressive looks. But does such a trifle as this enter into the imaginations of the readers of that wild and wonderful scene? Does not the mind dismiss the feasters as rapidly as it can? Does it care about the gracefulness of doing it? But by acting, and judging of acting, all these non-essentials are raised into an importance injurious to the main interest of the play.

I have confined my observations to the tragic parts of Shakespeare. It would be no very difficult task to extend the inquiry to his comedies, and to show why Falstaff, Shallow, Sir Hugh Evans, and the rest, are equally incompatible with stage representation. The length to which this essay has run will make it, I am afraid, sufficiently distasteful to the amateurs of the theatre, without going any deeper into the subject at present.

Reflector, 1811.

C. L. IS NOT MUSICAL

To Clara N[ovello]

The Gods have made me most unmusical,
With feelings that respond not to the call
Of stringéd harp or voice – obtuse and mute
To hautboy, sackbut, dulcimer, and flute;
King David's lyre, that made the madness flee
From Saul, had been but a jew's-harp to me:
Theorbos, violins, French horns, guitars,
Leave in my wounded ears inflicted scars;
I hate those trills, and shakes, and sounds that float
Upon the captive air; I know no note,
Nor ever shall, whatever folks may say,
Of the strange mysteries of *Sol* and *Fa*;
I sit at oratorios like a fish,
Incapable of sound, and only wish
The thing was over. Yet do I admire,

O tuneful daughter of a tuneful sire,
Thy painful labours in a science which
To your deserts I pray may make you rich
As much as you are loved, and add a grace
To the most musical Novello race.
Women lead men by the nose, some cynics say;
You draw them by the ear – a delicater way.

Athenæum, July 1834

A Chapter on Ears

I have no ear. –

Mistake me not, reader – nor imagine that I am by nature destitute of those exterior twin appendages, hanging ornaments, and (architecturally speaking) handsome volutes to the human capital. Better my mother had never borne me. – I am, I think, rather delicately and copiously provided with those conduits; and I feel no disposition to envy the mule for his plenty, or the mole for her exactness, in those ingenious labyrinthine inlets – those indispensable side-intelligencers.

Neither have I incurred, or done anything to incur, with Defoe, that hideous disfigurement, which constrained him to draw upon assurance – to feel 'quite unabashed',[1] and at ease upon that article. I was never, I thank my stars, in the pillory; nor, if I read them aright, is it within the compass of my destiny, that I ever should be.

When therefore I say that I have no ear, you will understand me to mean – *for music.* To say that this heart never melted at the concord of sweet sounds, would be a foul self-libel. *'Water parted from the sea'* never fails to move it strangely. So does *'In infancy'*. But they were used to be sung at her harpsichord (the old-fashioned instrument in vogue in those days) by a gentlewoman – the gentlest, sure, that ever merited the appellation – the sweetest – why should I hesitate to name Mrs S[pinkes], once the blooming Fanny

---

[1] 'Earless on high stood, unabashed, Defoe.' – *Dunciad.*

Weatheral of the Temple – who had power to thrill the soul of Elia, small imp as he was, even in his long coats; and to make him glow, tremble, and blush with a passion, that not faintly indicated the dayspring of that absorbing sentiment which was afterwards destined to overwhelm and subdue his nature quite for Alice W—n.

I even think that *sentimentally* I am disposed to harmony. But *organically* I am incapable of a tune. I have been practising 'God save the King' all my life; whistling and humming of it over to myself in solitary corners; and am not yet arrived, they tell me, within many quavers of it. Yet hath the loyalty of Elia never been impeached.

I am not without suspicion, that I have an undeveloped faculty of music within me. For thrumming, in my wild way, on my friend A[yrton]'s piano, the other morning, while he was engaged in an adjoining parlour, – on his return he was pleased to say, *'he thought it could not be the maid!'* On his first surprise at hearing the keys touched in somewhat an airy and masterful way, not dreaming of me, his suspicions had lighted on *Jenny.* But a grace, snatched from a superior refinement, soon convinced him that some being – technically perhaps deficient, but higher informed from a principle common to all the fine arts – had swayed the keys to a mood which Jenny, with all her (less cultivated) enthusiasm, could never have elicited from them. I mention this as a proof of my friend's penetration, and not with any view of disparaging Jenny.

Scientifically I could never be made to understand (yet have I taken some pains) what a note in music is; or how one note should differ from another. Much less in voices can I distinguish a soprano from a tenor. Only sometimes the thorough-bass I contrive to guess at, from its being supereminently harsh and disagreeable. I tremble, however, for my misapplication of the simplest terms of *that* which I disclaim. While I profess my ignorance, I scarce know what to *say* I am ignorant of. I hate, perhaps, by misnomers. *Sostenuto* and *adagio* stand in the like relation of obscurity to me; and *Sol, Fa, Mi, Re*, is as conjuring as *Baralipton.*

It is hard to stand alone in an age like this, – (constituted to the quick and critical perception of all harmonious combinations, I verily believe, beyond all preceding ages, since Jubal stumbled upon the gamut), to remain, as it were, singly unimpressible to the magic influences of an art, which is said to have such an especial stroke at soothing, elevating, and refining the passions. – Yet, rather than break the candid current of my confessions, I must avow to you that I have received a great deal more pain than pleasure from this so cried-up faculty.

I am constitutionally susceptible of noises. A carpenter's hammer, in a warm summer noon, will fret me into more than midsummer madness. But those unconnected, unset sounds, are nothing to the measured malice of music. The ear is passive to those single strokes; willingly enduring stripes while it hath no task to con. To music it cannot be passive. It will strive – mine at least will – spite of its in-aptitude, to thrid the maze; like an unskilled eye painfully poring upon hieroglyphics. I have sat through an Italian Opera, till, for sheer pain, and inexplicable anguish, I have rushed out into the noisiest places of the crowded streets, to solace myself with sounds, which I was not obliged to follow, and get rid of the distracting torment of endless, fruitless, barren attention! I take refuge in the unpretending assemblage of honest common-life sounds; – and the purgatory of the Enraged Musician becomes my paradise.

I have sat at an Oratorio (that profanation of the purposes of the cheerful playhouse) watching the faces of the auditory in the pit (what a contrast to Hogarth's Laughing Audience!) immoveable, or affecting some faint emotion – till (as some have said, that our occupations in the next world will be but a shadow of what delighted us in this) I have imagined myself in some cold Theatre in Hades, where some of the *forms* of the earthly one should be kept up, with none of the *enjoyment*; or like that

> — Party in a parlour
> All silent, and all DAMNED.

Above all, those insufferable concertos, and pieces of music, as they are called, do plague and embitter my apprehension. – Words are something; but to be exposed to an endless battery of mere sounds; to be long a dying; to lie stretched upon a rack of roses; to keep up languor by un-intermitted effort; to pile honey upon sugar, and sugar upon honey, to an interminable tedious sweetness; to fill up sound with feeling, and strain ideas to keep pace with it; to gaze on empty frames, and be forced to make the pictures for yourself; to read a book, *all stops*, and be obliged to supply the verbal matter; to invent extempore tragedies to answer to the vague gestures of an inexplicable rambling mime – these are faint shadows of what I have undergone from a series of the ablest-executed pieces of this empty *instrumental music*.

I deny not, that in the opening of a concert, I have ex-perienced something vastly lulling and agreeable: – after-wards followeth the languor and the oppression. – Like that disappointing book in Patmos; or, like the comings on of melancholy, described by Burton, doth music make her first insinuating approaches: – 'Most pleasant it is to such as are melancholy given, to walk alone in some solitary grove, betwixt wood and water, by some brook side, and to meditate upon some delightsome and pleasant subject, which shall effect him most, *amabilis insania*, and *mentis gratissimus error*. A most incomparable delight to build castles in the air, to go smiling to themselves, acting an infinite variety of parts, which they suppose, and strongly imagine, they act, or that they see done. – So delightsome these toys at first, they could spend whole days and nights without sleep, even whole years in such contemplations, and fantastical meditations, which are like so many dreams, and will hardly be drawn from them – winding and unwinding themselves as so many clocks, and still pleasing their humours, until at the last the 'scene turns upon a sudden', and they being now habituated to such meditations and solitary places, can endure no company, can think of noth-ing but harsh and distasteful subjects. Fear, sorrow, sus-picion, *subrusticus pudor*, discontent, cares, and weariness of life, surprise them on a sudden, and they can think of noth-ing else: continually suspecting, no sooner are their eyes open, but this infernal plague of melancholy seizeth on them, and terrifies their souls, representing some dismal object to their minds; which now, by no means, no labour, no persuasions, they can avoid, they cannot be rid of, they cannot resist.'

Something like this 'scene turning' I have experienced at the evening parties, at the house of my good Catholic friend *Nov[ello]*; who, by the aid of a capital organ, himself the most finished of players, converts his drawing-room into a chapel, his week days into Sundays, and these latter into minor heavens.[1]

When my friend commences upon one of those solemn anthems, which peradventure struck upon my heedless ear, rambling in the side aisles of the dim Abbey, some five-and-thirty years since, waking a new sense, and putting a soul of old religion into my young apprehension – (whether it be *that*, in which the Psalmist, weary of the persecutions of bad men, wisheth to himself dove's wings – or *that other* which, with a like measure of sobriety and pathos, inquireth by what means the young man shall best cleanse his mind) – a holy calm pervadeth me. – I am for the time

————rapt above earth,—
And possess joys not promised at my birth.

But when this master of the spell, not content to have laid a soul prostrate, goes on, in his power, to inflict more bliss than lies in her capacity to receive – impatient to overcome her 'earthly' with his 'heavenly', – still pouring in, for protracted hours, fresh waves and fresh from the sea of sound, from that inexhausted *German* ocean, above which, in triumphant progress, dolphin-seated, ride those Arions *Haydn* and *Mozart*, with their attendant Tritons, *Bach*, *Beethoven*, and a countless tribe, whom to attempt to reckon up would but plunge me again in the deeps, – I stagger under the weight of harmony, reeling to and fro at my wits' end; – clouds, as of frankincense, oppress me – priests, altars,

[1] I have been there, and still would go –
'Tis like a little heaven below. – Dr. Watts.

I

censers, dazzle before me – the genius of *his* religion hath me in her toils – a shadowy triple tiara invests the brow of my friend, late so naked, so ingenuous – he is Pope, – and by him sits, like as in the anomaly of dreams, a she-Pope too, – tri-coronated like himself! – I am converted, and yet a Protestant ; – at once *malleus hereticorum,* and myself grand heresiarch : or three heresies centre in my person : – I am Marcion, Ebion, and Cerinthus – Gog and Magog – what not? – till the coming in of the friendly supper-tray dissipates the figment, and a draught of true Lutheran beer (in which chiefly my friend shows himself no bigot) at once reconciles me to the rationalities of a purer faith ; and restores to me the genuine unterrifying aspects of my pleasant-countenanced host and hostess.

ELIA.

London Magazine, March 1821.

Free Thoughts on Several Eminent Composers

Some cry up Haydn, some Mozart,
Just as the whim bites ; for my part,
I do not care a farthing candle
For either of them, or for Handel.
Cannot a man live free and easy
Without admiring Pergolese?
Or through the world with comfort go
That never heard of Doctor Blow?
So help me Heaven, I hardly have ;
And yet I eat, and drink, and shave,
Like other people, if you watch it,
And know no more of stave or crotchet
Than did the primitive Peruvians ;
Or those old ante-queer-diluvians
That lived in the unwashed world with Jubal,
Before that dirty blacksmith Tubal,
By stroke on anvil, or by summat,
Found out, to his great surprise, the gamut.

I care no more for Cimarosa
Than he did for Salvator Rosa,
Being no painter; and bad luck
Be mine, if I can bear that Gluck!
Old Tycho Brahe and modern Herschel
Had something in them; but who's Purcell?
The devil, with his foot so cloven,
For aught I care, may take Beethoven;
And, if the bargain does not suit,
I'll throw him Weber in to boot!
There's not the splitting of a splinter
To choose 'twixt him last named, and Winter.
Of Doctor Pepusch old Queen Dido
Knew just as much, God knows, as I do.
I would not go four miles to visit
Sebastian Bach (or Batch, which is it?)
No more I would for Bononcini.
As for Novello, or Rossini,
I shall not say a word to grieve 'em,
Because they're living; so I leave 'em.

                                        1830.

The *Free Thoughts* were entered by Lamb in Vincent Novello's album with the following footnote, supposedly by Mary Lamb, but, more probably, by Charles — in her name:

The reason why my brother's so severe,
Vincentio, is — my brother has no *ear*:
And Caradori her mellifluous throat
Might stretch in vain to make him learn a note.
Of common tunes he knows not anything,
Nor 'Rule, Britannia' from 'God save the King'.
He rail at Handel! He the gamut quiz!
I'd lay my life he knows not what it is.
His spite at music is a pretty whim —
He loves not it, because it loves not him.

A GOOD JUDGE OF PRINTS AND PICTURES

*Barrenness of the Imaginative Faculty in the
Productions of Modern Art*

Hogarth excepted, can we produce any one painter within
the last fifty years, or since the humour of exhibiting began,
that has treated a story *imaginatively*? By this we mean, upon
whom his subject has so acted, that it has seemed to direct
him – not to be arranged by him? Any upon whom
its leading or collateral points have impressed themselves so tyrannically, that he dared not treat it otherwise,
lest he should falsify a revelation? Any that has imparted to
his compositions, not merely so much truth as is enough to
convey a story with clearness, but that individualizing property, which should keep the subject so treated distinct in
feature from every other subject, however similar, and to
common apprehensions almost identical; so that we might
say, this and this part could have found an appropriate
place in no other picture in the world but this? Is there
anything in modern art – we will not demand that it should
be equal – but in any way analogous to what Titian has
effected, in that wonderful bringing together of two times
in the 'Ariadne', in the National Gallery? Precipitous,
with his reeling satyr rout about him, re-peopling and re-
illuming suddenly the waste places, drunk with a new fury
beyond the grape, Bacchus, born in fire, fire-like flings himself at the Cretan. This is the time present. With this telling
of the story, an artist, and no ordinary one, might remain
richly proud. Guido, in his harmonious version of it, saw
no farther. But from the depths of the imaginative spirit
Titian has recalled past time, and laid it contributory with
the present to one simultaneous effect. With the desert all
ringing with the mad cymbals of his followers, made lucid
with the presence and new offers of a god, – as if unconscious of Bacchus, or but idly casting her eyes as upon some

unconcerning pageant – her soul undistracted from Theseus – Ariadne is still pacing the solitary shore in as much heart-silence, and in almost the same local solitude, with which she awoke at daybreak to catch the forlorn last glances of the sail that bore away the Athenian.

Here are two points miraculously co-uniting; fierce society, with the feeling of solitude still absolute; noonday revelations, with the accidents of the dull gray dawn unquenched and lingering; the *present* Bacchus, with the *past* Ariadne: two stories, with double Time; separate, and harmonizing. Had the artist made the woman one shade less indifferent to the God; still more, had she expressed a rapture at his advent, where would have been the story of the mighty desolation of the heart previous? merged in the insipid accident of a flattering offer met with a welcome acceptance. The broken heart for Theseus was not likely to be pieced up by a God.

We have before us a fine rough print, from a picture by Raphael in the Vatican. It is the Presentation of the new-born Eve to Adam by the Almighty. A fairer mother of mankind we might imagine, and a goodlier sire perhaps of men since born. But these are matters subordinate to the conception of the *situation*, displayed in this extraordinary production. A tolerable modern artist would have been satisfied with tempering certain raptures of connubial anticipation, with a suitable acknowledgment to the Giver of the blessing, in the countenance of the first bridegroom: something like the divided attention of the child (Adam was here a child-man) between the given toy, and the mother who had just blest it with the bauble. This is the obvious, the first-sight view, the superficial. An artist of a higher grade, considering the awful presence they were in, would have taken care to subtract something from the expression of the more human passion, and to heighten the more spiritual one. This would be as much as an exhibition-goer, from the opening of Somerset House to last year's show, has been encouraged to look for. It is obvious to hint at a lower expression yet, in a picture that, for respects of drawing and colouring, might be deemed not wholly inadmissible within these art-fostering walls, in which the raptures should be as ninety-nine, the gratitude as one, or perhaps zero! By neither the one passion nor the other has Raphael expounded the situation of Adam. Singly upon his brow sits the absorbing sense of wonder at the created miracle. The *moment* is seized by the intuitive artist, perhaps not self-conscious of his art, in which neither of the conflicting emotions – a moment now abstracted! – have had time to spring up, or to battle for indecorous mastery. – We have seen a landscape of a justly-admired neoteric, in which he aimed at delineating a fiction, one of the most severely beautiful in antiquity – the gardens of the Hesperides. To do Mr T[urner] justice, he had painted a laudable orchard, with fitting seclusion, and a veritable dragon (of which a Polypheme, by Poussin, is somehow a fac-simile for the situation), looking over into the world shut out backwards, so that none but a 'still-climbing Hercules' could hope to catch a peep at the admired Ternary of Recluses. No conventual porter could keep his keys better than this custos with the 'lidless eyes'. He not only sees that none *do* intrude into that privacy, but, as clear as daylight, that none but *Hercules aut Diabolus* by any manner of means *can*. So far all is well. We have absolute solitude here or nowhere. *Ab extra*, the damsels are snug enough. But here the artist's courage seems to have failed him. He began to pity his pretty charge, and, to comfort the irksomeness, has peopled their solitude with a bevy of fair attendants, maids of honour, or ladies of the bed-chamber, according to the approved etiquette at a court of the nineteenth century; giving to the whole scene the air of a *fête-champêtre*, if we will but excuse the absence of the gentlemen. This is well, and Watteauish. But what is become of the solitary mystery – the

> Daughters three,
> That sing around the golden tree?

This is not the way in which Poussin would have treated this subject.

The paintings, or rather the stupendous architectural

designs, of a modern artist[1] have been urged as objections
to the theory of our motto. They are of a character, we confess, to stagger it. His towered structures are of the highest
order of the material sublime. Whether they were dreams,
or transcripts of some elder workmanship – Assyrian ruins
old – restored by this mighty artist, they satisfy our most
stretched and craving conceptions of the glories of the
antique world. It is a pity that they were ever peopled. On
that side, the imagination of the artist halts, and appears
defective. Let us examine the point of the story in the 'Belshazzar's Feast'. We will introduce it by an apposite
anecdote.

The court historians of the day record, that at the first
dinner given by the late King (then Prince Regent) at the
Pavilion, the following characteristic frolic was played
off. The guests were select and admiring; the banquet
profuse and admirable; the lights lustrous and oriental;
the eye was perfectly dazzled with the display of plate,
among which the great gold salt-cellar, brought from the
regalia in the Tower for this especial purpose, itself a tower!
stood conspicuous for its magnitude. And now the Rev.
* * *, the then admired court Chaplain, was proceeding
with the grace, when, at a signal given, the lights were suddenly overcast, and a huge transparency was discovered,
in which glittered in gold letters –

'BRIGHTON – EARTHQUAKE – SWALLOW-UP-ALIVE!'

Imagine the confusion of the guests; the Georges and garters,
jewels, bracelets, moulted upon the occasion! The fans
dropped, and picked up the next morning by the sly court-
pages! Mrs Fitz-what's-her-name[2] fainting, and the Countess
of * * * holding the smelling-bottle, till the good-humoured
Prince caused harmony to be restored, by calling in fresh
candles, and declaring that the whole was nothing but a
pantomime *hoax*, got up by the ingenious Mr Farley, of
Covent Garden, from hints which his Royal Highness him-

[1 John Martin.]   [2 Mrs Fitzherbert.]

self had furnished! Then imagine the infinite applause that
followed, the mutual rallyings, the declarations that 'they
were not much frightened', of the assembled galaxy.

The point of time in the picture exactly answers to the
appearance of the transparency in the anecdote. The huddle,
the flutter, the bustle, the escape, the alarm, and the mock
alarm; the prettinesses heightened by consternation; the
courtier's fear which was flattery; and the lady's which was
affectation; all that we may conceive to have taken place
in a mob of Brighton courtiers, sympathising with the well-
acted surprise of their sovereign; all this, and no more, is
exhibited by the well-dressed lords and ladies in the Hall of
Belus. Just this sort of consternation we have seen among a
flock of disquieted wild geese at the report only of a gun
having gone off!

But is this vulgar fright, this mere animal anxiety for the
preservation of their persons – such as we have witnessed at
a theatre, when a slight alarm of fire has been given – an
adequate exponent of a supernatural terror? the way in
which the finger of God, writing judgments, would have
been met by the withered conscience? There is a human
fear, and a divine fear. The one is disturbed, restless, and
bent upon escape; the other is bowed down, effortless,
passive. When the spirit appeared before Eliphaz in the
visions of the night, and the hair of his flesh stood up, was
it in the thoughts of the Temanite to ring the bell of his
chamber, or to call up the servants? But let us see in the text
what there is to justify all this huddle of vulgar consternation.

From the words of Daniel it appears that Belshazzar had
made a great feast to a thousand of his lords, and drank
wine before the thousand. The golden and silver vessels are
gorgeously enumerated, with the princes, the king's con-
cubines, and his wives. Then follows –

'In the same hour came forth fingers of a man's hand,
and wrote over against the candlestick upon the plaster of
the wall of the king's palace; and the *king* saw the part of
the hand that wrote. Then the *king's* countenance was
changed, and his thoughts troubled him, so that the joints

of his loins were loosened, and his knees smote one against another.'

This is the plain text. By no hint can it be otherwise inferred, but that the appearance was solely confined to the fancy of Belshazzar, that his single brain was troubled. Not a word is spoken of its being seen by any else there present, not even by the queen herself, who merely undertakes for the interpretation of the phenomenon, as related to her, doubtless, by her husband. The lords are simply said to be astonished; *i.e.* at the trouble and the change of countenance in their sovereign. Even the prophet does not appear to have seen the scroll, which the king saw. He recalls it only, as Joseph did the Dream to the King of Egypt. 'Then was the part of the hand sent from him [the Lord], and this writing was written.' He speaks of the phantasm as past.

Then what becomes of this needless multiplication of the miracle? this message to a royal conscience, singly expressed – for it was said, 'Thy kingdom is divided', – simultaneously impressed upon the fancies of a thousand courtiers, who were implied in it neither directly nor grammatically?

But, admitting the artist's own version of the story, and that the sight was seen also by the thousand courtiers – let it have been visible to all Babylon – as the knees of Belshazzar were shaken, and his countenance troubled, even so would the knees of every man in Babylon, and their countenances, as of an individual man, have been troubled; bowed, bent down, so would they have remained, stupor-fixed, with no thought of struggling with that inevitable judgment.

Not all that is optically possible to be seen, is to be shown in every picture. The eye delightedly dwells upon the brilliant individualities in a 'Marriage at Cana', by Veronese, or Titian, to the very texture and colour of the wedding garments, the ring glittering upon the bride's finger, the metal and fashions of the wine-pot; for at such seasons there is leisure and luxury to be curious. But in a 'day of judgment', or in a 'day of lesser horrors, yet divine', as at the impious feast of Belshazzar, the eye should see, as the actual eye of an agent or patient in the immediate scene would see, only in masses and indistinction. Not only the female attire and jewelry exposed to the critical eye of the fashion, as minutely as the dresses in a Lady's Magazine, in the criticized picture – but perhaps the curiosities of anatomical science, and studied diversities of posture, in the falling angels and sinners of Michael Angelo, – have no business in their great subjects. There was no leisure for them.

By a wise falsification, the great masters of painting got at their true conclusions; by not showing the actual appearances, that is, all that was to be seen at any given moment by an indifferent eye, but only what the eye might be supposed to see in the doing or suffering of some portentous action. Suppose the moment of the swallowing up of Pompeii. There they were to be seen – houses, columns, architectural proportions, differences of public and private buildings, men and women at their standing occupations, the diversified thousand postures, attitudes, dresses, in some confusion truly, but physically they were visible. But what eye saw them at that eclipsing moment, which reduces confusion to a kind of unity, and when the senses are upturned from their proprieties, when sight and hearing are a feeling only? A thousand years have passed, and we are at leisure to contemplate the weaver fixed standing at his shuttle, the baker at his oven, and to turn over with antiquarian coolness the pots and pans of Pompeii.

'Sun, stand thou still upon Gibeon, and thou, Moon, in the valley of Ajalon.' Who, in reading this magnificent Hebraism, in his conception, sees aught but the heroic son of Nun, with the out-stretched arm, and the greater and lesser light obsequious? Doubtless there were to be seen hill and dale, and chariots and horsemen, on open plain, or winding by secret defiles, and all the circumstances and stratagems of war. But whose eyes would have been conscious of this array at the interposition of the synchronic miracle? Yet in the picture of this subject by the artist of the 'Belshazzar's Feast' – no ignoble work, either – the marshalling and landscape of the war is everything, the miracle sinks into an anecdote of the day; and the eye may

'dart through rank and file traverse' for some minutes,
before it shall discover, among his armed followers, *which
is Joshua!* Not modern art alone, but ancient, where only
it is to be found if anywhere, can be detected erring, from
defect of this imaginative faculty. The world has nothing
to show of the preternatural in painting, transcending the
figure of Lazarus bursting his grave-clothes, in the great
picture of Angerstein's. It seems a thing between two beings.
A ghastly horror at itself struggles with newly-apprehending
gratitude at second life bestowed. It cannot forget that it
was a ghost. It has hardly felt that it is a body. It has to tell of
the world of spirits. – Was it from a feeling, that the crowd
of half-impassioned bystanders, and the still more irrelevant
herd of passers-by at a distance, who have not heard, or but
faintly have been told of the passing miracle, admirable as
they are in design and hue – for it is a glorified work – do
not respond adequately to the action – that the single
figure of the Lazarus has been attributed to Michael Angelo,
and the mighty Sebastian unfairly robbed of the fame of the
greater half of the interest? Now that there were not indifferent passers-by within actual scope of the eyes of those
present at the miracle, to whom the sound of it had but
faintly, or not at all, reached, it would be hardihood to
deny; but would they see them? or can the mind in the conception of it admit of such unconcerning objects; can it
think of them at all? or what associating league to the
imagination can there be between the seers and the seers
not, of a presential miracle?

Were an artist to paint upon demand a picture of a
Dryad, we will ask whether, in the present low state of
expectation, the patron would not, or ought not be fully
satisfied with a beautiful naked figure recumbent under
wide-stretched oaks? Dis-seat those woods, and place the
same figure among fountains, and falls of pellucid water,
and you have a – Naïad! Not so in a rough print we have
seen after Julio Romano,[1] we think – for it is long since –
there, by no process, with mere change of scene, could the

1 Giulio Pippi, 1492–1546, a pupil of Raphael.

figure have reciprocated characters. Long, grotesque, fantastic, yet with a grace of her own, beautiful in convolution and distortion, linked to her connatural tree, co-twisting with its limbs her own, till both seemed either - these, animated branches; those, disanimated members - yet the animal and vegetable lives sufficiently kept distinct - *his* Dryad lay - an approximation of two natures, which to conceive, it must be seen; analogous to, not the same with, the delicacies of Ovidian transformations.

To the lowest subjects, and, to a superficial comprehension the most barren, the Great Masters gave loftiness and fruitfulness. The large eye of genius saw in the meanness of present objects their capabilities of treatment from their relations to some grand Past or Future. How has Raphael - we must still linger about the Vatican - treated the humble craft of the ship-builder, in *his* 'Building of the Ark'? It is in that scriptural series, to which we have referred, and which, judging from some fine rough old graphic sketches of them which we possess, seem to be of a higher and more poetic grade than even the Cartoons. The dim of sight are the timid and the shrinking. There is a cowardice in modern art. As the Frenchman, of whom Coleridge's friend made the prophetic guess at Rome, from the beard and horns of the Moses of Michael Angelo collected no inferences beyond that of a He Goat and a Cornuto; so from this subject, of mere mechanic promise, it would instinctively turn away, as from one incapable of investiture with any grandeur. The dock-yards at Woolwich would object derogatory associations. The depôt at Chatham would be the mote and the beam in its intellectual eye. But not to the nautical preparations in the ship-yards of Civita Vecchia did Raphael look for instructions, when he imagined the building of the Vessel that was to be conservatory of the wrecks of the species of drowned mankind. In the intensity of the action he keeps ever out of sight the meanness of the operation. There is the Patriarch, in calm forethought, and with holy prescience, giving directions. And there are his agents - the solitary but sufficient Three - hewing, sawing, every one with the might and earnestness

of a Demiurgus; under some instinctive rather than tech-
nical guidance! giant-muscled; every one a Hercules; or
liker to those Vulcanian Three, that in sounding caverns
under Mongibello wrought in fire — Brontes, and black
Steropes, and Pyracmon. So work the workmen that should
repair a world!

Artists again err in the confounding of *poetic* with *pictorial*
subjects. In the latter, the exterior accidents are nearly
everything, the unseen qualities as nothing. Othello's colour
— the infirmities and corpulence of a Sir John Falstaff — do
they haunt us perpetually in the reading? or are they obtruded upon our conceptions one time for ninety-nine that
we are lost in admiration at the respective moral or intellectual attributes of the character? But in a picture Othello
is *always* a Blackamoor; and the other only Plump Jack.
Deeply corporealized, and enchained hopelessly in the
grovelling fetters of externality, must be the mind, to which,
in its better moments, the image of the high-souled, high-
intelligenced Quixote — the errant Star of Knighthood, made
more tender by eclipse — has never presented itself divested
from the unhallowed accompaniment of a Sancho, or a
rabblement at the heels of Rosinante. That man has read
his book by halves; he has laughed, mistaking his author's
purport, which was — tears. The artist that pictures Quixote
(and it is in this degrading point that he is every season
held up at our Exhibitions) in the shallow hope of exciting
mirth, would have joined the rabble at the heels of his
starved steed. We wish not to see *that* counterfeited, which
we would not have wished to see in the reality. Conscious
of the heroic inside of the noble Quixote, who, on hearing
that his withered person was passing, would have stepped
over his threshold to gaze upon his forlorn habiliments, and
the 'strange bed-fellows which misery brings a man
acquainted with'? Shade of Cervantes! who in thy Second
Part could put into the mouth of thy Quixote those high
aspirations of a super-chivalrous gallantry, where he replies
to one of the shepherdesses, apprehensive that he would
spoil their pretty net-works, and inviting him to be a guest
with them, in accents like these: 'Truly, fairest Lady,

Actæon was not more astonished when he saw Diana bath-
ing herself at the fountain, than I have been in beholding
your beauty: I commend the manner of your pastime, and
thank you for your kind offers; and, if I may serve you, so
I may be sure you will be obeyed, you may command me:
for my profession is this, To show myself thankful, and a
doer of good to all sorts of people, especially of the rank
that your person shows you to be; and if those nets, as they
take up but a little piece of ground, should take up the
whole world, I would seek out new worlds to pass through,
rather than break them: and (he adds) that you may give
credit to this my exaggeration, behold at least he that
promiseth you this, is Don Quixote de la Mancha, if haply
his name hath come to your hearing.' Illustrious Romancer!
were the 'fine frenzies', which possessed the brain of thy
own Quixote, a fit subject, as in this Second Part, to be
exposed to the jeers of Duennas and Serving-men? to be
monstered, and shown up at the heartless banquets of great
men? Was that pitiable infirmity, which in thy First Part
misleads him, *always from within*, into half-ludicrous, but
more than half-compassionable and admirable errors, not
infliction enough from heaven, that men by studied artifices
must devise and practise upon the humour, to inflame where
they should soothe it? Why, Goneril would have blushed
to practise upon the abdicated king at this rate, and the
she-wolf Regan not have endured to play the pranks upon
his fled wits, which thou first made thy Quixote suffer in
Duchesses' halls, and at the hands of that unworthy noble-
man.[1]

In the First Adventures, even, it needed all the art of the
most consummate artist in the Book way that the world
hath yet seen, to keep up in the mind of the reader the heroic
attributes of the character without relaxing; so as absolutely
that they shall suffer no alloy from the debasing fellowship
of the clown. If it ever obtrudes itself as a disharmony, are
we inclined to laugh; or not, rather, to indulge a contrary
emotion? – Cervantes, stung, perchance, by the relish

[1] Yet from this Second Part, our cried-up pictures are mostly
selected; the waiting-women with beards, etc.

CRITICAL AND ANTI-CRITICAL   271

with which *his* Reading Public had received the fooleries
of the man, more to their palates than the generosities of
the master, in the sequel let his pen run riot, lost the harmony and the balance, and sacrificed a great idea to the
taste of his contemporaries. We know that in the present
day the Knight has fewer admirers than the Squire. Anticipating, what did actually happen to him — as afterwards
it did to his scarce inferior follower, the Author of *Guzman
de Alfarache* — that some less knowing hand would prevent
him by a spurious Second Part; and judging that it would
be easier for his competitor to outbid him in the comicalities,
than in the *romance*, of his work, he abandoned his Knight,
and has fairly set up the Squire for his Hero. For what else
has he unsealed the eyes of Sancho? and instead of that
twilight state of semi-insanity — the madness at second-hand
— the contagion, caught from a stronger mind infected —
that war between native cunning, and hereditary deference,
with which he has hitherto accompanied his master — two
for a pair almost — does he substitute a downright Knave,
with open eyes, for his own ends only following a confessed
Madman; and offering at one time to lay, if not actually
laying, hands upon him! From the moment that Sancho
loses his reverence, Don Quixote is become — a treatable
lunatic. Our artists handle him accordingly.

This essay was originally written for inclusion in the *Englishman's Magazine* in 1831. That paper closed down before the
essay could appear and it was over a year before it appeared in
print in Moxon's *Reflector* (December 1832). Next month, January 1833, it was printed in four weekly parts in the *Athenaeum*.

NOTES ON
LAMB'S FRIENDS AND CONTEMPORARIES

ALLEN, Robert (1772–1803) — Schoolfellow of Lamb, journalist and Army Surgeon.

ASBURY, Jacob Vale — The Lambs' doctor at Enfield.

AYRTON, William (1777–1858) — Music critic, director of King's Theatre, Haymarket. Introduced to the Lambs by the BURNEYS 1803.

BANNISTER, John (1760–1836) — Comedian. 'He gave you the idea of a good fellow, whom it would be most pleasant and profitable to live with; and this was his real character.' Leigh Hunt.

BARNES, Thomas (1786–1841) — Educated at Christ's Hospital and Cambridge. Editor of *The Times* 1807–41.

BARTON, Bernard (1784–1849) — Quaker poet. First met Lamb in 1822 at a *London Magazine* dinner.

BARTRUM — ANN SIMMONS married a BARTRAM, pawnbroker in Leicester Square.

BATTLE, Mrs — See Elia essay *Mrs Battle on Whist* (not included in this edition). Either Mrs PLUMER or SARAH BURNEY (q.v.).

BOYER, Rev James (d. 1816) — Headmaster of Christ's Hospital 1776–99.

BURNEY, Admiral James (1750–1821) — Brother of FANNY BURNEY, sailed round the world with Captain Cook. His wife SARAH is a possible candidate for Mrs Battle. His son MARTIN was a barrister. The whole family first met the Lambs in 1803 and became close friends.

CARLYLE, Thomas (1795–1881)

Historian and critic. He visited the Lambs in 1824.

CARY, Rev. H. F. (1772–1844)

Published translation of Dante's *Inferno* (1805) and the whole *Divina Commedia* (1814). Also translated Pindar's *Odes* and Aristophane's *Birds*. One of Lamb's *London Magazine* associates.

CHAMBERS, The

'Old MR CHAMBERS, the sensible clergyman in Warwickshire,' was the Rev THOMAS, vicar of Radway. His two sons CHARLES and JOHN were at school with Lamb and JOHN was one of his colleagues at the E.I.H.

CLARKSON, Thomas (1760–1846)

A leader of the anti-slavery movement.

COLERIDGE, Hartley (1796–1849)

SAMUEL TAYLOR's eldest son. Brought up in the SOUTHEY family. Journalist and poet.

COLERIDGE, Samuel Taylor (1772–1834)

'The finest dreamer, the most eloquent talker, and the most original thinker of his day.' Leigh Hunt.

COLLIER, John Dyer

He, his wife, and their son, JOHN PAYNE COLLIER (1789–1883), critic, Parliamentary correspondent and literary forger, were friends and admirers of the Lambs from 1808.

DE QUINCEY, Thomas (1785–1859)

His 'Confessions of an Opium Eater' appeared in the *London Magazine* at the same time as Lamb's Elia essays.

DYER, George (1755–1841)

Educated Christ's Hospital and Cambridge. Wrote *History of the University of Cambridge* (1814) and *Privileges of the University of Cambridge* (1824). Prolific hack-writer, 'poet', and translator. The major work of his life was his share of Valpy's monumental edition of the classics upon which he worked 1819–30. During his last years he was totally blind.

FENWICK, John (d. 1820)

Editor of the *Albion* and of the *Plough*. Author of a farce *The Indian*. Bigod of *The Two Races of Men*.

FIELD, Barron (1786–1840)

Essayist, dramatic critic. Judge of the Supreme Court of New South Wales and Chief Justice of Gibraltar, was introduced to Lamb in 1809 by his brother FRANCIS FIELD at the E.I.H.

FIELDE, Francis (d. 1809)

Lamb's godfather.

FITZHERBERT, Mrs Maria (1756–1837)

Morganatic wife of the Prince Regent.

FORSTER, John (1812–1876)

Biographer of Goldsmith, Landor, Dickens and Swift. First met Lamb when he was editor of Moxon's *Reflector* in 1832.

GODWIN, William (1756–1836)

Philosopher, novelist, and publisher (of *Tales from Shakespeare* and *Adventures of Ulysses*.) Introduced to Lamb by Coleridge 1800. Married first MARY WOLLSTONECROFT (1759–97), the feminist and then in 1801 Mrs CLAREMONT – 'the Bitch'. His daughter, MARY WOLLSTONECROFT (1797–1851) married SHELLEY and was the authoress of *Frankenstein*.

HAZLITT, William (1778–1830)

Unsuccessful portrait painter and successful critic, essayist and lampoon writer. His 'Table Talk' appeared in the *London Magazine* at the same time as Lamb's Elia essays. He first met Lamb in 1798 and painted his portrait in 1804. He married SARAH STODDART in 1808. They were divorced in 1822, but she remained a friend and correspondent of the Lambs.

HESSEY, James (1781–1870)

Partner in the publishing firm Taylor and Hessey.

HETTY

The Lambs' servant.

HOLCROFT, Thomas (1745–1809)

Dramatist. First met Lamb about 1800. His widow later married JAMES KENNEY (q.v.) and she and his daughters FANNY and LOUISA (MRS BADDAMS) were friends of the Lambs to the end.

HOOD, Thomas (1799–1845)

First met Lamb when he was sub-editor of the *London Magazine* 1821, and was his neighbour in Islington 1823–27. Editor of *The Gem* 1829, in which he published *Eugene Aram*; Editor of yearly *Comic Annuals* 1830–39; *New Monthly Magazine* in 1841; *Hoods Own* 1844. His 'Literary Reminiscences' originally appeared scattered through the pages of *Hoods Own* and provide some of the most fascinating and perceptive information about Lamb in all the writings of Lamb's contemporaries.

HUNT, J. H. Leigh (1784–1859).

Son of Isaac Hunt, a Barbadian and Philadelphia Tory. Like Lamb educated at C.H.; like Lamb debarred from a university exhibition by a stammer and, for a short time, like Lamb clerk in a public office, in his case the War Office. The editor or co-editor of various short-lived radical papers of which the best known are *The Reflector*, *The Examiner*, *The Liberal* (with BYRON and SHELLEY). He was sentenced to two years imprisonment for libels against the Prince Regent in 1813. He was a friend of Lamb, from his schooldays until Lamb's death. Though his work as poet, essayist, critic and translator is overshadowed by his great contemporaries, he is an outstanding figure in literary history not only for his own convictions and qualities, but also because his friendship forms a link between Coleridge and Lamb on the one hand and Byron and Shelley on the other.

HUTCHINSON, Sarah
ISOLA, Emma

Wordsworth's sister-in-law.
The Lambs' adopted daughter. Later wife to Edward Moxon.

KELLY, Fanny (1790–1882)

Comedienne. Made first appearance Drury Lane 1797. Lamb's essay 'Barbara S —' is taken from the story of her childhood and, although supposedly referring to his earlier love, Ann Simmons, it is possible that his recent refusal by Fanny Kelly may have occasioned the wistfulness which is the inspiration of 'Dream Children'.

KEMBLE, John Philip (1757–1823)

Actor, brother of SARAH SIDDONS (d.v.). 'His power was all studied acquirement,' Leigh Hunt. His brothers CHARLES and STEPHEN were also actors of first rank. CHARLES in particular was a friend of Lamb's.

KENNEY, James (1780–1849)

Dramatist. His son CHARLES LAMB KENNEY was a librettist.

KEYMER, J.

Stationer of Cheapside.

LAMB, John (1763–1821)

Charles's brother. Clerk at the South Sea House, Contributor to 'Poetry for Children'.

LAMB, Mary (1764–1847)

Charles's sister, collaborator and favourite companion.

LE GRICE, Rev. Charles Valentine (1773–1858)

Translator of Longus 1803. On leaving C.H. went to Trinity College, Cambridge. Became tutor to the son of a rich widow. He married the widow.

LE GRICE, Samuel

After leaving C.H. joined the army and died 1802 in Jamaica of yellow fever.

LLOYD, Charles (1775–1839)

Poet. An early friend and collaborator of Coleridge and Lamb. Went mad and died in an asylum in France.

MANNING, Thomas (1772–1840)

Mathematician, physician and orientalist. Met Lamb in 1799, became one of his most frequent companions until in 1806 he sailed for China. From where he did not return until 1817. The first Englishman to enter Lhassa. (1811).

MARTIN, John (1789–1854) — He painted a series of lurid works of 'Immeasurable spaces, innumerable multitudes, and gorgeous prodiges'. 'Belshazzar's Feast' was exhibited at the British Institution 1816.

MONTAGU, Basil (1770–1851) — Lawyer. His third wife, a Mrs Skepper, was the mother of Ann Skepper (q.v.). First met Lamb about 1798.

MOXON, Edward (1801–58) — Publisher, versifier and EMMA ISOLA's husband.

NOVELLOS, The: Vincent (1781–1861) — Organist, music publisher, and composer. Married Mary Hehl, and they had eleven children. A daughter CLARA (1818–1908) became an outstanding singer. The whole family were friends of the Lambs who they met in 1816.

PALMER, John — Comedian 'In sock or buskin there was an air of swaggering gentility about Jack Palmer'. 'On Some of the Old Actors.' Elia.

PLUMERS — Owners of Blakesware House and New Place (Gilston Park).

PORSON, Richard (1759–1808) — Regius Professor of Greek at Cambridge.

ROBINSON, Henry Crabb (1775–1867) — Lawyer and diarist. He accompanied the army in Spain 1807–9 as war correspondent and was probably the first newspaperman accredited to an armed force. A founder of London University and one of the earliest members of the Athenaeum.

ROGERS, Samuel
(1763–1855)

Millionaire – poet and wit.

SALT, Samuel

M.P. Employer of John Lamb, senior. Governor of Christ's Hospital and a Director of the South Sea Company and the East India Company.

SIDDONS, Sarah
(1775–1831)

Sister of John Kemble (q.v.). One of the greatest tragic actresses of all times.

SIMMONS, Ann

Alice W —.

SKEPPER, Ann

Step daughter of Basil Montague (q.v.).

SOUTHEY, Robert
(1774–1843)

Poet laureate from 1813. Brother-in-law of Coleridge who introduced him to Lamb in 1795.

STODDART, John
(1773–1856)

HAZLITT's brother-in-law. Leader writer on *The Times* and later Chief Justice of Malta.

STUART, Daniel
(1766–1846)

Proprietor and editor of the *Morning Post* and of *The Courier*.

TALFOURD, Sir Thomas
(1795–1854)

Lawyer, M.P., essayist, tragedian. He first met Lamb in 1815 and was later executor of his will and his official biographer (1848). Drafted the Copyright Act of 1842.

TALMA, François Joseph
(1763–1826)

French tragedian.

TURNER, J. M. W.
(1775–1851)

The great landscape painter. His *Garden of the Hesperedes* was shown at the British Institute 1806.

WHITE, James
(1775–1820)

Educated C.H. and on leaving school served in the Treasurer's Office of the foundation. Later established his own advertising agency and instituted the feast for chimney sweeps, which inspired the Elia essay 'The Praise of Chimney-Sweepers'. One of Lamb's bondsmen at the E. I. H. and co-author of the *Falstaff Letters*.

WORDSWORTH, William (1770–1850)

Collaborator with COLERIDGE, who introduced him to Lamb in 1797. He married MARY HUTCHINSON in 1802. Poet Laureate 1843. The journals of his sister DOROTHY (1771–1855) are among the most delightful records in English literature, and, among other things, particularly valuable for the account of their friendship with the Lambs and Coleridge.

PENGUIN PLAYWRIGHTS

SHAKESPEARE

The text of the Penguin Shakespeare is not a reprint of existing texts, but a new text specially prepared for this edition from the original quartos and folios. Each volume contains the following introductory matter:

1. Chronological list of Shakespeare's works.
2. A short life of Shakespeare.
3. A note on the Elizabethan theatre, with a drawing.
4. A brief introduction to the play.

There are also notes and a glossary at the end of each volume, but the distraction of notes and references in the text itself has been avoided.

Volumes at present available are:

TWELFTH NIGHT	B 1
HAMLET	B 2
AS YOU LIKE IT	B 5
THE TEMPEST	B 7
HENRY THE FOURTH Part 2	B14
CORIOLANUS	B20
TROYLUS AND CRESSIDA	B21

*

SHAW

Of the ten volumes of Mr Shaw's works issued as Penguins in honour of his ninetieth birthday in 1946 the following volumes are now available in reprint:

MAN AND SUPERMAN	563
PLAYS UNPLEASANT	561
THE DOCTOR'S DILEMMA	564
PYGMALION	300
SAINT JOAN	565

and two others,

PLAYS PLEASANT

PLAYS FOR PURITANS, will shortly be reprinted.

In every case the texts are complete and unabridged, and the Prefaces and other supplementary matter are included.

All these are Penguin volumes at 1/6

OSCAR WILDE

Two of Wilde's plays, *The Importance of Being Earnest* and *Lady Windermere's Fan*, were published together as a Penguin in 1940. There have been many requests for Penguin editions of Wilde's other works, and there have now been added to the Penguin List

SALOME AND OTHER PLAYS

A Woman of No Importance

and

An Ideal Husband

600

Salome was written in French in 1891, translated into English by Lord Alfred Douglas, and published in 1894. It was to have been played at the Palace Theatre by Sarah Bernhardt in 1892, but the censor intervened. With its odd, moonlit beauty and the ramping luxuriance of its language, it is nearer akin to a modern prose poem than to drama proper.

A Woman of No Importance and *An Ideal Husband* are true Wildean comedies. In each a serious theme is seriously treated – in the first a woman betrayed and forgotten, in the second the idolising of a man with feet of clay. There is no curb on feeling in the presentation of the chief characters, while the lesser sparkle with the brilliance of Wilde's wit. The character of Lord Goring in *An Ideal Husband* is the reconciliation of Wilde's two worlds, the good and the delightful, and may be an idealised self-portrait. Like the plays of Bernard Shaw these two can be enjoyed both as pure comedy and as food for thought.

THE PICTURE OF DORIAN GRAY

616

Perhaps the masterpiece of 'symbolist' fiction in English, Wilde's novel sparkles with the wit that is more familiar in his plays. 'His principles were out of date, but there was a good deal to be said for his prejudices'; '"The East End" is the problem of slavery, and we try to solve it by amusing the slaves'; 'Nowadays people know the price of everything, and the value of nothing'; 'One of those characteristic British faces, that, once seen, are never remembered'; with such gems as these, many of which have become almost proverbial, this brilliant book is profusely set.

1s. 6d. each

WILLIAM COBBETT

W. Baring Pemberton

680

From whatever angle William Cobbett is regarded, whether as a reformer, author, polemical writer, Rural Rider, farmer or pater-familias, a man is revealed for whom it is impossible not to feel genuine affection. If he was the grandest hater of his day and the last consummate master of prose invective, Cobbett was also one of the most sincere, warm-hearted and single-minded men who ever lived and wrote.

Born, as he was never tired of boasting, the son of a farmer and bred at the tail of the plough, Cobbett was every inch an English yeoman, in appearance, in manner, in character – 'the pattern John Bull of his century', was Carlyle's delineation. He hated cant and affectation, he abominated and distrusted cities (which he called 'wens'), bankers, stockjobbers, paper money and political economists; he adored all forms of sport, was perfectly at home in a cattle market or at a farmers' 'ordinary', and for one blow was ready to return half a dozen. Indeed his whole life from ploughboy to Member of Parliament was little more than a series of fights, and controversies, and personalities.

But of all objects worth fighting for, there was none closer to Cobbett's heart than the preservation of the rural England he had known in his boyhood and its bold independent peasantry, with their full bellies and neat Sunday coats. In his evergreen *Rural Rides* Cobbett has left not only an inimitable picture of a vanished countryside but a testament at once literary, economic and agrarian. To-day, when agriculture is rightly coming to be recognised as one of Britain's principal industries, the life of this turbulent peasant champion and philosopher acquires especial interest.

Mr Pemberton's new study is one of that growing number of books which has not previously appeared in any other form, but makes its first bow to the world as a *Penguin*.

One shilling and sixpence

THE PENGUIN CLASSICS

A LIBRARY OF NEW TRANSLATIONS

EDITED BY E. V. RIEU

HOMER: THE ODYSSEY* – *translated by E. V. Rieu*

'I had forgotten how easy it was for the Greekless reader to enjoy the two epics (*The Wrath of Achilles* and *The Return of Odysseus*) until Mr Rieu's translation of *The Odyssey* reminded me ...' Desmond McCarthy in *The Sunday Times*

SOPHOCLES: THE THEBAN PLAYS

– translated by E. F. Watling

'Mr Watling is to be congratulated not only on the lucidity and sound scholarship of the translation but on his success in enabling the reader to grasp the character of these great dramas and the atmosphere in which they were first enacted.' *Free Verse.*

VOLTAIRE: CANDIDE – *translated by John Butt*

'Mr Butt has given a pleasing modern English translation, and an informative introduction on Voltaire's work, his aims and the factual basis of *Candide*.' *British Book News*

TACITUS: ON BRITAIN AND GERMANY

– translated by H. Mattingly

A version in contemporary prose of the greatest Roman historian's description of 'the noble savage' of two thousand years ago as seen by a cultivated gentleman of the world metropolis.

DANTE: THE INFERNO – *translated by Dorothy L. Sayers*

APULEIUS: THE GOLDEN ASS – *translated by Robert Graves*

XENOPHON: THE PERSIAN EXPEDITION

– translated by Rex Warner

—

* *A double volume, two shillings: the other volumes 1/6 each*

A SHORT HISTORY
OF ENGLISH LITERATURE

B. Ifor Evans

A72

'*Pelicanus in Solitudine*, that Peerless Pelican' is the way in which the discreet and discriminating *Tablet* describes this book, which, in 1940, Dr B. Ifor Evans wrote specially for Pelican Books and which is once again reprinted. It has already become a classic work in literary criticism. Covering the whole of English literature from Beowulf to James Joyce, a period of over a thousand years, and crowded with facts, it remains a volume easy to read and full of original judgements.

Commenting in *The Observer* on its leisurely movement combined with masterly compression, Ivor Brown described the book as written 'to the classical model, as brief as lucid.'

A SHORT HISTORY OF
ENGLISH DRAMA

B. Ifor Evans

A172

Dr Evans has also written this companion volume, which covers the whole sweep of English drama from the miming 'joculator' of the early Middle Ages to Noel Coward and J. B. Priestley in his own day. A history of drama is more than a catalogue of playwrights, and the author shows with great clarity the external factors that have limited and stimulated our theatre. In reviewing it *Punch* says:

'What makes this attractive little book doubly useful is the fact that Dr Evans sees his subject through the theatre , not, as is more usual with Professors of Literature, in terms of the study.'

Each volume 1s. 6d.

A BOOK OF ENGLISH ESSAYS

Selected by W. E. Williams

A99

One of the most notable and attractive forms of Eng. Litt. is the Essay which, through the last three and a half centuries, has prospered abundantly in all periods. In his Introduction to this selection, first made for Pelicans in 1942, Mr W. E. Williams points out that the Essay 'has a multitude of forms and manners, and scarcely any rules and regulations', and being so free from literary convention it has developed a wide variety of styles'.

One aim in this selection has been to show how, in successive Ages of Eng. Litt., the Essay reflects in miniature the prose-manners of the day. The influence of the Press upon the Essay is particularly emphasised by the inclusion of many examples taken from such famous 18th-century periodicals as the *Spectator* and the *Tatler*.

Although many of the pieces chosen for this volume are such well-known ones as Charles Lamb's 'In Praise of Chimney Sweepers' or De Quincey's memorable commentary on an episode in 'Macbeth', an endeavour has been made to remind readers that Addison, for example, wrote other and better essays than the few which are usually anthologised. Modern writers, moreover, such as Belloc, Priestley, Aldous Huxley, Robert Lynd and Ivor Brown, are given a fair share of representation. And in Maurice Hewlett's 'The Maypole and the Column', also included, the reader will find one of the best essays on the English Essay ever written.

This popular Pelican has been reprinted and is again available at one shilling and sixpence.

ENGLISH LETTERS
OF
THE EIGHTEENTH AND NINETEENTH
CENTURIES

Selected by James Aitken

The student of manners – or of human nature – in the past finds
no better quarry for his researches than the private letter –
written not, or at least seldom, with an eye on its publication,
but as a sincere and personal outpouring of the writer's heart.

The letter-writer of the 18th, and almost equally of the 19th,
century spent often more thought and care on his letters than
we are apt to spend on ours. He wrote, perhaps, less often, and
deemed it worth while to bestow some care on style and expression. But human nature is the same in all the centuries, and
behind the occasional formality we can see plainly the same
common interests as our own corerspondence would reveal, the
same sympathies and affections, the same varieties of character
and circumstance, the same gleams of humour and fancy.

The letters in these two volumes are selected from the correspondence of

VOLUME ONE	VOLUME TWO
Alexander Pope	Dr Thomas Arnold
Lady Mary Wortley Montagu	Sir Samuel Romilly
Joseph Addison	John Keats
Mrs Delany	The Carlyles
Rev. Patrick Delany	William Wilberforce
James Thomson	W. E. Gladstone
Samuel Johnson	William Frend
Horace Walpole	Hannah More
William Cowper	Robert Southey
Fanny Burney	Benjamin Disraeli
Edmund Burke	Lord Nelson
William Blake	Harriet Martineau
Charles Lamb	Sir Walter Scott
Lord Byron	The Duke of Wellington

Two Volumes at 1/6 each (Pelican A163, A164)